GCSE Statistics Vocabulary Workbook

By Lewis Morris

Copyright © Network4Learning, Inc. 2019.

www.insiderswords.com/GCSE-Statistics

ISBN-13: 978-1694092533

Copyright © 2019, Network4Learning, inc.
All rights reserved. No part of this publication may be reproduced, distributed, or transmitted in any form or by any means, including photocopying, recording, or other electronic or mechanical methods, without the prior written permission of the publisher, except in the case of brief quotations embodied in critical reviews and certain other noncommercial uses permitted by copyright law. For permission requests, write to the publisher, addressed
"Attention: Permissions Coordinator," at the address below.
Network4Learning, inc.
109 E 17th St STE 63
Cheyenne, WY 82001-4584

www.InsidersWords.com

We hope you find this vocabulary workbook helpful with your studies. If you do, please consider leaving a brief review at this link:

http://www.amazon.com/review/create-review?&asin=1694092534

Table of Contents

Introduction	5
Crossword Puzzles	24
Multiple Choice	74
Matching	118
Word Search	142

What is "Insider Language"?

Recent research has confirmed what we have known for decades: The strongest students and leaders in industry have a mastered an Insider Language in their subject and field. This Insider language is made up of the technical terms and vocabulary necessary to communicate effectively in classes or the workplace. For those who master it, learning is easier, faster, and much more enjoyable.

Most students who are surveyed report that the greatest challenge to any course of study is learning the vocabulary. When we examine typical college courses, we discover that there is, on average, 250 Insider Terms a student must learn over the course of a semester. Further, most exams rely heavily on this set of words for assessment purposes. The structure of multiple choice exams lends itself perfectly to the testing of this Insider Language. Students who can differentiate between Insider Language terms can handle challenging exam questions with ease and confidence.

From recent research on learning and vocabulary we have learned:

- Your knowledge of any subject is contained in the content-specific words you know. The more of these terms that you know, the easier it is to understand and recall important information; the easier it will be to communicate your ideas to peers, professors, supervisors, and co-workers. The stronger your content-area vocabulary is, the higher your scores will be on your exams and written assignments.

- Students who develop a strong Insider Language perform better on tests, learn faster, retain more information, and express greater satisfaction in learning.

- Familiarizing yourself with subject-area vocabulary before formal study (pre-learning) is the most effective way to learn this language and reap the most benefit.

- The vocabulary on standardized exams come directly from the stated objectives of the test-makers. This means that the vocabulary found on standardized exams is predictable. Our books focus on this vocabulary.

- Most multiple-choice exams are glorified vocabulary quizzes. Think about the format of a multiple-choice question. The question stem is a definition of a term and the choices (known as distractors) are 4 or 5 similar words. Your task is to differentiate between the meanings of those terms and choose the correct word.

- It takes a person several exposures to a new word to be able to use it with confidence in conversation or in writing. You need to process these words several different ways to make them part of your long-term memory.

The goals of this book are:
- To give you an "Insider Language" for your subject.
- Pre-teach the most important words before you set out on a traditional course of review or study.
- Teach you the most important words in your subject area.
- Teach you strategies for learning subject-area words on your own.
- Boost your confidence in your ability to master this language and support you in your study.
- Reduce the stress of studying and provide you with fun activities that work.

How it works:
The secret to mastering Insider Language is through repetition and exposure. We have eleven steps for you to follow:

1. Read the word and definition in the glossary out loud. "See it, Say it"
2. Identify the part of speech the word belongs to such as noun, verb, adverb, or adjective. This will help you group the word and identify similar words.
3. Place the word in context by using it in a sentence. Write this sentence down and read it aloud.
4. Use "Chunking" to group the words. Make a diagram or word cloud using these groups.
5. Make connections to the words by creating analogies.
6. Create mnemonics that help you recognize patterns and orders of words by substituting the words for more memorable items or actions.
7. Examine the morphology of the word, that is, identify the root, prefix, and suffix that make up the word. Identify similar and related words.
8. Complete word games and puzzles such as crosswords and word searches.
9. Complete matching questions that require you to differentiate between related words.
10. Complete Multiple-choice questions containing the words.
11. Create a visual metaphor or "memory cartoon" to make a mental picture of the word and related processes.

By completing this word study process, you will be exposed to the terminology in various ways that will activate your memory and create a lasting understanding of this language.

The strategies in this book are designed to make you an independent expert at learning insider language. These strategies include:

- Verbalizing the word by reading it and its definition aloud ("See It, Say It"). This allows you to make visual, auditory, and speech connections with its meaning.

- Identifying the type of word (Noun, verb, adverb, and adjective). Making this distinction helps you understand how to visualize the word. It helps you "chunk" the words into groups, and gives you clues on how to use the word.

- Place the word in context by using it in a sentence. Write this sentence down and read it aloud. This will give you an example of how the word is used.

- "Chunking". By breaking down the word list into groups of closely related words, you will learn them better and be able to remember them faster. Once you have group the terms, you can then make word clouds using a free online service. These word clouds provide visual cues to remembering the words and their meanings.

- Analogies. By creating analogies for essential words, you will be making connections that you can see on paper. These connections can trigger your memory and activate your ability to use the word in your writing as you begin to use them. Many of these analogies also use visual cues. In a sense, you can make a mental picture from the analogy.

- Mnemonics. A device such as a pattern of letters, ideas, or associations that assists in remembering something. A mnemonic is especially useful for remembering the order of a set of words or the order of a process.

- Morphology. The study of word roots, prefixes, and suffixes. By examining the structure of the words, you will gain insight into other words that are closely related, and learn how to best use the word.

- Visual metaphors. This is the most sophisticated and entertaining strategy for learning vocabulary. Create a "memory cartoon" using one or more of the vocabulary terms. This activity triggers the visual part of your memory and makes fast, permanent, imprints of the word on your memory. By combining the terms in your visual metaphor, you can "chunk" the entire set of vocabulary terms into several visual metaphors and benefit from the brain's tendency to group these terms.

The activities in this book are designed to imprint the words and their meanings in your memory in different ways. By completing each activity, you will gain the necessary exposures to the word to make it a permanent part of your vocabulary. Each activity uses a different part of your memory. The result is that you will be comfortable using these words and be able to tell the difference between closely related words. The activities include:

A. Crossword Puzzles and Word Searches- These are proven to increase test scores and improve comprehension. Students frequently report that they are fun and engaging, while requiring them to analyze the structure and meaning of the words.

B. Matching- This activity is effective because it forces you to differentiate between many closely related terms.

C. Multiple Choice- This classic question format lends itself to vocabulary study perfectly. Most exams are in this format because they are simple to make, easy to score, and are a reliable type of assessment. (Perfect for the Vocabulary Master!) One strategy to use with multiple choice questions that enhance their effectiveness is to cover the answer choices while you read the question. After reading the question, see if you can answer it before looking at the choices. Then look at the choices to see if you match one of them.

Conducting a thorough "word study" of your insider language will take time and effort, but the rewards will be well worth it. By following this guide and completing the exercises thoughtfully, you will become a stronger, more effective, and satisfied student. Best of luck on your mastery of this Insider Language!

Insider Language Strategies

"See It, Say It!" Reading your Insider Language set aloud

"IT IS BETTER TO FAIL IN ORIGINALITY THAN TO SUCCEED IN IMITATION."
–HERMAN MELVILLE

Reading aloud is the foundation for the development of an Insider Language. It is the single most important thing you can do for vocabulary acquisition. Done correctly, it engages the visual, auditory, and speech centers of the brain and hastens its storage in your long-term memory.

Reading aloud demonstrates the relationship between the printed word and its meaning.

You can read aloud on a higher level than you can initially understand, so reading aloud makes complex ideas more accessible and exposes you to vocabulary and patterns that are not part of your typical speech. Reading aloud helps you understand the complicated text better and makes more challenging text easier to grasp and understand. Reading aloud helps you to develop the "habits of mind" the strongest students use.

Reading aloud will make connections to concepts in the reading that requires you to relate the new vocabulary to things you already know. Go to the glossary at the end of this book and for each word complete the five steps outlined below:

1. Read the word and its definition aloud. Focus on the sound of the word and how it looks on the paper.
2. Read the word aloud again try to say three or four similar words; this will help you build connections to closely related words.
3. Read the word aloud a third time. Try to make a connection to something you have read or heard.
4. Visualize the concept described in the term. Paint a mental picture of the word in use.
5. Try to think of the opposite of the word. Discovering a close antonym will help you place this word in context.

Create a sentence using the word in its proper context

"OPPORTUNITIES DON'T HAPPEN. YOU CREATE THEM." –CHRIS GROSSER

Context means the circumstances that form the setting for an event, statement, or idea, and which it can be fully understood and assessed. Synonyms for context include conditions, factors, situation, background, and setting.

Place the word in context by using it in a sentence. Write this sentence down and read it aloud. By creating sentences, you are practicing using the word correctly. If you strive to make these sentences interesting and creative, they will become more memorable and effective in activating your long-term memory.

Identify the Parts of Speech

"SUCCESS IS NOT FINAL; FAILURE IS NOT FATAL: IT IS THE COURAGE TO CONTINUE THAT COUNTS." –WINSTON S. CHURCHILL

Read through each term in the glossary and make a note of what part of speech each term is. Studying and identifying parts of speech shows us how the words relate to each other. It also helps you create a visualization of each term. Below are brief descriptions of the parts of speech for you to use as a guide.

VERB: A word denoting action, occurrence, or existence. Examples: walk, hop, whisper, sweat, dribbles, feels, sleeps, drink, smile, are, is, was, has.

NOUN: A word that names a person, place, thing, idea, animal, quality, or action. Nouns are the subject of the sentence. Examples: dog, Tom, Florida, CD, pasta, hate, tiger.

ADJECTIVE: A word that modifies, qualifies, or describes nouns and pronouns. Generally, adjectives appear immediately before the words they modify. Examples: smart girl, gifted teacher, old car, red door.

ADVERB: A word that modifies verbs, adjectives and other adverbs. An "ly" ending almost always changes an adjective to an adverb. Examples: ran swiftly, worked slowly, and drifted aimlessly. Many adverbs do not end in "ly." However, all adverbs identify when, where, how, how far, how much, etc. Examples: run hot, lived hard, moved right, study smart.

Chunking

"YOUR POSITIVE ACTION COMBINED WITH POSITIVE THINKING RESULTS IN SUCCESS." SHIV KHERA

Chunking is when you take a set of words and break it down into groups based on a common relationship. Research has shown that our brains learn by chunking information. By grouping your terms, you will be able to recall large sets of these words easily. To help make your chunking go easily use an online word cloud generator to make a set of word clouds representing your chunks.

1. Study the glossary and decide how you want to chunk the set of words. You can group by part of speech, topic, letter of the alphabet, word length, etc. Try to find an easy way to group each term.
2. Once you have your different groups, visit www.wordclouds.com to create a custom word cloud for each group. Print each one of these clouds and post it in a prominent place to serve as constant visual aids for your learning.

Analogies

"CHOOSE THE POSITIVE. YOU HAVE CHOICE, YOU ARE MASTER OF YOUR ATTITUDE, CHOOSE THE POSITIVE, THE CONSTRUCTIVE. OPTIMISM IS A FAITH THAT LEADS TO SUCCESS."– BRUCE LEE

An analogy is a comparison in which an idea or a thing is compared to another thing that is quite different from it. Analogies aim at explaining an idea by comparing it to something that is familiar. Metaphors and similes are tools used to create analogies.

Analogies are useful for learning vocabulary because they require you to analyze a word (or words), and then transfer that analysis to another word. This transfer reinforces the understanding of all the words.

As you analyze the relationships between the analogies you are creating, you will begin to understand the complex relationships between the seemingly unrelated words.

  A   is to   B   as   C   is to   D

This can be written using colons in place of the terms "is to" and "as."

 A:B::C:D

The two items on the left (items A & B) describe a relationship and are separated by a single colon. The two items on the right (items C & D) are shown on the right and are also separated by a colon. Together, both sides are then separated by two colons in the middle, as shown here: Tall: Short :: Skinny: Fat. The relationship used in this analogy is the antonym.

How to create an analogy

Start with the basic formula for an analogy:

____ : ____ :: ____ : ____

Next, we will examine a simple synonym analogy:

automobile : car :: box : crate

The key to figuring out a set of word analogies is determining the relationship between the paired set of words.

Here is a list of the most common types of Analogies and examples

Synonym	Scream : Yell :: Push : Shove
Antonym	Rich : Poor :: Empty : Full
Cause is to Effect	Prosperity : Happiness :: Success : Joy
A Part is to its Whole	Toe : Foot :: Piece : Set
An Object to its Function	Car : Travel :: Read : Learn
A Item is to its Category	Tabby : House Cat :: Doberman : Dog
Word is a symptom of the other	Pain : Fracture :: Wheezing : Allergy
An object and it's description	Glass : Brittle :: Lead : Dense
The word is lacking the second word	Amputee : Limb :: Deaf : Hearing
The first word Hinders the second word	Shackles : Movement :: Stagger : Walk
The first word helps the action of the second	Knife : Bread :: Screwdriver : Screw
This word is made up of the second word	Sweater : Wool :: Jeans : Denim
A word and it's definition	Cede: Break Away :: Abolish : To get rid of

Using words from the glossary, make a set of analogies using each one. As a bonus, use more than one glossary term in a single analogy.

_____ : _____ :: _____ : _____

Name the relationship between the words in your analogy:_____

_____ : _____ :: _____ : _____

Name the relationship between the words in your analogy:_____

_____ : _____ :: _____ : _____

Name the relationship between the words in your analogy:_____

13

Mnemonics

> "IT ISN'T THE MOUNTAINS AHEAD TO CLIMB THAT WEAR YOU OUT; IT'S THE PEBBLE IN YOUR SHOE."   –MUHAMMAD ALI

A mnemonic is a learning technique that helps you retain and remember information. Mnemonics are one of the best learning methods for remembering lists or processes in order. Mnemonics make the material more meaningful by adding associations and creating patterns. Interestingly, mnemonics may work better when they utilize absurd, startling, or shocking examples and references. Mnemonics help organize the information so that you can easily retrieve it later. By giving you associations and cues, mnemonics allow you to form a mental structure ordering a list or process to help you remember it better. This mental structure allows you to create a structure of association between items that may not appear to have any relationship. Mnemonics typically use references that are easy to visualize and thus easier to remember. Through visualization of vivid images and references, the information is much easier to imprint into long-term memory. The power of making mnemonics lies in converting dull, inert and uninspiring information into something vibrant and memorable.

How to make simple and effective mnemonics
Some of the best mnemonics help us remember simple rules or lists in order.

Step 1. Take a list of terms you are trying to remember in order. For example, we will use the scientific method:

> observation, question, hypothesis, methods, results, and conclusion.

Next, we will replace each word on the list with a new word that starts with the same letter. These new words will together form a vivid sentence that is easy to remember:

> Objectionable Queens Haunted Macho Rednecks Creatively.

As silly as the above sentence seems, it is easy to remember, and now we can call on this sentence to remind us of the order of the scientific method.

Visit http://www.mnemonicgenerator.com/ and try typing in a list of words. It is fun to see the mnemonics that it makes and shows how easy it is to make great mnemonics to help your studying.

Using vivid words in your mnemonics allows you to see the sentence you are making. Words that are gross, scary, or name interesting animals are helpful. Profanity is also useful because the shock value can trigger memory. The following are lists of vivid words to use in your mnemonics:

Gross words
Moist, Gurgle, Phlegm, Fetus, Curd, Smear, Squirt, Chunky, Orifice, Maggots, Viscous, Queasy, Bulbous, Pustule, Putrid, Fester, Secrete, Munch, Vomit, Ooze, Dripping, Roaches, Mucus, Stink, Stank, Stunk, Slurp, Pus, Lick, Salty, Tongue, Fart, Flatulence, Hemorrhoid.

Interesting Animals
Aardvark, Baboon, Chicken, Chinchilla, Duck, Dragonfly, Emu, Electric Eel, Frog, Flamingo, Gecko, Hedgehog, Hyena, Iguana, Jackal, Jaguar, Leopard, Lynx, Minnow, Manatee, Mongoose, Neanderthal, Newt, Octopus, Oyster, Pelican, Penguin, Platypus, Quail, Racoon, Rattlesnake, Rhinoceros, Scorpion, Seahorse, Toucan, Turkey, Vulture, Weasel, Woodpecker, Yak, Zebra.

Superhero Words
Diabolical, Activate, Boom, Clutch, Dastardly, Dynamic, Dynamite, Shazam, Kaboom, Zip, Zap, Zoom, Zany, Crushing, Smashing, Exploding, Ripping, Tearing.

Scary Words
Apparition, Bat, Chill, Demon, Eerie, Fangs, Genie, Hell, Lantern, Macabre, Nightmare, Owl, Ogre, Phantasm, Repulsive, Scarecrow, Tarantula, Undead, Vampire, Wraith, Zombie.

There are several types of mnemonics that can help your memory.

1. Images
Visual mnemonics are a type of **mnemonic** that works by associating an image with characters or objects whose name sounds like the item that must be memorized. This is one of the easiest ways to create effective mnemonics. An example would be to use the shape of numbers to help memorize a long list of them. Numbers can be memorized by their shapes, so that: 0 -looks like an egg; 1 -a pencil, or a candle; 2 -a snake; 3 -an ear; 4 -a sailboat; 5 -a key; 6 -a comet; 7 -a knee; 8 -a snowman; 9 -a comma.

Another type of visual mnemonic is the word-length mnemonic in which the number of letters in each word corresponds to a digit. This simple mnemonic gives pi to seven decimal places:

3.141582 becomes "How I wish I could calculate pi."

Of course, you could use this type of mnemonic to create a longer sentence showing the digits of an important number. Some people have used this type of mnemonic to memorize thousands of digits.

Using the hands is also an important tool for creating visual objects. Making the hands into specific shapes can help us remember the pattern of things or the order of a list of things.

2. Rhyming
Rhyming mnemonics are quick ways to make things memorable. A classic example is a mnemonic for the number of days in each month:
"30 days hath September, April, June, and November.
All the rest have 31
Except February, my dear son.
It has 28, and that is fine
But in Leap Year it has 29."

Another example of a rhyming mnemonic is a common spelling rule:
"I before e except after c
or when sounding like a
in neighbor and weigh."

Use **rhymer.com** to get large lists of rhyming words.

3. Homonym
A homonym is one of a group of words that share the same pronunciation but have different meanings, whether spelled the same or not.

Try saying what you're attempting to remember out loud or very quickly, and see if anything leaps out. If you know other languages, using similar-sounding words from those can be effective.

You could also browse this list of homonyms at http://www.cooper.com/alan/homonym_list.html.

4. Onomatopoeia
An Onomatopeia is a word that phonetically imitates, resembles or suggests the source of the sound that it describes. Are there any noises made by the thing you're trying to memorize? Is it often associated with some other sound? Failing that, just make up a noise that seems to fit.

Achoo, ahem, baa, bam, bark, beep, beep beep, belch, bleat, boo, boo hoo, boom, burp, buzz, chirp, click clack, crash, croak, crunch, cuckoo, dash, drip, ding dong, eek, fizz, flit, flutter, gasp, grrr, ha ha, hee hee, hiccup, hiss, hissing, honk, icky, itchy, jiggly, jangle, knock knock, lush, la la la, mash, meow, moan, murmur, neigh, oink, ouch, plop, pow, quack, quick, rapping, rattle, ribbit, roar, rumble, rustle, scratch, sizzle, skittering, snap crackle pop, splash, splish splash, spurt, swish, swoosh, tap, tapping, tick tock, tinkle, tweet, ugh, vroom, wham, whinny, whip, whooping, woof.

5. Acronyms

An acronym is a word or name formed as an abbreviation from the initial components of a word, such as NATO, which stands for North Atlantic Treaty Organization. If you're trying to memorize something involving letters, this is often a good bet. A lot of famous mnemonics are acronyms, such as ROYGBIV which stands for the order of colors in the light spectrum (Red, Orange, Yellow, Green, Blue, Indigo, and Violet).

A great acronym generator to try is: www.all-acronyms.com.

A different spin on an acronym is a backronym. A **backronym** is a specially constructed phrase that is supposed to be the source of a word that is an acronym. A backronym is constructed by creating a new phrase to fit an already existing word, name, or acronym.

The word is a combination of *backward* and *acronym*, and has been defined as a "reverse acronym." For example, the United States Department of Justice assigns to their Amber Alert program the meaning "**A**merica's **M**issing: **B**roadcast **E**mergency **R**esponse." The process can go either way to make good mnemonics.

Visit: https://arthurdick.com/projects/backronym/ to try out a simple backronym generator.

6. Anagrams

An anagram is a direct word switch or word play, the result of rearranging the letters of a word or phrase to produce a new word or phrase, using all the original letters exactly once; for example, the word anagram can be rearranged into nag-a-ram.

Try re-arranging letters or components and see if anything memorable emerges. Visit http://www.nameacronym.net/ to use a simple anagram generator.

One particularly memorable form of anagram is the spoonerism, where you swap the initial syllables or letters of words to make new phrases. These are usually humorous, and this makes them easier to remember. Here are some examples:

"Is it kisstomary to cuss the bride?" (as opposed to "customary to kiss")
"The Lord is a shoving leopard." (instead of "a loving shepherd")
"A blushing crow." ("crushing blow")
"A well-boiled icicle" ("well-oiled bicycle")
"You were fighting a liar in the quadrangle." ("lighting a fire")
"Is the bean dizzy?" (as opposed to "is the dean busy?")

7. Stories

Make up quick stories or incidents involving the material you want to memorize. For larger chunks of information, the stories can get more elaborate. Structured stories are particularly good for remembering lists or other sequenced information. Have a look at https://en.wikipedia.org/wiki/Method_of_loci for a more advanced memory sequencing technique.

Visual Metaphors

"Limits, like fear, is often an illusion." –Michael Jordan

What is a Metaphor?

A metaphor is a figure of speech that refers to one thing by mentioning another thing. Metaphors provide clarity and identify hidden similarities between two seemingly unrelated ideas. A visual metaphor is an image that creates a link between different ideas.

Visual metaphors help us use our understanding of the world to learn new concepts, skills, and ideas. Visual metaphors help us relate new material to what we already know. Visual metaphors must be clear and simple enough to spark a connection and understanding. Visual metaphors should use familiar things to help you be less fearful of new, complex, or challenging topics. Metaphors trigger a sense of familiarity so that you are more accepting of the new idea. Metaphors work best when you associate a familiar, easy to understand idea with a challenging, obscure, or abstract concept.

How to make a visual metaphor

1. Brainstorm using the words of the concept. Use different fonts, colors, or shapes to represent parts of the concept.

2. Merge these images together

3. Show the process using arrows, accents, etc.

4. Think about the story line your metaphor projects.

Examples of visual metaphors:

A skeleton used to show a framework of something.

A cloud showing an outline.

A bodybuilder whose muscles represent supporting ideas and details.

A sandwich where the meat, tomato, and lettuce represent supporting ideas.

A recipe card to show a process.

Your metaphor should be accurate. It should be complex enough to convey meaning, but simple and clear enough to be easily understood.

Morphology
"SCIENCE IS THE CAPTAIN, AND PRACTICE THE SOLDIERS." LEONARDO DA VINCI

Morphology is the study of the origin, roots, suffixes, and prefixes of the words. Understanding the meaning of prefixes, suffixes, and roots make it easier to decode the meaning of new vocabulary. Having the ability to decode using morphology increases text comprehension when initially reading as well.

The capability of identifying meaningful parts of words (morphemes), including prefixes, suffixes, and roots can be helpful. Identifying morphemes improves decoding accuracy and fluency. Reading speed improves when you can decode larger chunks of text quickly. When you can recognize morphemes in words, you will be better able to make sense of new words in context. Below are charts containing the most common prefixes, suffixes, and root words. Use them to help you decode your vocabulary terms.

Prefixes

Prefix	Meaning	Example words and meanings	
a, ab, abs	away from	absent abdicate	not to be present, to give up an office or throne.
ad, a, ac, af, ag, an, ar, at, as	to, toward	Advance advantage	To move forward To have the upper hand
anti	against	Antidote antisocial antibiotic	To repair poisoning refers to someone who's not social
bi, bis	two	bicycle binary biweekly	two-wheeled cycle two number system every two weeks
circum, cir	around	circumnavigate circle	Travel around the world a figure that goes all around
com, con, co, col	with, together	Complete Complement	To finish To go along with
de	away from, down, the opposite of	depart detour	to go away from to go out of your way
dis, dif, di	apart	dislike dishonest distant	not to like not honest away
En-, em-	Cause to	Entrance	the way in.
epi	upon, on top of	epitaph epilogue epidemic	writing upon a tombstone speech at the end, on top of the rest
equ, equi	equal	equalize equitable	to make equal fair, equal
ex, e, ef	out, from	exit eject exhale	to go out to throw out to breathe out
Fore-	Before	Forewarned	To have prior warning

Prefix	Meaning	Example Words and Meanings	
in, il, ir, im, en	in, into	Infield Imbibe	The inner playing field to take part in
in, il, ig, ir, im	not	inactive ignorant irreversible irritate	not active not knowing not reversible to put into discomfort
inter	between, among	international interact	among nations to mix with
mal, male	bad, ill, wrong	malpractice malfunction	bad practice fail to function, bad function
Mid	Middle	Amidships	In the middle of a ship
mis	wrong, badly	misnomer	The wrong name
mono	one, alone, single	monocle	one lensed glasses
non	not, the reverse of	nonprofit	not making a profit
ob	in front, against, in front of, in the way of	Obsolete	No longer needed
omni	everywhere, all	omnipresent omnipotent	always present, everywhere all powerful
Over	On top	Overdose	Take too much medication
Pre	Before	Preview	Happens before a show.
per	through	Permeable pervasive	to pass through, all encompassing
poly	many	Polygamy polygon	many spouses figure with many sides
post	after	postpone postmortem	to do after after death
pre	before, earlier than	Predict Preview	To know before To view before release
pro	forward, going ahead of, supporting	proceed pro-war promote	to go forward supporting the war to raise or move forward
re	again, back	retell recall reverse	to tell again to call back to go back
se	apart	secede seclude	to withdraw, become apart to stay apart from others
Semi	Half	Semipermeable	Half-permeable

Prefix	Meaning	Example Words and Meanings	
Sub	under, less than	Submarine	under water
super	over, above, greater	superstar superimpose	a start greater than her stars to put over something else
trans	across	transcontinental transverse	across the continent to lie or go across
un, uni	one	unidirectional unanimous unilateral	having one direction sharing one view having one side
un	not	uninterested unhelpful unethical	not interested not helpful not ethical

Roots

Root	Meaning	Example words & meanings	
act, ag	to do, to act	Agent Activity	One who acts as a representative Action
Aqua	Water	Aquamarine	The color of water
Aud	To hear	Auditorium	A place to hear music
apert	open	Aperture	An opening
bas	low	Basement Basement	Something that is low, at the bottom A room that is low
Bio	Living thing	Biological	Living matter
cap, capt, cip, cept, ceive	to take, to hold, to seize	Captive Receive Capable Recipient	One who is held To take Able to take hold of things One who takes hold or receives
ced, cede, ceed, cess	to go, to give in	Precede Access Proceed	To go before Means of going to To go forward
Cogn	Know	Cognitive	Ability to think
cred, credit	to believe	Credible Incredible Credit	Believable Not believable Belief, trust
curr, curs, cours	to run	Current Precursory Recourse	Now in progress, running Running (going) before To run for aid
Cycle	Circle	Lifecycle	The circle of life
dic, dict	to say	Dictionary Indict	A book explaining words (sayings)

Root	Meaning	Examples and meanings	
duc, duct	to lead	Induce Conduct Aqueduct	To lead to action To lead or guide Pipe that leads water somewhere
equ	equal, even	Equality Equanimity	Equal in social, political rights Evenness of mind, tranquility
fac, fact, fic, fect, fy	to make, to do	Facile Fiction Factory Affect	Easy to do Something that is made up Place that makes things To make a change in
fer, ferr	to carry, bring	Defer Referral	To carry away Bring a source for help/information
Gen	Birth	Generate	To create something
graph	write	Monograph Graphite	A writing on a particular subject A form of carbon used for writing
Loc	Place	Location	A place
Mater	Mother	Maternity	Expecting birth
Mem	Recall	Memory	The recall experiences
mit, mis	to send	Admit Missile	To send in Something sent through the air
Nat	Born	Native	Born in a place
par	equal	Parity Disparate	Equality No equal, not alike
Ped	Foot	Podiatrist	Foot doctor
Photo	Light	Photograph	A picture
plic	to fold, to bend, to turn	Complicate Implicate	To fold (mix) together To fold in, to involve
pon, pos, posit, pose	to place	Component Transpose Compose Deposit	A part placed together with others A place across To put many parts into place To place for safekeeping
scrib, script	to write	Describe Transcript Subscription	To write about or tell about A written copy A written signature or document
sequ, secu	to follow	Sequence	In following order

Root	Meaning	Examples and Meanings	
Sign	Mark	Signal	to alert somebody
spec, spect, spic	to appear, to look, to see	Specimen Aspect	An example to look at One way to see something
sta, stat, sist, stit, sisto	to stand, or make stand Stable, steady	Constant Status Stable Desist	Standing with Social standing Steady (standing) To stand away from
Struct	To build	Construction	To build a thing
tact	to touch	Contact Tactile	To touch together To be able to be touched
ten, tent, tain	to hold	Tenable Retentive Maintain	Able to be held, holding Holding To keep or hold up
tend, tens, tent	to stretch	Extend Tension	To stretch or draw out Stretched
Therm	Temperature	Thermometer	Detects temperature
tract	to draw	Attract Contract	To draw together An agreement drawn up
ven, vent	to come	Convene Advent	To come together A coming
Vis	See	Invisible	Cannot be seen
ver, vert, vers	to turn	Avert Revert Reverse	To turn away To turn back To turn around

Crossword Puzzles

1.

ACROSS

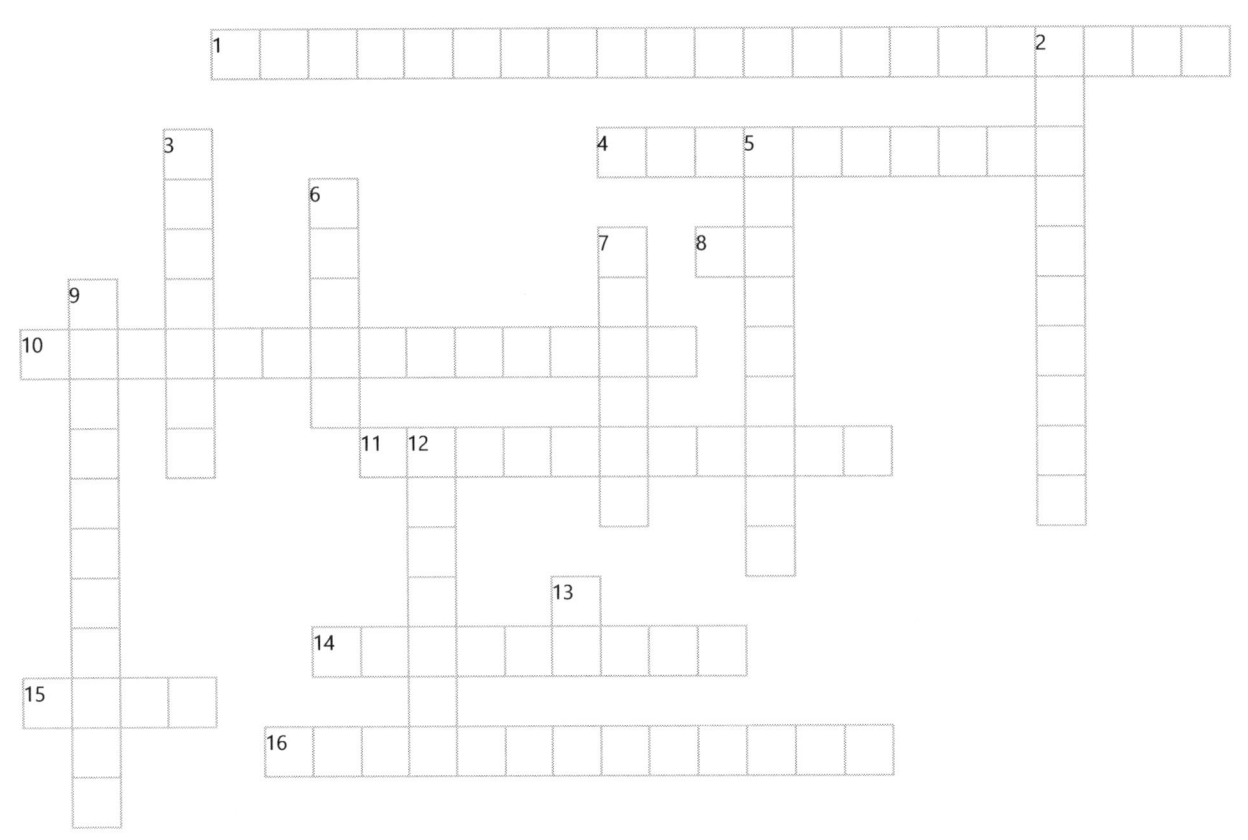

1. Numerical and graphical summaries of data.
4. Each of the 100 equal groups into which a population can be divided according to the distribution of values of a variable.
8. Population mean.
10. Type of cohort where measurements are taken at one point in time.
11. Cause surprise or confusion, especially by acting against an expectation.
14. Relating to or denoting a statistical method assessing the goodness of fit between observed values and those expected theoretically.
15. Any problem in the design or conduct of a statistical study that tends to favor certain results.
16. Calculating a value outside the range of known values.

DOWN

2. The procedures applied to each experimental unit.
3. All of the information collected.
5. The act of making something happen.
6. The probability of correctly rejecting the null hypothesis.
7. The probability of obtaining a value of the test statistic equal to or more extreme than that observed.
9. Type of cohort study where the subjects are followed over time.
12. Scores that differ so markedly from the main body of data that their accuracy is questioned.
13. Degrees of freedom.

A. Bias
B. Outlier
C. Descriptive Statistics
D. Power
E. Cross Sectional
F. Data Set
G. Extrapolation
H. Prospective
I. Nu
J. Mu
K. Causation
L. Chi square
M. Percentile
N. Treatments
O. P value
P. Confounding

2.

ACROSS

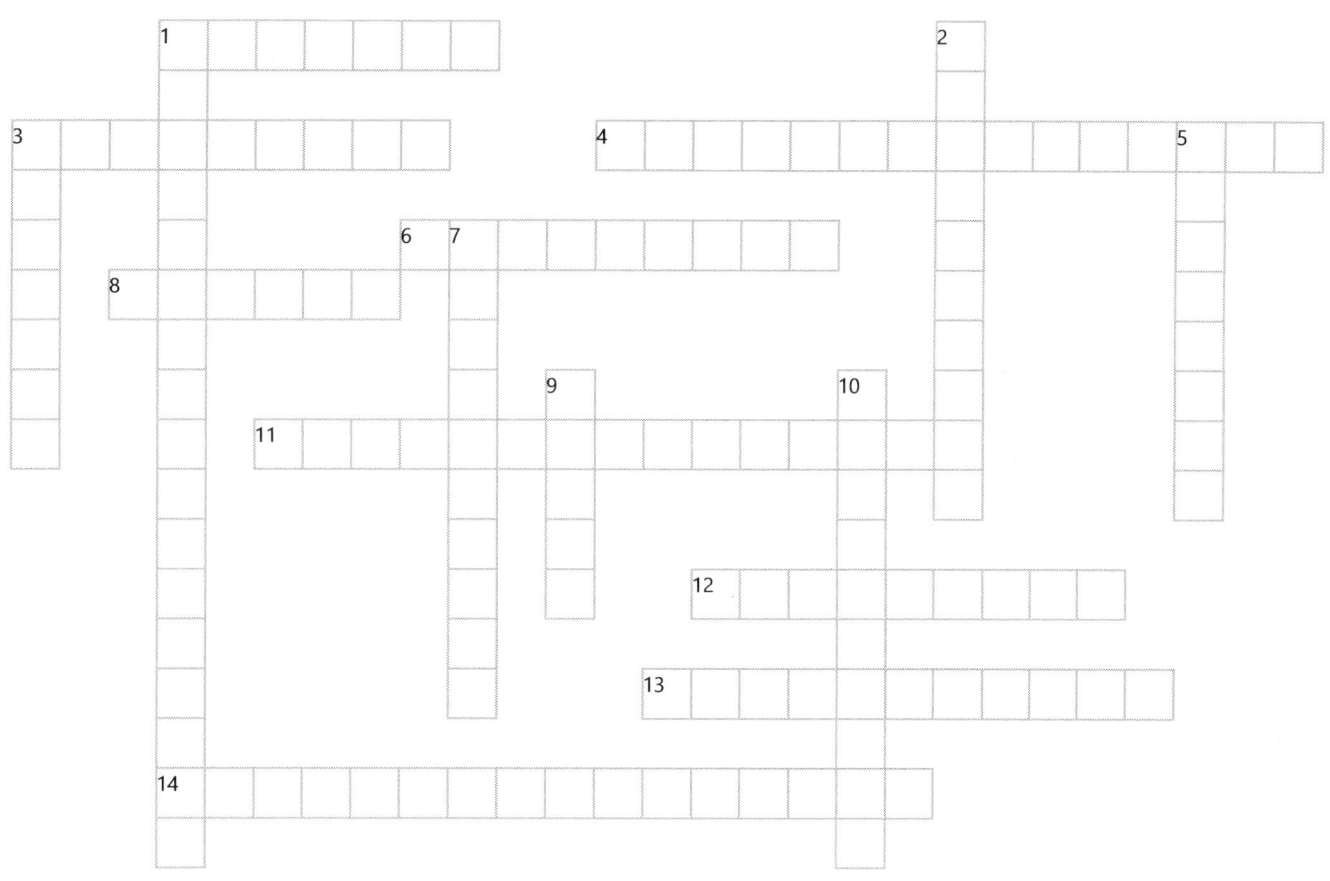

1. When the experimental units are people.
3. Having two variables.
4. The relationship between rankings of different ordinal variables.
6. Relating to or denoting a statistical method assessing the goodness of fit between observed values and those expected theoretically.
8. Made, done, happening, or chosen without method or conscious decision.
11. Population is divided into groups that are randomly sampled, and all the members of the selected from the sample.
12. The act of making something happen.
13. Group of subjects is studied to determine whether various factors of interest are associated with an outcome.
14. Type of qualitative variable. Have a natural ordering, but have no mathematically value.

DOWN

1. The square root of the variance.
2. A proportion in relation to a whole.
3. Two clearly distinct modes.
5. A set containing all points between two given endpoints.
7. A supposition or proposed explanation based on limited evidence as a starting point for further investigation.
9. Any number of entities members considered as a unit.
10. A series of values of a variable at successive times.

A. Causation	B. Subject	C. Group	D. Cohort Study
E. percentage	F. Chi square	G. Bimodal	H. Cluster Sampling
I. Time series	J. Standard Deviation	K. Hypothesis	L. Interval
M. Rank Correlation	N. Bivariate	O. Random	P. Ordinal Variables

25

3.

ACROSS

1. Matching each participant in the experimental condition with a participant in the control condition.
3. Studies conducted by a procedure that produces the correct result on average.
5. Relating to or denoting a statistical method assessing the goodness of fit between observed values and those expected theoretically.
8. Type of cohort study where the subjects are followed over time.
11. The relationship between rankings of different ordinal variables.
12. Only one mode.
14. Arranged into groups.
15. A procedure for determining how much of the variability among scores to attribute to a range of sources of variation.
16. Drawing inferences from sample data to a population.

DOWN

2. Graphical representation of frequency distribution for quantitative data. Rectangle for each class.
4. Any problem in the design or conduct of a statistical study that tends to favor certain results.
6. A subset of a population.
7. A part, share, or number considered in comparative relation to a whole.
9. Extending without break or irregularity.
10. Explain the meaning of information, words, or actions.
13. The score or qualitative category that occurs with greatest frequency.

A. Interpret
B. Matched sample
C. Mode
D. Chi square
E. Proportion
F. Rank Correlation
G. Inferential Statistics
H. Analysis of variance
I. Histogram
J. Grouped
K. Sample
L. Unimodal
M. Unbiased
N. Continuous
O. Bias
P. Prospective

4.

ACROSS

1. A quantity whose value depends on another quantity.
3. Make or place alongside something.
7. The probability of correctly rejecting the null hypothesis.
9. Significance level; probability of a type I error.
11. Minimum, 1st Quartile, Median, 3rd Quartile, Maximum.
13. Only one mode.
14. Each of four equal groups into which a population can be divided according to the distribution of values of a variable.
15. The random variable is a statistic based on the results of more than one trial.

DOWN

2. Collection of propositions to illustrate the principles of a subject.
4. Group of subjects is studied to determine whether various factors of interest are associated with an outcome.
5. As great, high, or intense as possible or permitted.
6. Each of the 100 equal groups into which a population can be divided according to the distribution of values of a variable.
8. The number designating place in an ordered sequence.
10. Make a detailed inspection of; for statistical purposes.
12. Population mean.

A. parallel
B. Cohort Study
C. Quartile
D. Theory
E. Alpha
F. Dependent variable
G. Survey
H. Mu
I. Sampling distribution
J. Five Number Summary
K. Power
L. ordinal
M. Unimodal
N. Maximum
O. Percentile

5.

ACROSS

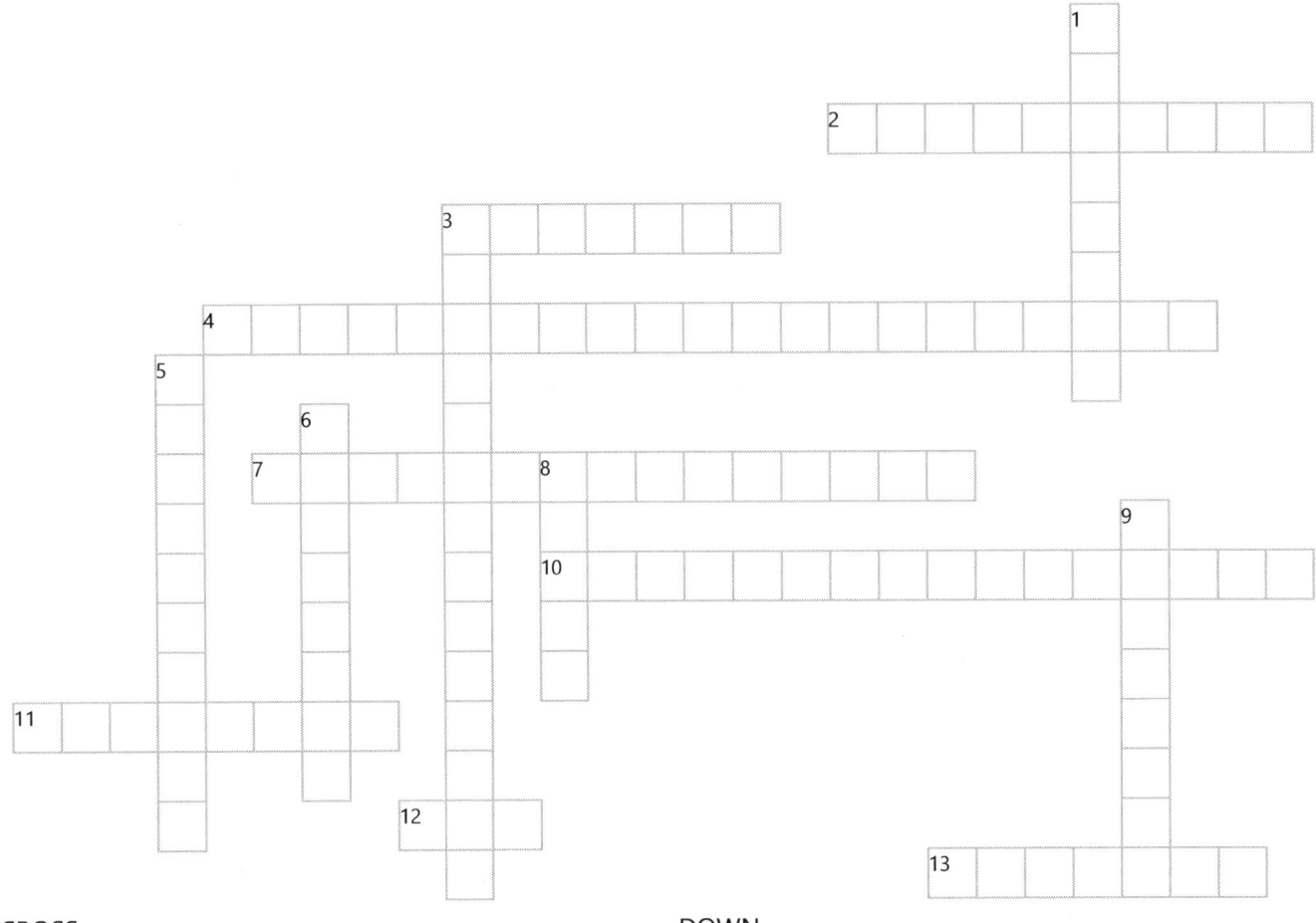

2. Increasing by successive addition.
3. Intervals of equal width that cover all values observed in the data set.
4. Tells how much or many of something there is.
7. The relationship between rankings of different ordinal variables.
10. Longer tail extends to the left
11. Studies conducted by a procedure that produces the correct result on average.
12. A very small circular shape.
13. A graphic way to display the median, quartiles, and extremes of a data set on a number line to show the distribution of the data.

DOWN

1. Each of four equal groups into which a population can be divided according to the distribution of values of a variable.
3. The region for rejecting the null hypothesis.
4. Semi interquartile range.
5. A part, share, or number considered in comparative relation to a whole.
6. Make or place alongside something.
8. The difference between the largest and the smallest value.
9. The difference between actual score and predicted score.

A. Critical region
B. Rank Correlation
C. Dot
D. Boxplot
E. Q
F. Negatively skewed
G. Quantitative Variables
H. Cumulative
I. Quartile
J. Proportion
K. Residual
L. Unbiased
M. parallel
N. Classes
O. Range

6.

ACROSS

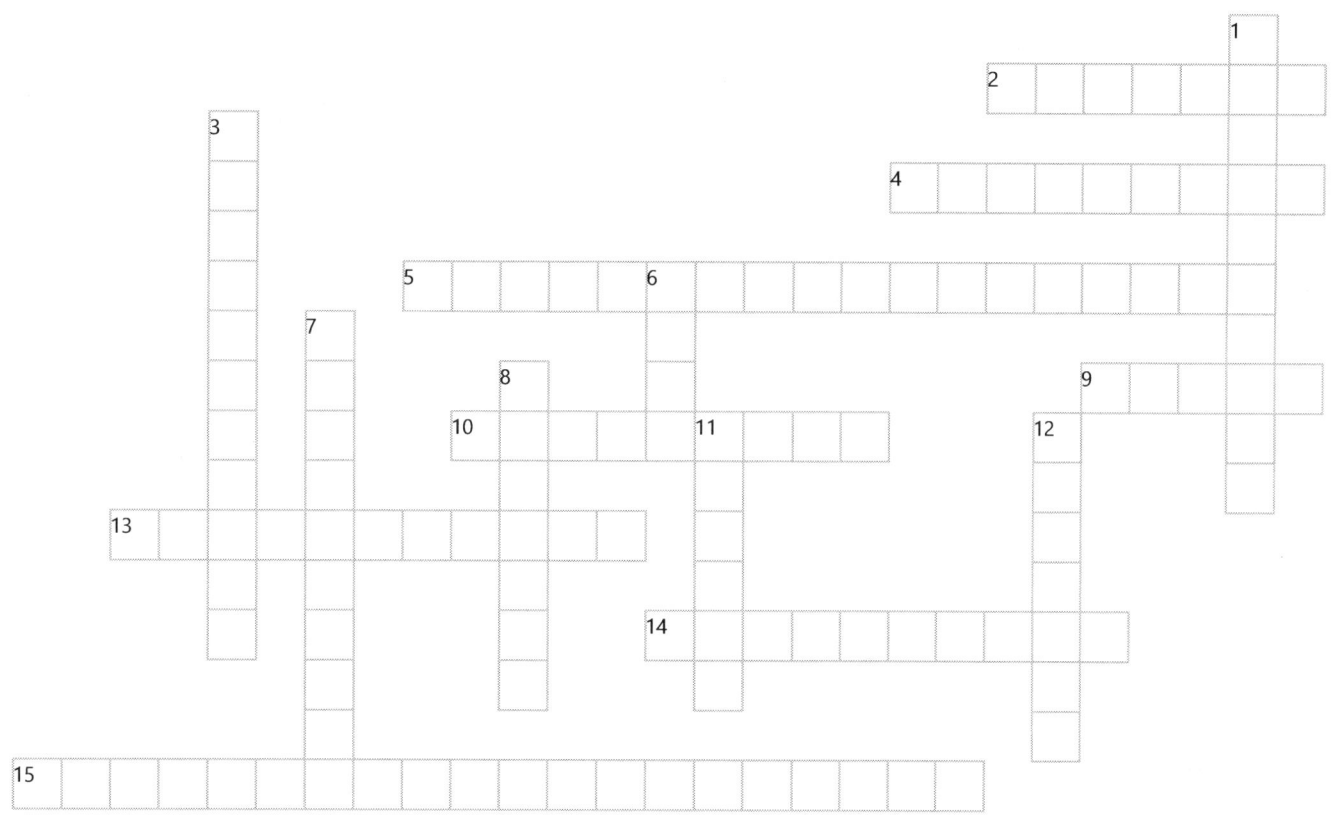

2. Bar graph that shows frequencies or relative frequencies in categories for more than one group frequencies within each category.
4. The number of times a variable occurs in a data set.
5. Distributions that are asymmetrical.
9. The quantitative relation between two amounts showing the number of times one value contains or is contained within the other.
10. The act of making something happen.
13. An experiment where neither the investigator nor the subjects know who has been assigned to which treatment.
14. A series of values of a variable at successive times.
15. The random variable is a statistic based on the results of more than one trial.

DOWN

1. Each of the 100 equal groups into which a population can be divided according to the distribution of values of a variable.
3. Group of subjects is studied to determine whether various factors of interest are associated with an outcome.
6. The values of the variables that we obtain.
7. The collection of all people, objects, or events having one or more specified characteristics.
8. As great, high, or intense as possible or permitted.
11. An error retaining a false null hypothesis.
12. When the experimental units are people.

A. Double Blind
B. Cohort Study
C. Type II
D. Population
E. Sampling distribution
F. Maximum
G. Percentile
H. Time series
I. Ratio
J. Subject
K. Stacked
L. Frequency
M. Data
N. Skewed distribution
O. Causation

7.

ACROSS

1. A graphic way to display the median, quartiles, and extremes of a data set on a number line to show the distribution of the data.
3. A response where the opinions of non-responders tend to differ from the opinions of those who do respond.
5. Type of qualitative variable. Have no natural ordering.
6. Actual measurements or observations collected from the sample.
9. Found by subtracting the 1st quartile from the 3rd quartile. One method for detecting outliers.
12. Items are ordered, and every nth item is chosen to be included in the sample.
13. Tells how many standard deviations that value is from its population mean.
14. The number of times a variable occurs in a data set.
15. Histogram with single mode the near center of the data and are approximately symmetric.

DOWN

2. When the first class has no lower limit, or the last class has no upper limit.
4. Calculating a value outside the range of known values.
7. A circular chart divided into triangular areas proportional to the percentages of the whole.
8. Make a detailed inspection of; for statistical purposes.
10. Semi interquartile range.
11. Bar graph that shows frequencies or relative frequencies in categories for more than one group frequencies within each category.

A. Pie chart
B. Systematic Sampling
C. Q
D. Extrapolation
E. Bell Shaped
F. Interquartile Range
G. Non response
H. Stacked
I. Z Score
J. Boxplot
K. Raw data
L. Survey
M. Nominal Variables
N. Open Ended Classes
O. Frequency

8.

ACROSS

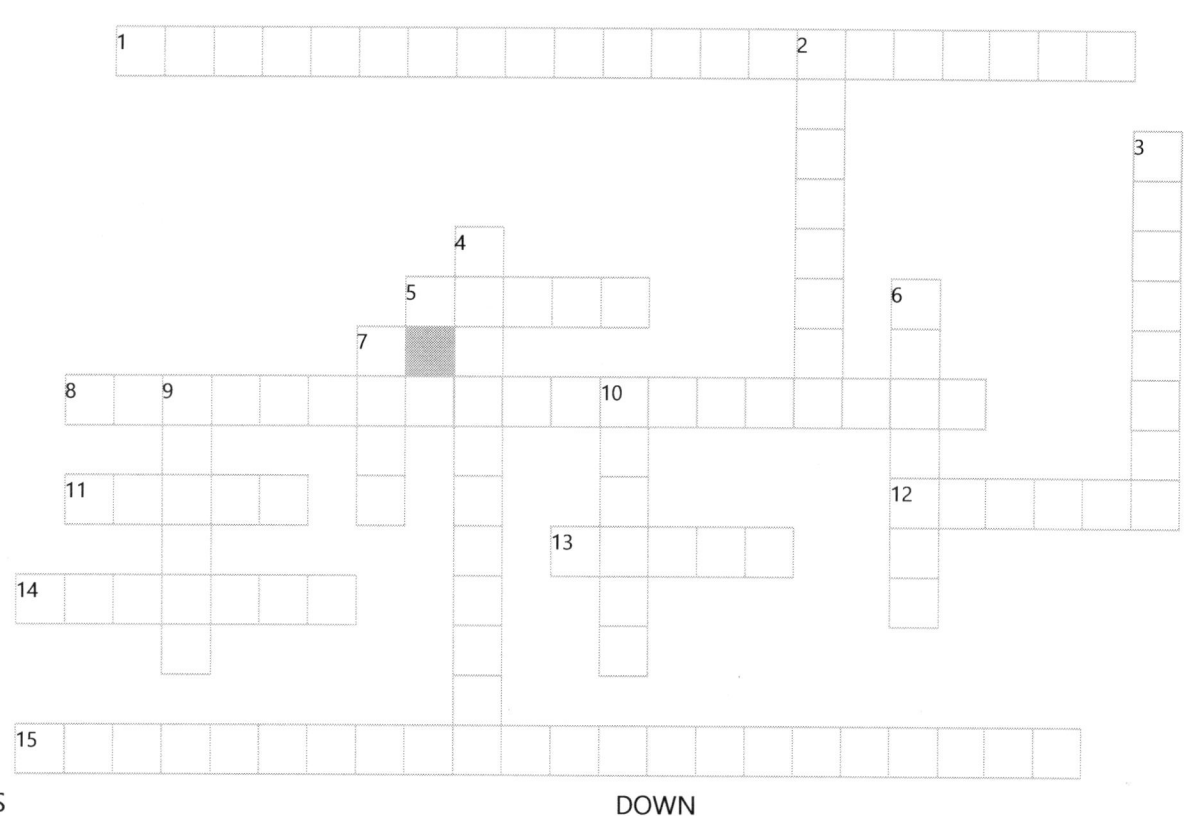

1. Tells how much or many of something there is.
5. Significance level; probability of a type I error.
8. A bias where people are reluctant to admit to behavior that may reflect negatively on them.
11. The difference between the largest and the smallest value.
12. A subset of a population.
13. The probability of correctly rejecting the null hypothesis.
14. Arranged into groups.
15. Tells how large the standard deviation is relative to the mean. It can be used to compare the spreads of data sets whose values have different units.

DOWN

1. Semi interquartile range.
2. The difference between actual score and predicted score.
3. A measure of how far the values in a data set are from the mean, on the average.
4. The quality of being unsteady and subject to changes.
6. All of the information collected.
7. The values of the variables that we obtain.
9. The collection of data from every member of the population.
10. Collection of propositions to illustrate the principles of a subject.

A. Residual
B. Quantitative Variables
C. Sample
D. Data
E. Alpha
F. Coefficient of Variation
G. Range
H. Variance
I. Census
J. Fluctuation
K. Grouped
L. Social Acceptability
M. Power
N. Q
O. Data Set
P. Theory

9.

ACROSS

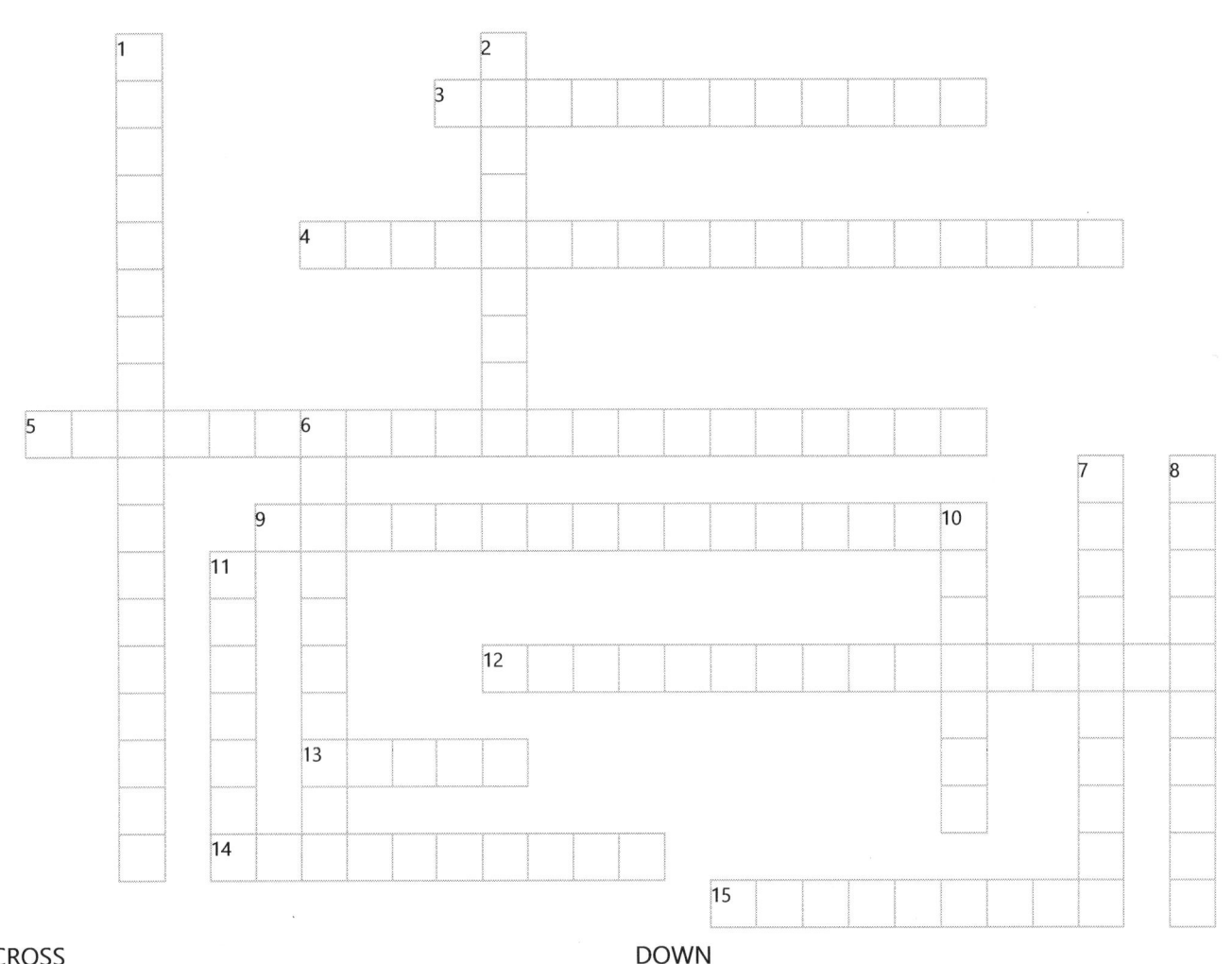

3. The way in which a variable's values are spread over all possible values.
4. The assignment to treatment groups is not made by the investigator.
5. Numerical and graphical summaries of data.
9. Type of qualitative variable. Have a natural ordering, but have no mathematically value.
12. The selection of participants in one sample is affected by the selection of participants in the other sample.
13. Significance level; probability of a type I error.
14. The procedures applied to each experimental unit.
15. The act of making something happen.

DOWN

1. A probability distribution that is unimodal and symmetrical.
2. Having two variables.
6. A proportion in relation to a whole.
7. The collection of all people, objects, or events having one or more specified characteristics.
8. A series of values of a variable at successive times.
10. People having the same social or economic status.
11. Come together and form a group or mass.

- A. percentage
- B. Population
- C. Causation
- D. Descriptive Statistics
- E. Observational Study
- F. Treatments
- G. Normal distribution
- H. Time series
- I. Collect
- J. Ordinal Variables
- K. Bivariate
- L. Distribution
- M. Stratum
- N. Dependent samples
- O. Alpha

10.

ACROSS
1. Arrange into a structured whole; order.
5. A circular chart divided into triangular areas proportional to the percentages of the whole.
6. Make a drawing that shows interactions among variables.
9. Ratio of a circle's circumference to its diameter, ≈ 3.1416
10. The act of making and recording a measurement.
12. Sometimes questions are worded in a way that suggest a particular response.
13. Observing the same participants under both the experimental and control conditions.
14. The selection of a random sample.

DOWN
1. The assignment to treatment groups is not made by the investigator.
2. The smallest value that can appear in that class.
3. Descriptive measure for a sample.
4. Longer tail extends to the left
7. An error rejecting a true null hypothesis.
8. A characteristic that differs from one subject to the next.
11. Come together and form a group or mass.

A. Pie chart
B. Collect
C. Organize
D. Statistic
E. Observational Study
F. Leading Question Bias
G. Variable
H. Type I
I. Pi
J. Observation
K. random sampling
L. Repeated measures
M. Plot
N. Lower Class Limit
O. Negatively skewed

11.

ACROSS
1. A branch of mathematics concerned with quantitative data.
3. probability of a success.
4. Any number of entities members considered as a unit.
6. An experiment where neither the investigator nor the subjects know who has been assigned to which treatment.
9. Tells how large the standard deviation is relative to the mean. It can be used to compare the spreads of data sets whose values have different units.
10. Arranged into groups.
12. Make or place alongside something.
13. A line on a graph indicating a statistical trend.
14. A measure of center in a data set.
15. The random variable is a statistic based on the results of more than one trial.

DOWN
2. When the experimental units are people.
3. Longer tail extends to the right
5. The middle value that divides the data into two equal groups.
7. Descriptive measure for a population represented by Greek letters.
8. Two clearly distinct modes.
11. As great, high, or intense as possible or permitted.

A. Maximum
B. Group
C. P
D. Trend line
E. Positively skewed
F. Subject
G. Sampling distribution
H. Parameter
I. Median
J. Mean
K. Statistics
L. Bimodal
M. parallel
N. Double Blind
O. Coefficient of Variation
P. Grouped

34

12.

ACROSS

2. Calculating a value outside the range of known values.
3. Semi interquartile range.
5. Every possible sample of a size has an equal chance of being selected.
6. The difference between the largest and the smallest value.
7. Histogram with single mode the near center of the data and are approximately symmetric.
8. population standard deviation.
9. Arrange into a structured whole; order.
10. Graphical representation of frequency distribution for quantitative data. Rectangle for each class.
11. Make or place alongside something.
12. Classify individuals into categories.
13. Any number of entities members considered as a unit.
14. The middle value that divides the data into two equal groups.

DOWN

1. Population is divided into groups that are randomly sampled, and all the members of the selected from the sample.
3. A form with a set of queries to gain statistical information.
4. A set containing all points between two given endpoints.
5. Made, done, happening, or chosen without method or conscious decision.

A. Random sampling B. Sigma C. Median D. Range
E. Interval F. Group G. Qualitative Variable H. Extrapolation
I. Histogram J. Q K. Random L. parallel
M. Organize N. Bell Shaped O. Questionnaire P. Cluster Sampling

35

13.

ACROSS

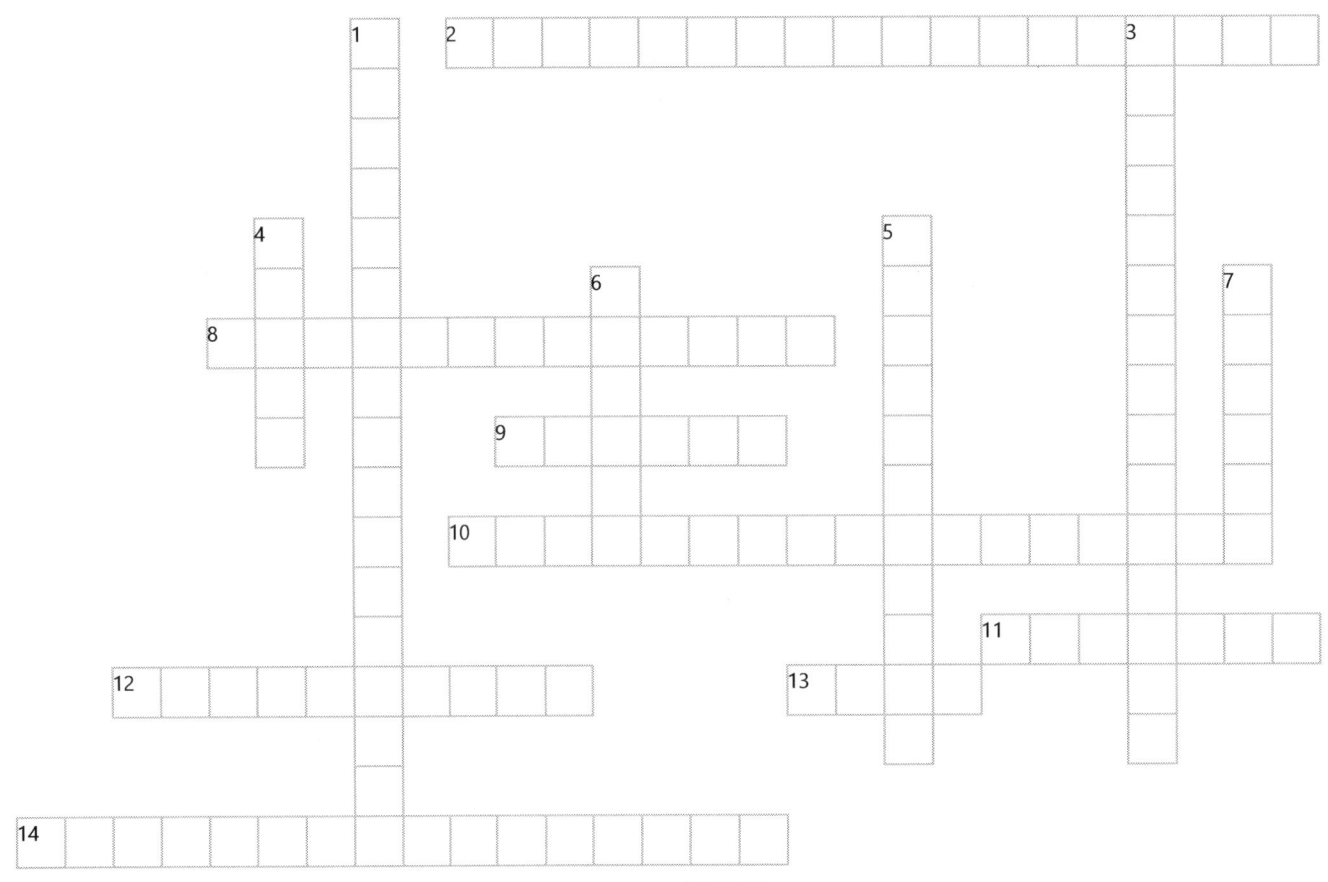

2. A range of values so defined that there is a specified probability that the value of a parameter lies within it.
8. Calculation of the value of a function between known values.
9. An error retaining a false null hypothesis.
10. Minimum, 1st Quartile, Median, 3rd Quartile, Maximum.
11. As great, high, or intense as possible or permitted.
12. Increasing by successive addition.
13. Any problem in the design or conduct of a statistical study that tends to favor certain results.
14. Longer tail extends to the right

DOWN

1. A quantity whose value depends on another quantity.
3. The relationship between rankings of different ordinal variables.
4. The difference between the largest and the smallest value.
5. Relating to or included in a class or classes.
6. A subset of a population.
7. Collection of propositions to illustrate the principles of a subject.

A. Categorical
D. Sample
G. Confidence interval
J. Range
M. Positively skewed

B. Maximum
E. Theory
H. Interpolation
K. Rank Correlation
N. Cumulative

C. Bias
F. Type II
I. Dependent variable
L. Five Number Summary

14.

ACROSS

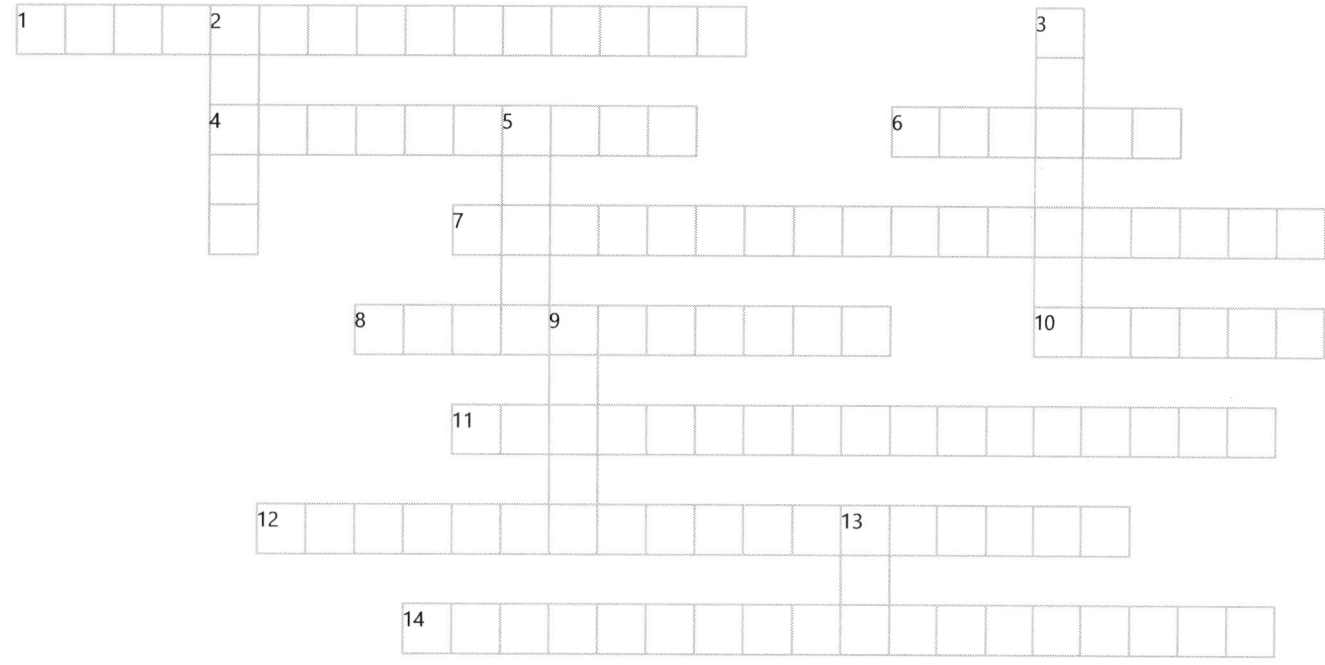

1. The smallest value that can appear in that class.
4. A series of values of a variable at successive times.
6. The probability of obtaining a value of the test statistic equal to or more extreme than that observed.
7. Found by subtracting the 1st quartile from the 3rd quartile. One method for detecting outliers.
8. Bar graph in which categories are represented in order of frequency.
10. Collection of propositions to illustrate the principles of a subject.
11. Things who are studied.
12. A procedure for determining how much of the variability among scores to attribute to a range of sources of variation.
14. The assignment to treatment groups is not made by the investigator.

DOWN

2. The quantitative relation between two amounts showing the number of times one value contains or is contained within the other.
3. Come together and form a group or mass.
5. The difference between the largest and the smallest value.
9. An error rejecting a true null hypothesis.
13. A non-parametric measure of rank correlation.

A. Theory
B. Rho
C. Time series
D. Type I
E. Experimental Units
F. Range
G. Collect
H. Lower Class Limit
I. Observational Study
J. Analysis of variance
K. Pareto Chart
L. P value
M. Interquartile Range
N. Ratio

37

15.

ACROSS

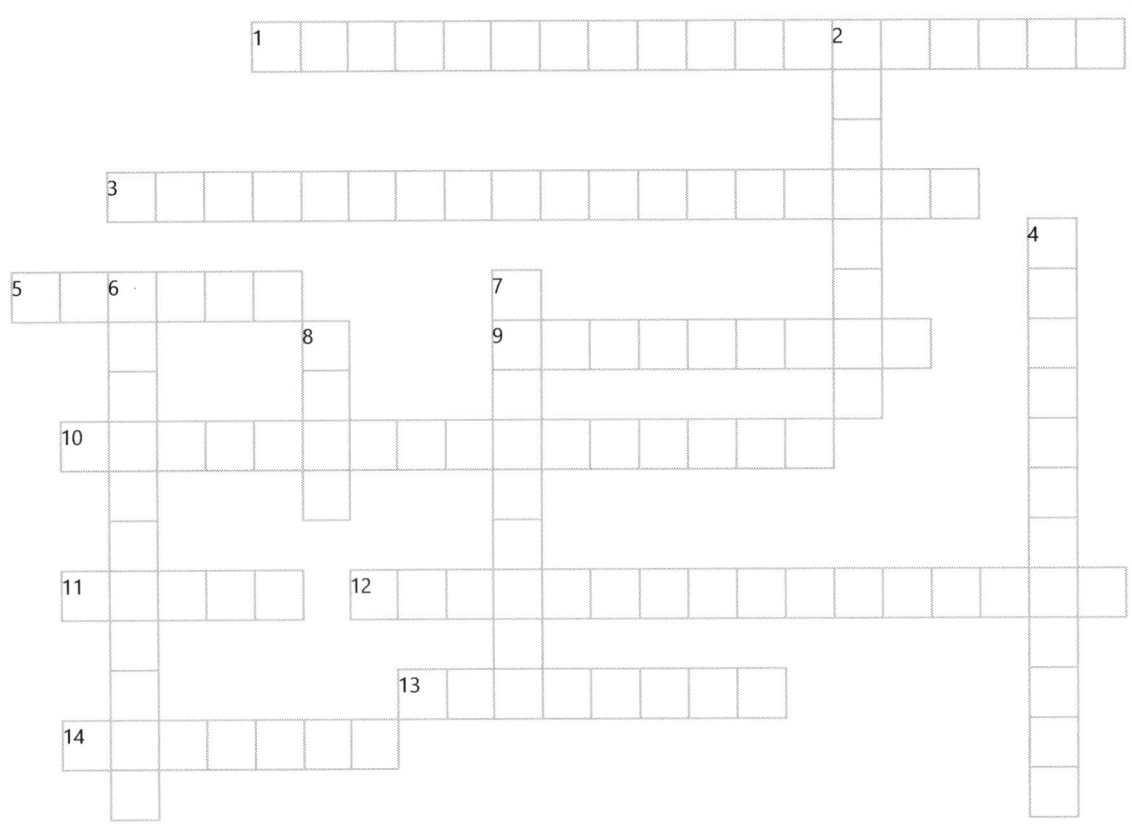

1. A procedure for determining how much of the variability among scores to attribute to a range of sources of variation.
3. Items are ordered, and every nth item is chosen to be included in the sample.
5. Tells how many standard deviations that value is from its population mean.
9. A bar graph used for quantitative variables.
10. The selection of participants in one sample is affected by the selection of participants in the other sample.
11. Any number of entities members considered as a unit.
12. Longer tail extends to the left
13. A circular chart divided into triangular areas proportional to the percentages of the whole.
14. As great, high, or intense as possible or permitted.

DOWN

2. The difference between actual score and predicted score.
4. A bias where people who have an interest in the outcome of an experiment have an incentive to use biased methods.
6. Relating to or included in a class or classes.
7. Relating to or denoting a statistical method assessing the goodness of fit between observed values and those expected theoretically.
8. The score or qualitative category that occurs with greatest frequency.

A. Chi square
B. Residual
C. Negatively skewed
D. Systematic Sampling
E. Self Interest
F. Mode
G. Z Score
H. Group
I. Analysis of variance
J. Pie chart
K. Categorical
L. Histogram
M. Maximum
N. Dependent samples

16.

ACROSS

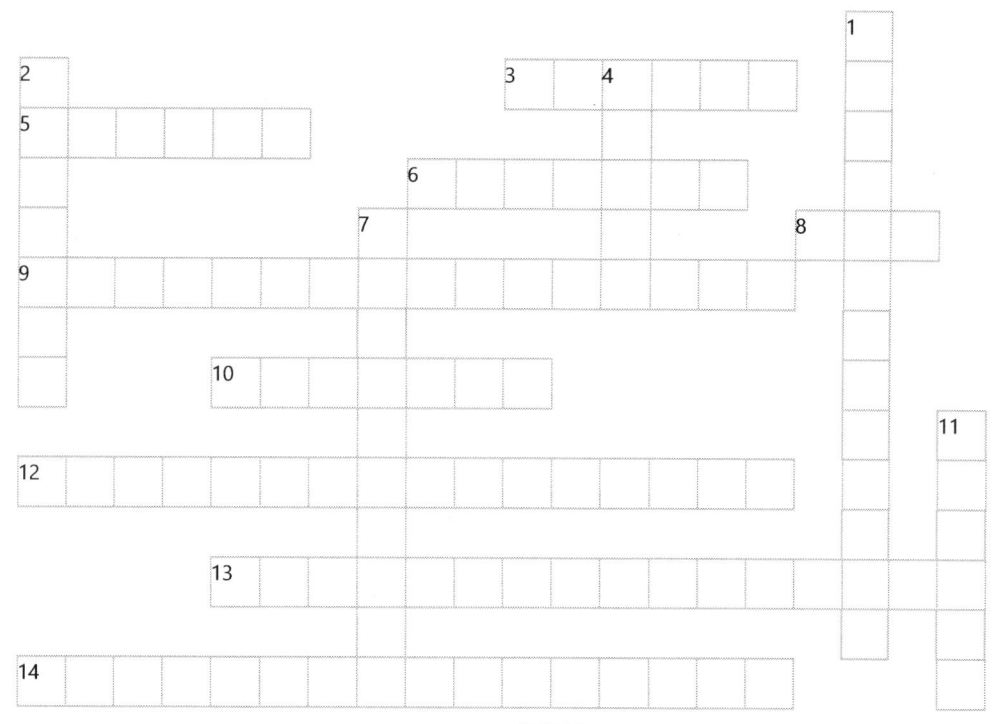

3. Make a detailed inspection of; for statistical purposes.
5. Made, done, happening, or chosen without method or conscious decision.
6. The number designating place in an ordered sequence.
8. A non-parametric measure of rank correlation.
9. Longer tail extends to the right
10. Bar graph that shows frequencies or relative frequencies in categories for more than one group frequencies within each category.
12. The selection of participants in one sample is affected by the selection of participants in the other sample.
13. Type of qualitative variable. Have no natural ordering.
14. Longer tail extends to the left

DOWN

1. Matching each participant in the experimental condition with a participant in the control condition.
2. Arranged into groups.
4. The difference between the largest and the smallest value.
7. Each of the 100 equal groups into which a population can be divided according to the distribution of values of a variable.
11. The collection of data from every member of the population.

A. Survey
B. Nominal Variables
C. Stacked
D. Grouped
E. ordinal
F. Dependent samples
G. Census
H. Percentile
I. Random
J. Negatively skewed
K. Positively skewed
L. Matched sample
M. Range
N. Rho

17.

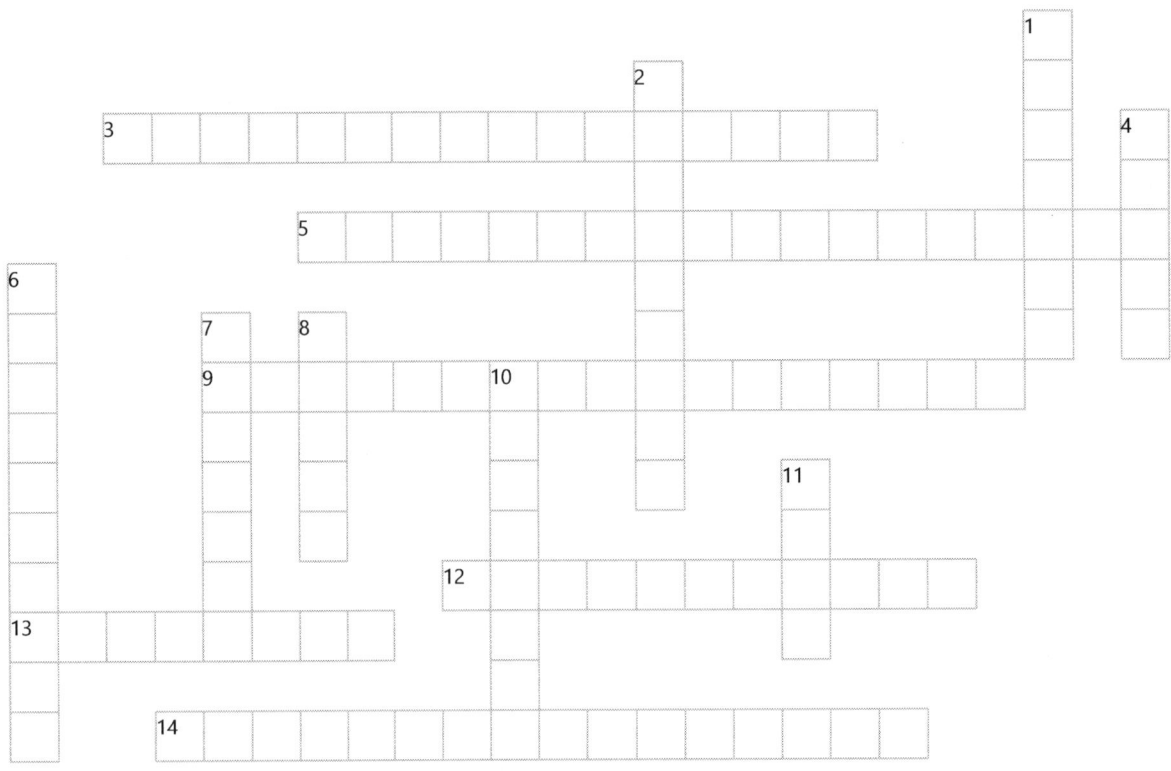

ACROSS
3. Type of quantitative variable whose possible values can be listed.
5. Items are ordered, and every nth item is chosen to be included in the sample.
9. A distribution that shows the proportion or percent frequency for each interval.
12. A type of study where two samples are drawn.
13. The selection of a suitable sample for study.
14. Longer tail extends to the right

DOWN
1. Scores that differ so markedly from the main body of data that their accuracy is questioned.
2. Graphical representation of frequency distribution for quantitative data. Rectangle for each class.
4. population standard deviation.
6. A supposition or proposed explanation based on limited evidence as a starting point for further investigation.
7. The number designating place in an ordered sequence.
8. Arrange or order by categories.
10. A characteristic that differs from one subject to the next.
11. The values of the variables that we obtain.

A. Sampling
B. Relative frequency
C. Data
D. Discrete Variable
E. Histogram
F. Case Control
G. Systematic Sampling
H. ordinal
I. Variable
J. Outlier
K. Sigma
L. Hypothesis
M. Positively skewed
N. Class

18.

ACROSS

1. The procedures applied to each experimental unit.
6. The selection of participants in one sample is not affected by the selection of participants in the other sample.
7. Its value is not affected much by extreme values in the data set.
8. A group.
9. Studies conducted by a procedure that produces the correct result on average.
11. The difference between the largest and the smallest value.
12. A number that represents the degree of association or strength of relationship between two variables.
14. Presented in a table that gives the frequency for each category.

DOWN

2. A line on a graph indicating a statistical trend.
3. The relationship between rankings of different ordinal variables.
4. A form with a set of queries to gain statistical information.
5. Intervals of equal width that cover all values observed in the data set.
10. Probability of a type II error.
13. An error retaining a false null hypothesis.

A. Correlation coefficient
B. Classes
C. Independent samples
D. Cohort
E. Rank Correlation
F. Unbiased
G. Type II
H. Trend line
I. Questionnaire
J. Frequency Distribution
K. Range
L. Beta
M. Treatments
N. Resistant Statistic

19.

ACROSS

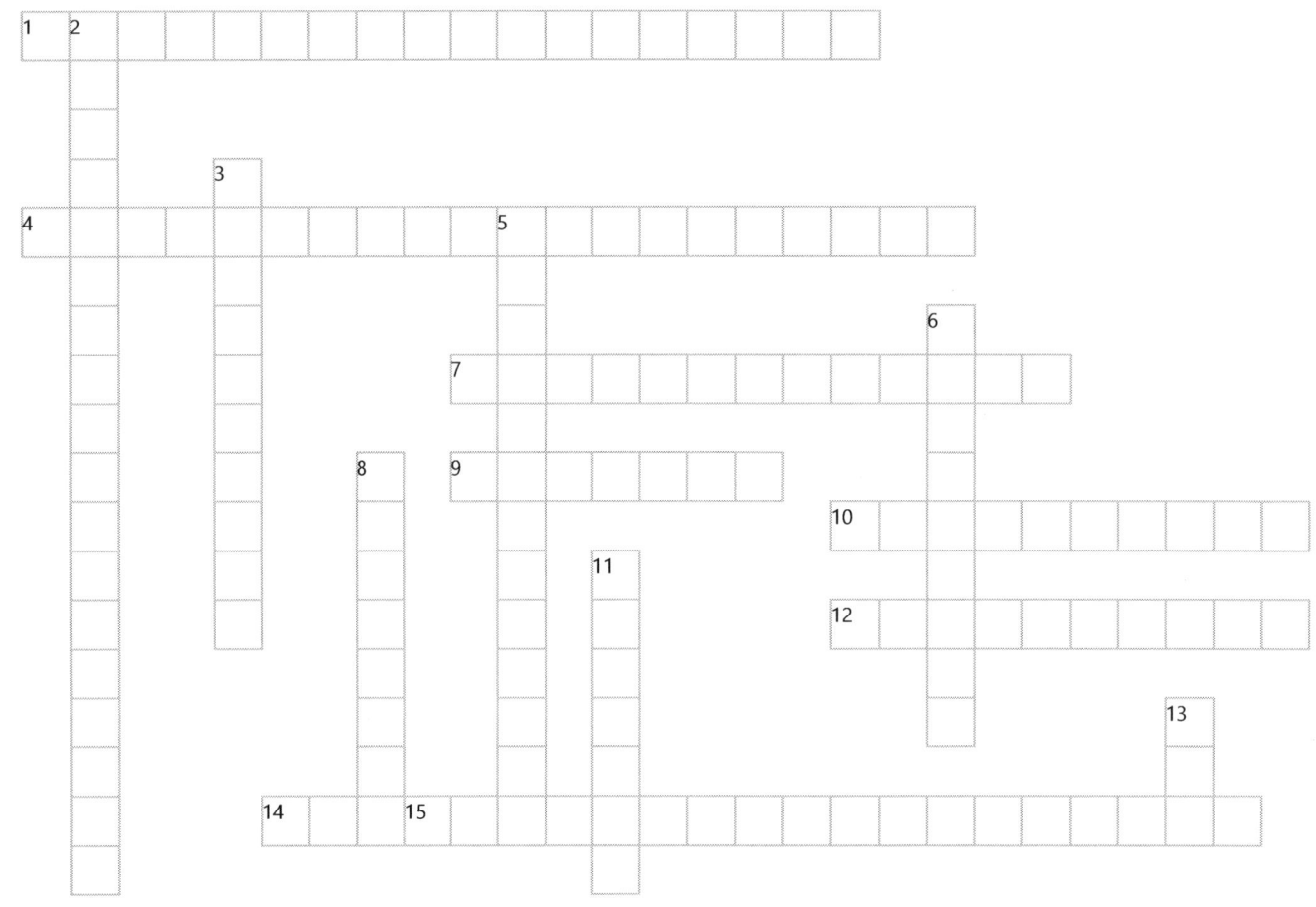

1. Found by subtracting the 1st quartile from the 3rd quartile. One method for detecting outliers.
4. The random variable is a statistic based on the results of more than one trial.
7. Calculation of the value of a function between known values.
9. As great, high, or intense as possible or permitted.
10. A part, share, or number considered in comparative relation to a whole.
12. Each of the 100 equal groups into which a population can be divided according to the distribution of values of a variable.
14. Presented in a table that gives the frequency for each category.

DOWN

2. A probability distribution that is unimodal and symmetrical.
3. The difference between consecutive lower class limits.
5. Expresses the value of a score relative to the mean and standard deviation of its distribution.
6. A bar graph used for quantitative variables.
8. Constituting a separate entity or part.
11. When the experimental units are people.
13. A non-parametric measure of rank correlation.
15. Semi interquartile range.

A. Standard score
B. Subject
C. Percentile
D. Proportion
E. Class Width
F. Maximum
G. Interquartile Range
H. Discrete
I. Frequency Distribution
J. Q
K. Histogram
L. Rho
M. Sampling distribution
N. Normal distribution
O. Interpolation

42

20.

ACROSS

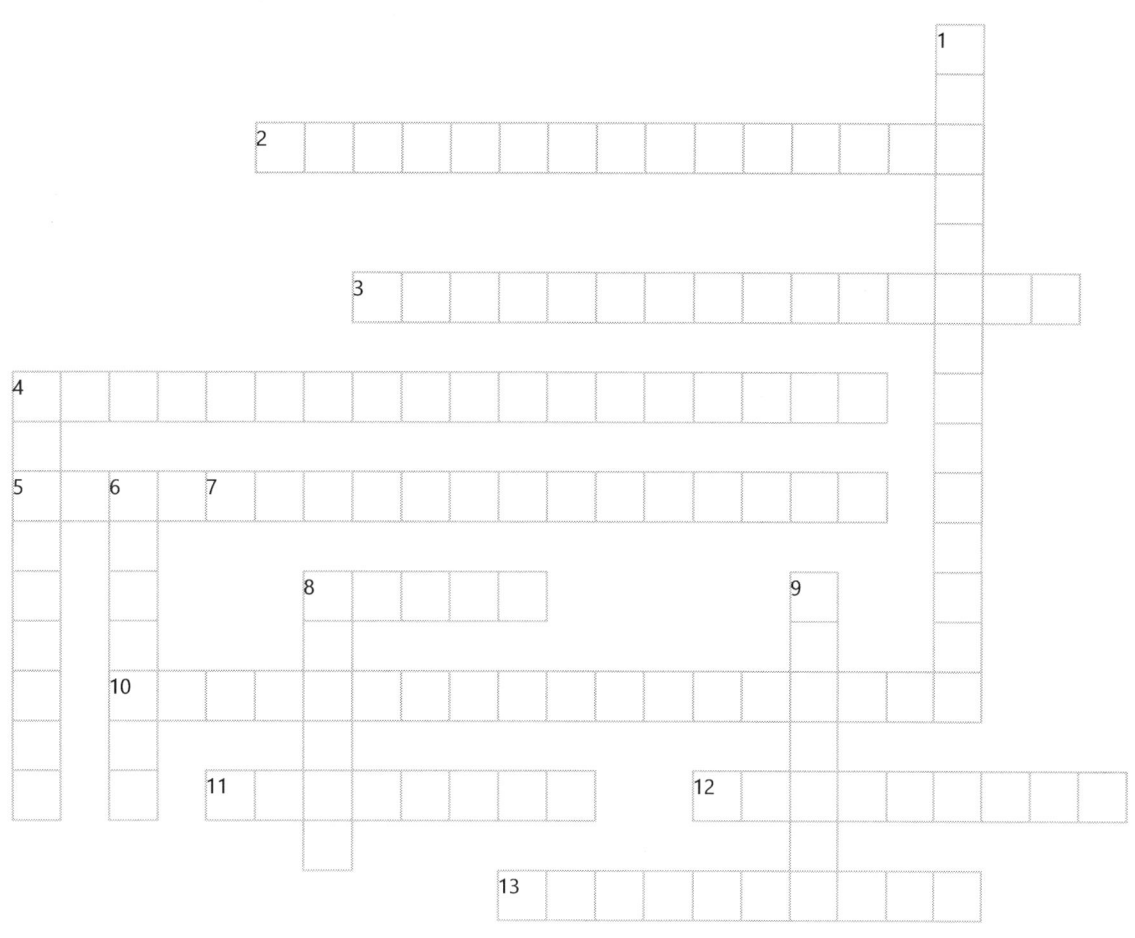

2. The relationship between rankings of different ordinal variables.
3. The largest value that can appear in that class.
4. A range of values so defined that there is a specified probability that the value of a parameter lies within it.
5. The selection of participants in one sample is not affected by the selection of participants in the other sample.
8. An error rejecting a true null hypothesis.
10. Items are ordered, and every nth item is chosen to be included in the sample.
11. Make or place alongside something.
12. The number of times a variable occurs in a data set.
13. Increasing by successive addition.

DOWN

1. The selection of a random sample.
4. Relating to or denoting a statistical method assessing the goodness of fit between observed values and those expected theoretically.
6. All of the information collected.
7. probability of a success.
8. Collection of propositions to illustrate the principles of a subject.
9. Come together and form a group or mass.

A. Cumulative
B. Data Set
C. Confidence interval
D. parallel
E. Rank Correlation
F. Chi square
G. Type I
H. P
I. Independent samples
J. Collect
K. random sampling
L. Frequency
M. Systematic Sampling
N. Upper Class Limit
O. Theory

21.

ACROSS

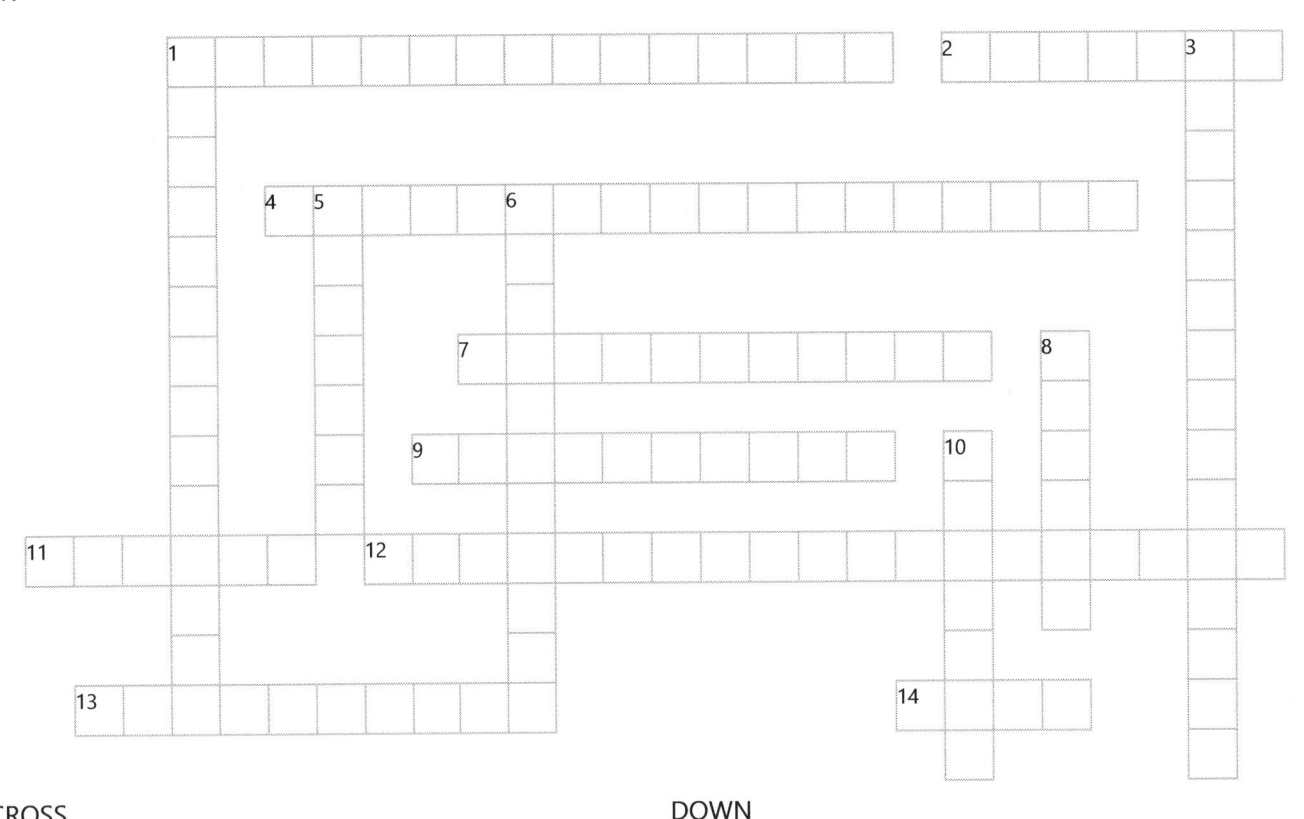

1. Population is divided into groups that are randomly sampled, and all the members of the selected from the sample.
2. As great, high, or intense as possible or permitted.
4. A range of values so defined that there is a specified probability that the value of a parameter lies within it.
7. The act of making and recording a measurement.
9. The procedures applied to each experimental unit.
11. Collection of propositions to illustrate the principles of a subject.
12. Classify individuals into categories.
13. Histogram with single mode the near center of the data and are approximately symmetric.
14. A measure of center in a data set.

DOWN

1. Type of cohort where measurements are taken at one point in time.
3. The largest value that can appear in that class.
5. Scores that differ so markedly from the main body of data that their accuracy is questioned.
6. An experiment where neither the investigator nor the subjects know who has been assigned to which treatment.
8. An error retaining a false null hypothesis.
10. Intervals of equal width that cover all values observed in the data set.

- A. Theory
- B. Cluster Sampling
- C. Mean
- D. Maximum
- E. Confidence interval
- F. Bell Shaped
- G. Treatments
- H. Cross Sectional
- I. Double Blind
- J. Upper Class Limit
- K. Outlier
- L. Type II
- M. Observation
- N. Qualitative Variable
- O. Classes

22.

ACROSS

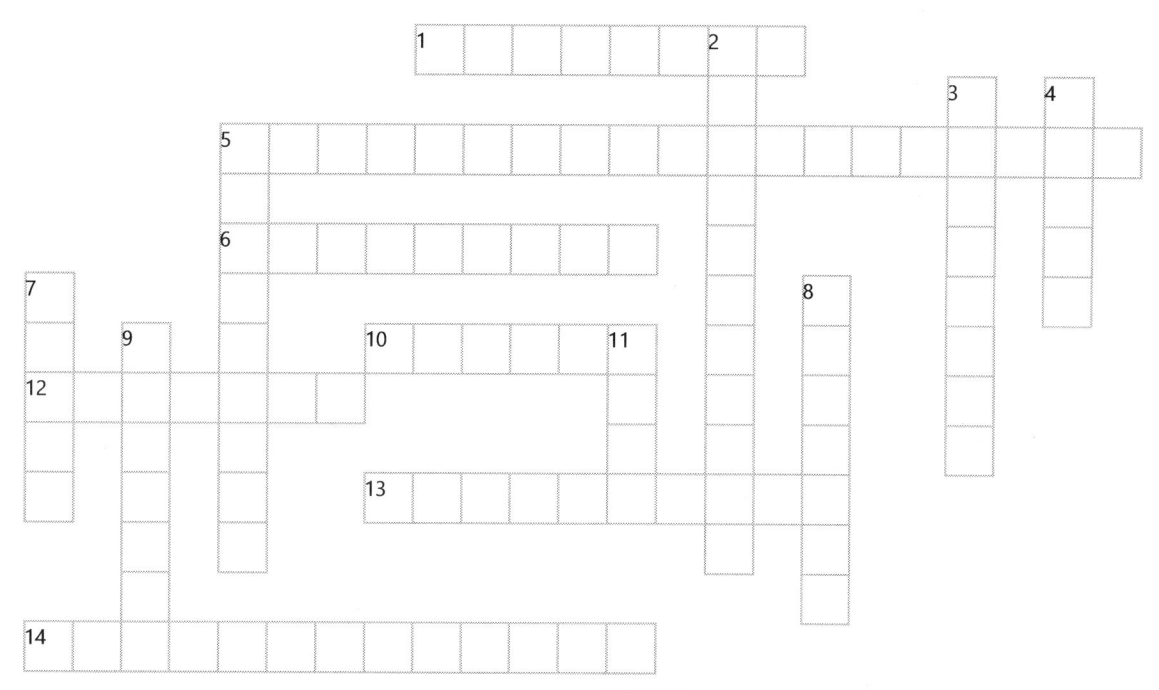

1. A measure of how far the values in a data set are from the mean, on the average.
5. A value that does not depend on changes in other values.
6. A line on a graph indicating a statistical trend.
10. Made, done, happening, or chosen without method or conscious decision.
12. Arranged into groups.
13. A proportion in relation to a whole.
14. Calculation of the value of a function between known values.

DOWN

2. Relating to or included in a class or classes.
3. Make or place alongside something.
4. Arrange or order by categories.
5. Explain the meaning of information, words, or actions.
7. population standard deviation.
8. When the experimental units are people.
9. Come together and form a group or mass.
11. A measure of center in a data set.

A. Collect
D. Grouped
G. Sigma
J. Trend line
M. Class

B. Independent variable
E. Interpolation
H. percentage
K. Variance
N. parallel

C. Categorical
F. Subject
I. Random
L. Mean
O. Interpret

23.

ACROSS

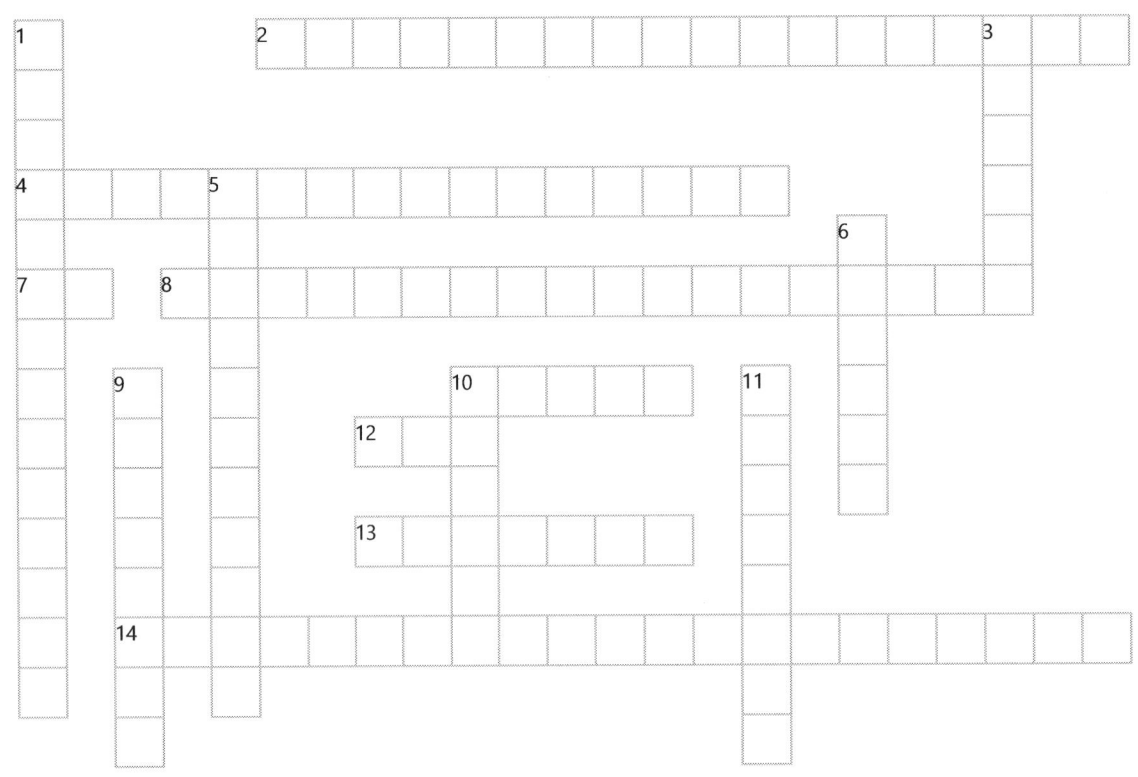

2. A sample is chosen by a method such that every member of the population is equally likely to be selected.
4. The selection of participants in one sample is affected by the selection of participants in the other sample.
7. Population mean.
8. A procedure for determining how much of the variability among scores to attribute to a range of sources of variation.
10. Arrange or order by categories.
12. A non-parametric measure of rank correlation.
13. Arranged into groups.
14. Numerical and graphical summaries of data.

DOWN

1. The selection of a random sample.
3. The probability of obtaining a value of the test statistic equal to or more extreme than that observed.
5. A response where the opinions of non-responders tend to differ from the opinions of those who do respond.
6. A subset of a population.
9. Only one mode.
10. A group.
11. A circular chart divided into triangular areas proportional to the percentages of the whole.

A. Rho
B. Unimodal
C. Class
D. Pie chart
E. Grouped
F. Dependent samples
G. Sample
H. Cohort
I. Simple Random Sample
J. Non response
K. random sampling
L. Analysis of variance
M. P value
N. Mu
O. Descriptive Statistics

24.

ACROSS

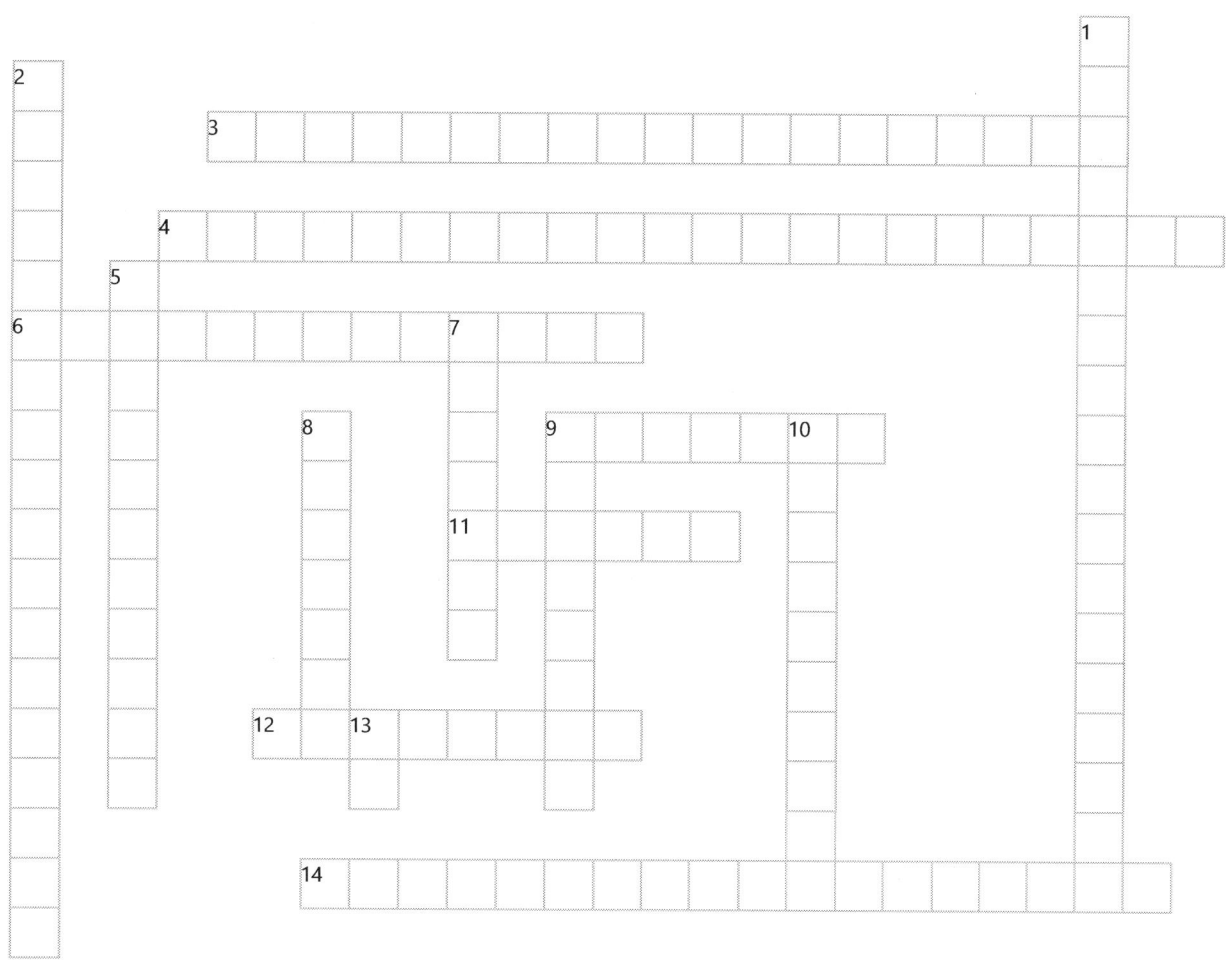

3. Classify individuals into categories.
4. A number that represents the degree of association or strength of relationship between two variables.
6. Expresses the value of a score relative to the mean and standard deviation of its distribution.
9. Come together and form a group or mass.
11. A subset of a population.
12. The selection of a suitable sample for study.
14. The population is divided into subpopulations and random samples are taken of each stratum.

DOWN

1. Distributions that are asymmetrical.
2. A procedure for determining how much of the variability among scores to attribute to a range of sources of variation.
5. Relating to or included in a class or classes.
7. Intervals of equal width that cover all values observed in the data set.
8. Actual measurements or observations collected from the sample.
9. Put or add together.
10. Extending without break or irregularity.
13. Population mean.

A. Correlation coefficient
B. Classes
C. Collect
D. Sample
E. Analysis of variance
F. Standard score
G. Stratified sampling
H. Raw data
I. Skewed distribution
J. Qualitative Variable
K. Sampling
L. Continuous
M. Mu
N. Categorical
O. Compound

25.

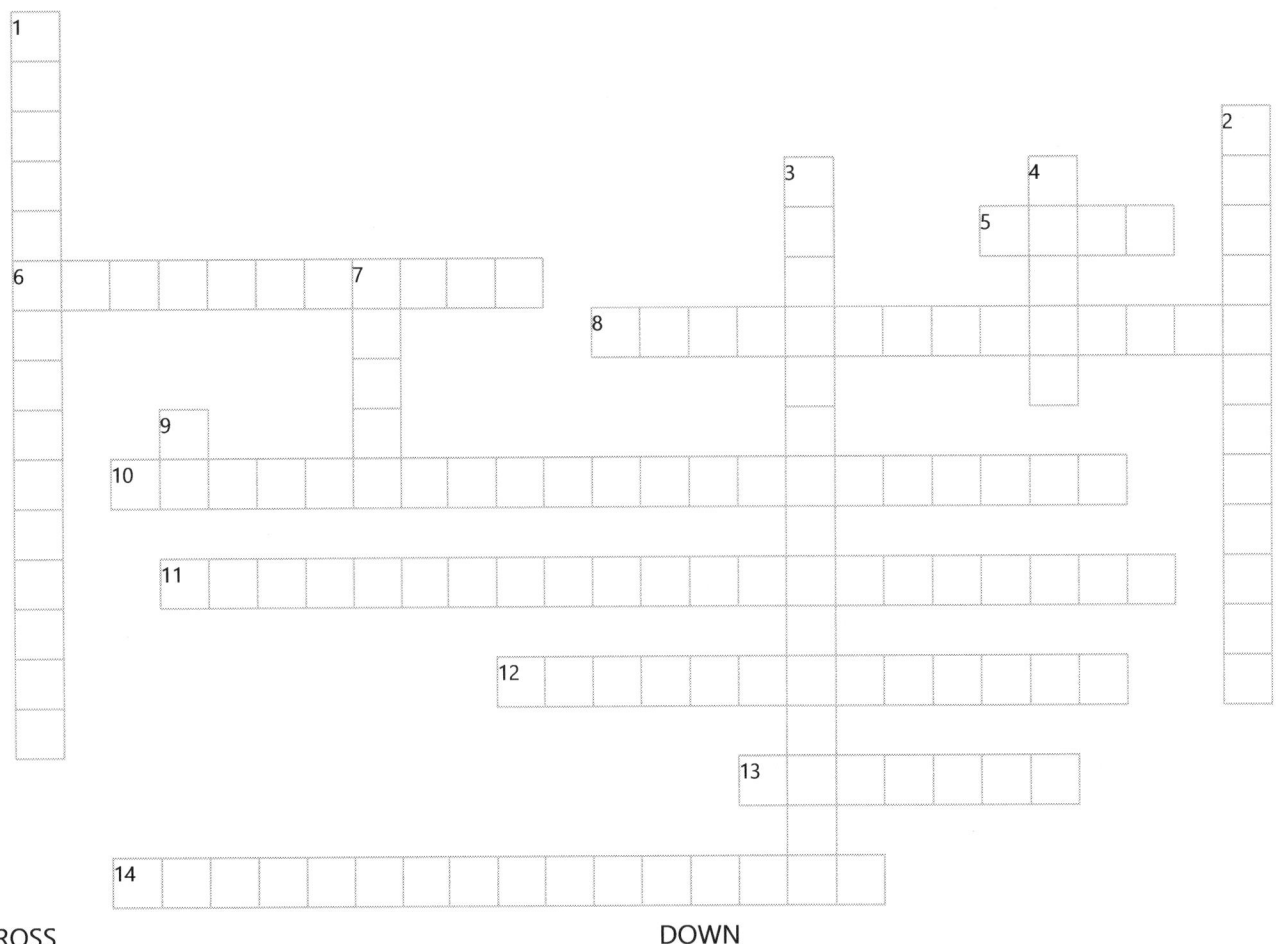

ACROSS
5. The values of the variables that we obtain.
6. Group of subjects is studied to determine whether various factors of interest are associated with an outcome.
8. Type of cohort where measurements are taken at one point in time.
10. Tells how much or many of something there is.
11. Drawing inferences from sample data to a population.
12. Type of cohort study where subjects are sampled after the outcome has occurred.
13. The least or smallest amount or quantity possible, attainable, or required.
14. A study in which the assignment of participants to treatment levels is completely random.

DOWN
1. The largest value that can appear in that class.
2. Occurs when some members in the population are more likely to be included in the sample than others.
3. Population is divided into groups that are randomly sampled, and all the members of the selected from the sample.
4. The quantitative relation between two amounts showing the number of times one value contains or is contained within the other.
7. An error rejecting a true null hypothesis.
9. Degrees of freedom.
10. Semi interquartile range.

A. Minimum
B. Sampling Bias
C. Inferential Statistics
D. Cohort Study
E. Ratio
F. Q
G. Cross Sectional
H. Quantitative Variables
I. Upper Class Limit
J. Retrospective
K. Nu
L. Type I
M. Randomized design
N. Cluster Sampling
O. Data

1.

			¹D	E	S	C	R	I	P	T	I	V	E	S	T	A	T	I	S	²T	I	C	S

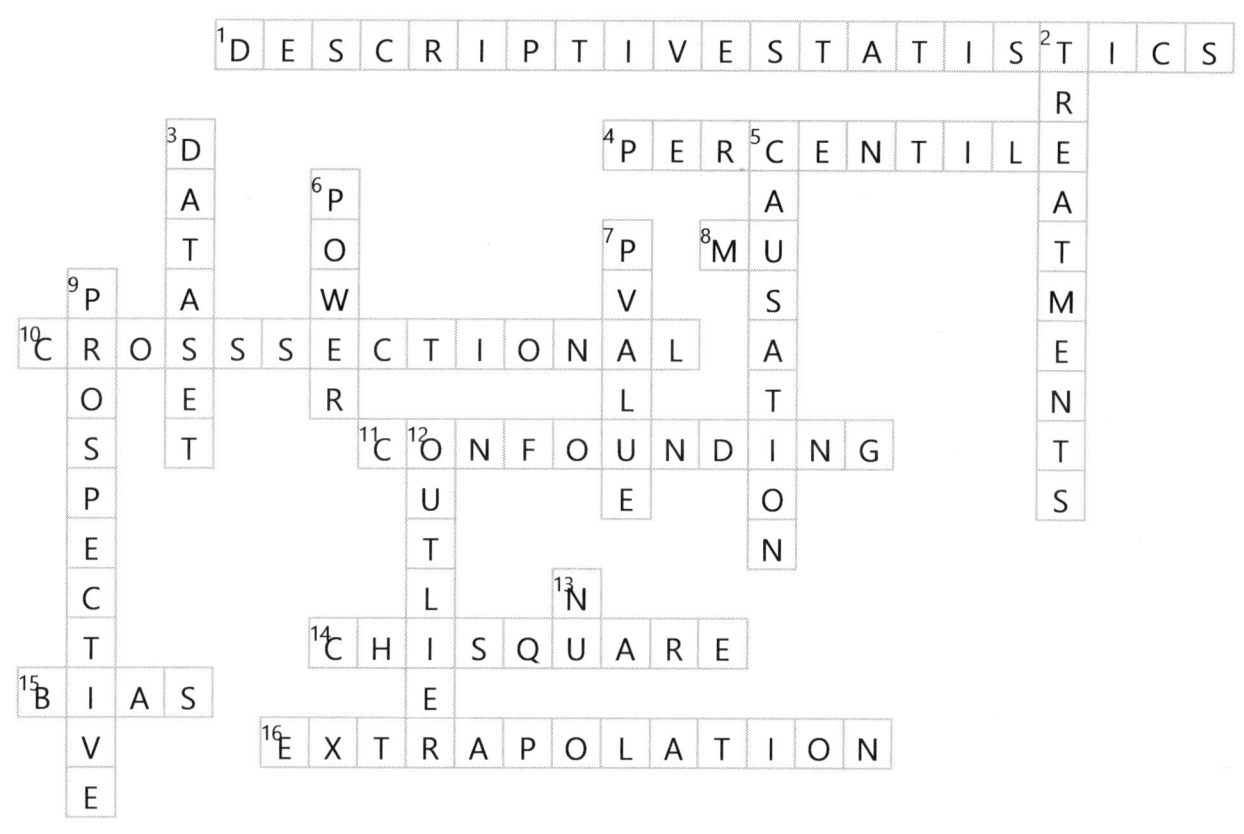

(Crossword puzzle with the following filled answers)

ACROSS
1. Numerical and graphical summaries of data.
4. Each of the 100 equal groups into which a population can be divided according to the distribution of values of a variable.
8. Population mean.
10. Type of cohort where measurements are taken at one point in time.
11. Cause surprise or confusion, especially by acting against an expectation.
14. Relating to or denoting a statistical method assessing the goodness of fit between observed values and those expected theoretically.
15. Any problem in the design or conduct of a statistical study that tends to favor certain results.
16. Calculating a value outside the range of known values.

DOWN
2. The procedures applied to each experimental unit.
3. All of the information collected.
5. The act of making something happen.
6. The probability of correctly rejecting the null hypothesis.
7. The probability of obtaining a value of the test statistic equal to or more extreme than that observed.
9. Type of cohort study where the subjects are followed over time.
12. Scores that differ so markedly from the main body of data that their accuracy is questioned.
13. Degrees of freedom.

A. Bias
B. Outlier
C. Descriptive Statistics
D. Power
E. Cross Sectional
F. Data Set
G. Extrapolation
H. Prospective
I. Nu
J. Mu
K. Causation
L. Chi square
M. Percentile
N. Treatments
O. P value
P. Confounding

Answers filled in puzzle:
1 Across: DESCRIPTIVE STATISTICS
4 Across: PERCENTILE
8 Across: MU
10 Across: CROSS SECTIONAL
11 Across: CONFOUNDING
14 Across: CHI SQUARE
15 Across: BIAS
16 Across: EXTRAPOLATION
2 Down: TREATMENTS
3 Down: DATA SET
5 Down: CAUSATION
6 Down: POWER
7 Down: P VALUE
9 Down: PROSPECTIVE
12 Down: OUTLIER
13 Down: NU

49

2.

```
        ¹S U B J E C T                          ²P
         T                                       E
  ³B I V A R I A T E        ⁴R A N K C O R R E L A T ⁵I O N
  I      N                                C           N
  M      D            ⁶C ⁷H I S Q U A R E E           T
  O   ⁸R A N D O M      Y                 N           E
  D      R              P                 T           R
  A      D              O    ⁹G      ¹⁰T  A           V
  L      D          ¹¹C L U S T E R S A M P L I N G   A
         E              H    O           M     E     L
         V              E    U           E
         I              S    P      ¹²C A U S A T I O N
         A              I               E
         T              S          ¹³C O H O R T S T U D Y
         I                              I
       ¹⁴O R D I N A L V A R I A B L E S
         N                              S
```

ACROSS

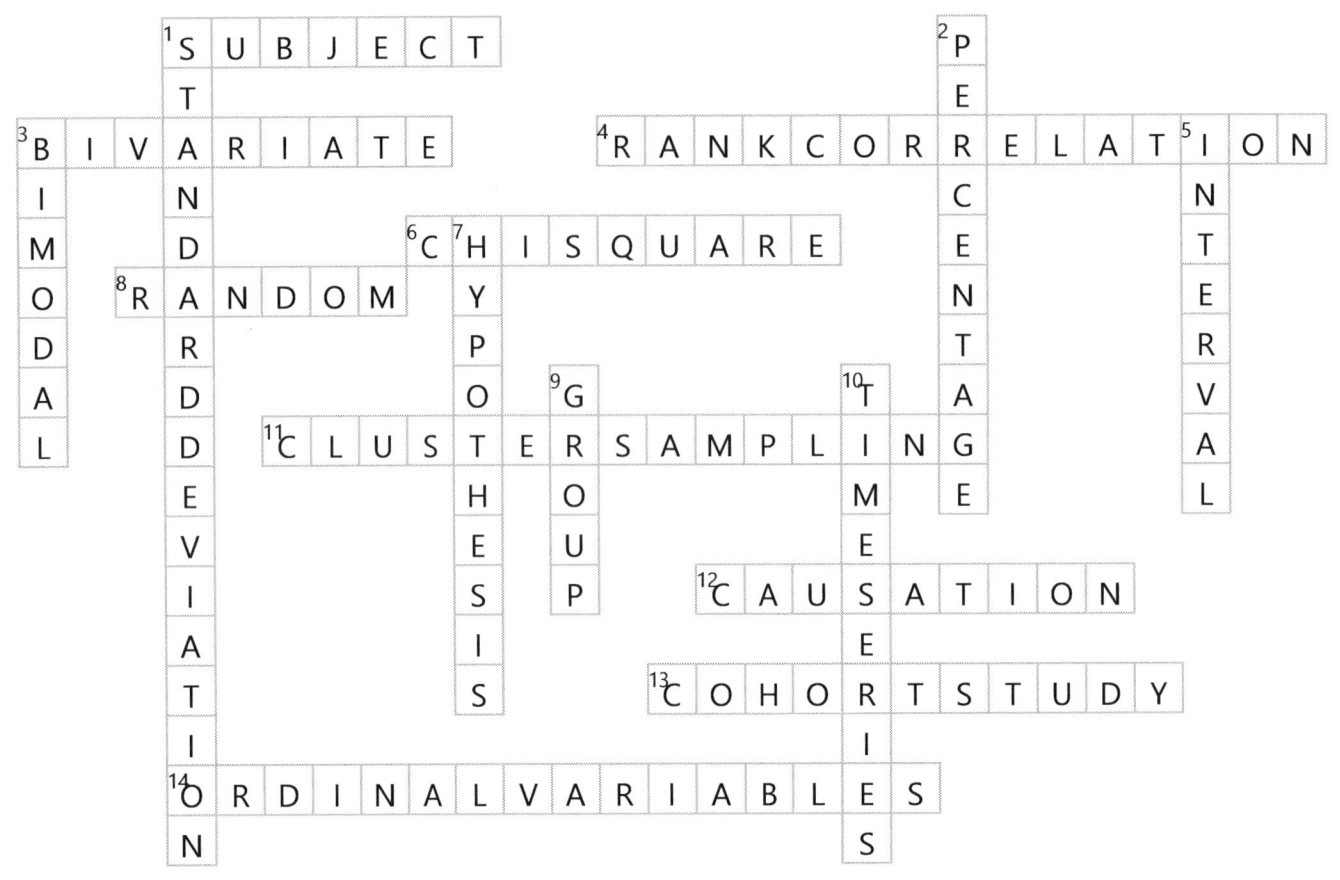

1. When the experimental units are people.
3. Having two variables.
4. The relationship between rankings of different ordinal variables.
6. Relating to or denoting a statistical method assessing the goodness of fit between observed values and those expected theoretically.
8. Made, done, happening, or chosen without method or conscious decision.
11. Population is divided into groups that are randomly sampled, and all the members of the selected from the sample.
12. The act of making something happen.
13. Group of subjects is studied to determine whether various factors of interest are associated with an outcome.
14. Type of qualitative variable. Have a natural ordering, but have no mathematically value.

DOWN

1. The square root of the variance.
2. A proportion in relation to a whole.
3. Two clearly distinct modes.
5. A set containing all points between two given endpoints.
7. A supposition or proposed explanation based on limited evidence as a starting point for further investigation.
9. Any number of entities members considered as a unit.
10. A series of values of a variable at successive times.

A. Causation
E. percentage
I. Time series
M. Rank Correlation

B. Subject
F. Chi square
J. Standard Deviation
N. Bivariate

C. Group
G. Bimodal
K. Hypothesis
O. Random

D. Cohort Study
H. Cluster Sampling
L. Interval
P. Ordinal Variables

50

3.

			¹M	A	T	²H	E	D	S	A	M	P	L	E			³U	N	⁴B	I	A	S	E	D
						I													I					
						S					⁵C	H	I	⁶S	Q	U	A	R	E					
						T								A					S					
⁷P			⁸P	R	O	S	P	E	⁹C	T	I	V	E											
R						O			O					M								¹⁰I		
O						G		¹¹R	A	N	K	C	O	R	R	E	L	A	T	I	O	N		
P						R			T					E								T		
O						A		¹²U	N	I	M	O	D	A	L		¹³M					E		
¹⁴G	R	O	U	P	E	D			N								O					R		
T									U								D					P		
I			¹⁵A	N	A	L	Y	S	I	S	O	F	V	A	R	I	A	N	C	E		R		
O									U													E		
¹⁶I	N	F	E	R	E	N	T	I	A	L	S	T	A	T	I	S	T	I	C	S		T		

ACROSS

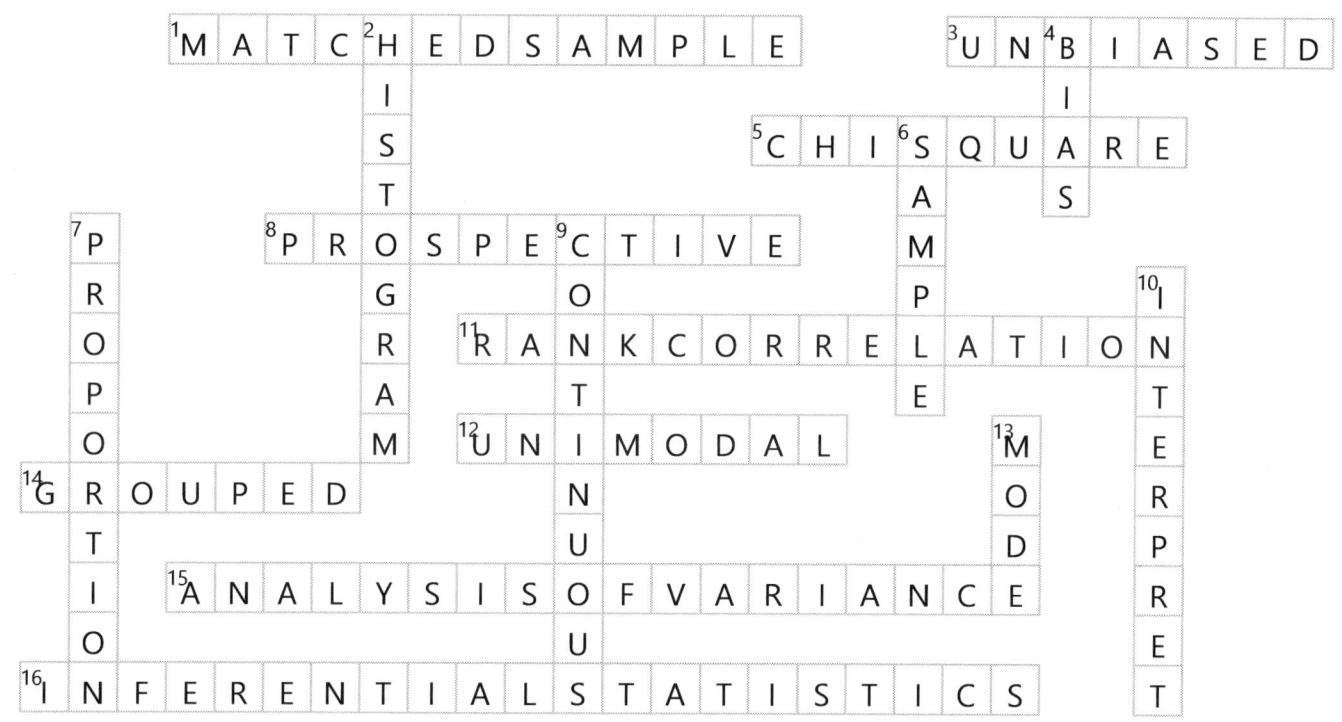

1. Matching each participant in the experimental condition with a participant in the control condition.
3. Studies conducted by a procedure that produces the correct result on average.
5. Relating to or denoting a statistical method assessing the goodness of fit between observed values and those expected theoretically.
8. Type of cohort study where the subjects are followed over time.
11. The relationship between rankings of different ordinal variables.
12. Only one mode.
14. Arranged into groups.
15. A procedure for determining how much of the variability among scores to attribute to a range of sources of variation.
16. Drawing inferences from sample data to a population.

DOWN

2. Graphical representation of frequency distribution for quantitative data. Rectangle for each class.
4. Any problem in the design or conduct of a statistical study that tends to favor certain results.
6. A subset of a population.
7. A part, share, or number considered in comparative relation to a whole.
9. Extending without break or irregularity.
10. Explain the meaning of information, words, or actions.
13. The score or qualitative category that occurs with greatest frequency.

A. Interpret
B. Matched sample
C. Mode
D. Chi square
E. Proportion
F. Rank Correlation
G. Inferential Statistics
H. Analysis of variance
I. Histogram
J. Grouped
K. Sample
L. Unimodal
M. Unbiased
N. Continuous
O. Bias
P. Prospective

4.

```
 1D E P E N D E N 2T V A R I A B L E
                 H
             3P A R A L L E L
                 O       4C       5M
 6P       7P 8O W E R    O        A           10S
  E        R      Y   9A L P H A  X            U
  R        D      O               I            U
  C      11F I V E N U 12M B E R S U M M A R Y
  E        N      U                U           V
13U N I M O D A L                  S           M    E
  T        L           14Q U A R T I L E       Y
  I                      U
  L      15S A M P L I N G D I S T R I B U T I O N
  E                      Y
```

ACROSS

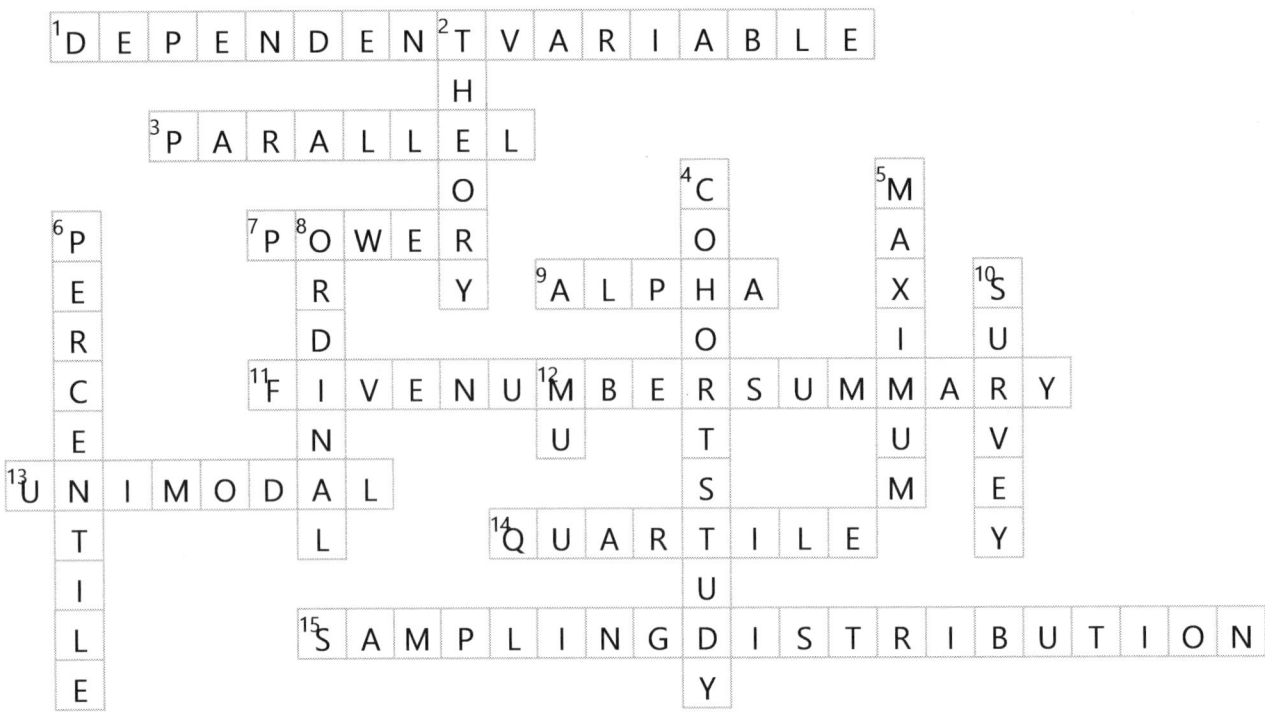

1. A quantity whose value depends on another quantity.
3. Make or place alongside something.
7. The probability of correctly rejecting the null hypothesis.
9. Significance level; probability of a type I error.
11. Minimum, 1st Quartile, Median, 3rd Quartile, Maximum.
13. Only one mode.
14. Each of four equal groups into which a population can be divided according to the distribution of values of a variable.
15. The random variable is a statistic based on the results of more than one trial.

DOWN

2. Collection of propositions to illustrate the principles of a subject.
4. Group of subjects is studied to determine whether various factors of interest are associated with an outcome.
5. As great, high, or intense as possible or permitted.
6. Each of the 100 equal groups into which a population can be divided according to the distribution of values of a variable.
8. The number designating place in an ordered sequence.
10. Make a detailed inspection of; for statistical purposes.
12. Population mean.

A. parallel
D. Theory
G. Survey
J. Five Number Summary
M. Unimodal

B. Cohort Study
E. Alpha
H. Mu
K. Power
N. Maximum

C. Quartile
F. Dependent variable
I. Sampling distribution
L. ordinal
O. Percentile

5.

```
                                            ¹Q
                                             U
                                         ²C  U  M  U  L  A  T  I  V  E
                                             R
                        ³C  L  A  S  S  E  S  T
                            R                  I
                     ⁴Q U A N T I T A T I V E V A R I A B L E S
                   ⁵P        T                       E
                    R    ⁶P  I
                    O  ⁷R A N K C O ⁸R R E L A T I O N
                    P    R    A    A                        ⁹R
                    O    A    L  ¹⁰N E G A T I V E L Y S K E W E D
                    R    L    R    G                        S
                    T    L    E    E                        I
        ¹¹U N B I A S E D    G                              D
                    O        L                              U
                    N       ¹²D O T                         A
                             N                ¹³B O X P L O T
```

ACROSS

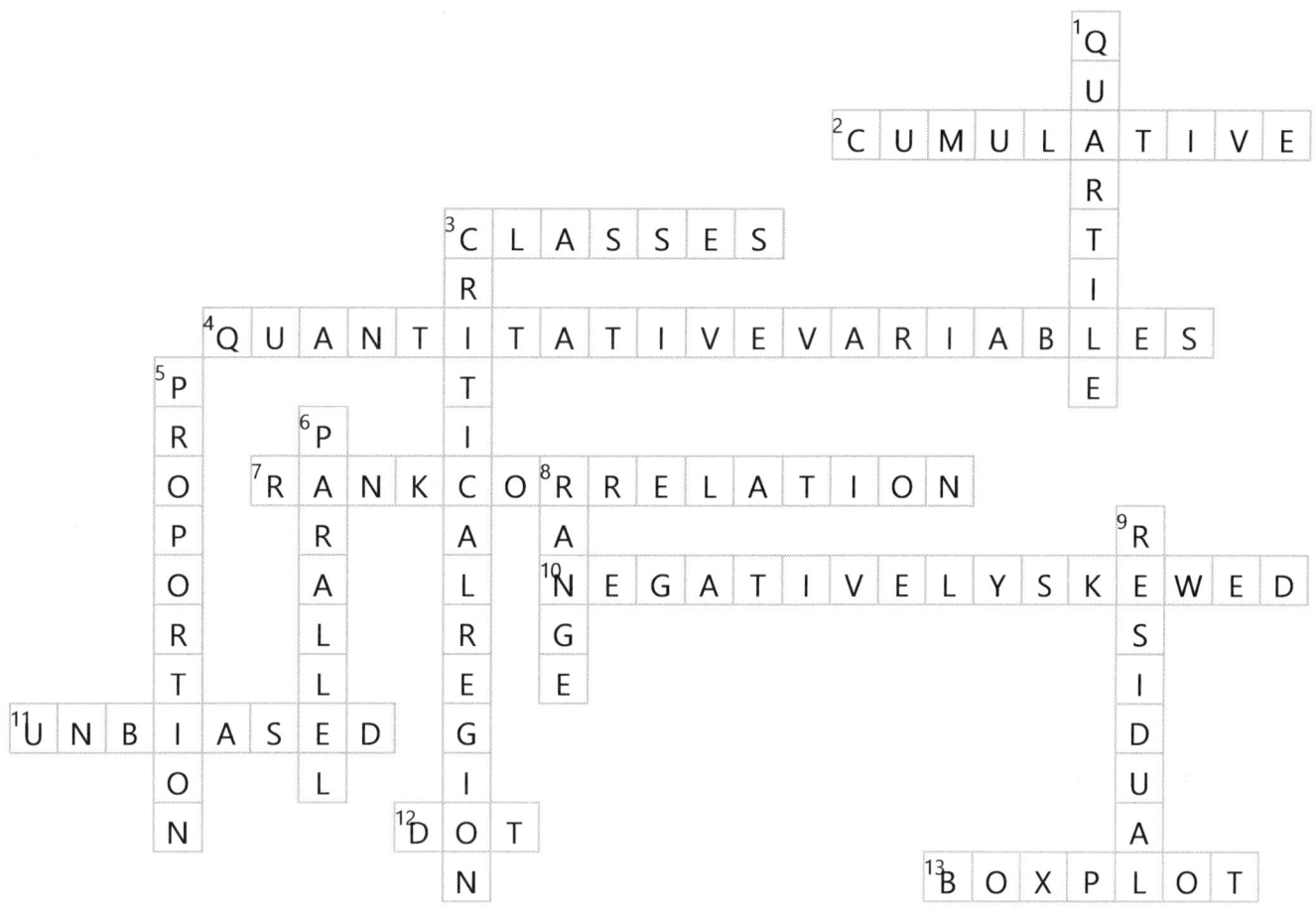

2. Increasing by successive addition.
3. Intervals of equal width that cover all values observed in the data set.
4. Tells how much or many of something there is.
7. The relationship between rankings of different ordinal variables.
10. Longer tail extends to the left
11. Studies conducted by a procedure that produces the correct result on average.
12. A very small circular shape.
13. A graphic way to display the median, quartiles, and extremes of a data set on a number line to show the distribution of the data.

DOWN

1. Each of four equal groups into which a population can be divided according to the distribution of values of a variable.
3. The region for rejecting the null hypothesis.
4. Semi interquartile range.
5. A part, share, or number considered in comparative relation to a whole.
6. Make or place alongside something.
8. The difference between the largest and the smallest value.
9. The difference between actual score and predicted score.

A. Critical region
B. Rank Correlation
C. Dot
D. Boxplot
E. Q
F. Negatively skewed
G. Quantitative Variables
H. Cumulative
I. Quartile
J. Proportion
K. Residual
L. Unbiased
M. parallel
N. Classes
O. Range

53

6.

																		¹P		
															²S	T	A	C	K	E	D
		³C																R		
		O										⁴F	R	E	Q	U	E	N	C	Y
		H																E		
		O				⁵S	K	E	W	E	⁶D	D	I	S	T	R	I	B	U	T	I	O	N
		R		⁷P							A							T		
		T		O			⁸M		T							⁹R	A	T	I	O
		S		P		¹⁰C	A	U	S	A	¹¹T	I	O	N		¹²S		L		
		T		U			X		Y							U		E		
	¹³D	O	U	B	L	E	B	L	I	N	D					B				
		D		A			M		E							J				
		Y		T			U		¹⁴T	I	M	E	S	E	R	I	E	S		
				I			M		I							C				
				O												T				
¹⁵S	A	M	P	L	I	N	G	D	I	S	T	R	I	B	U	T	I	O	N	

ACROSS

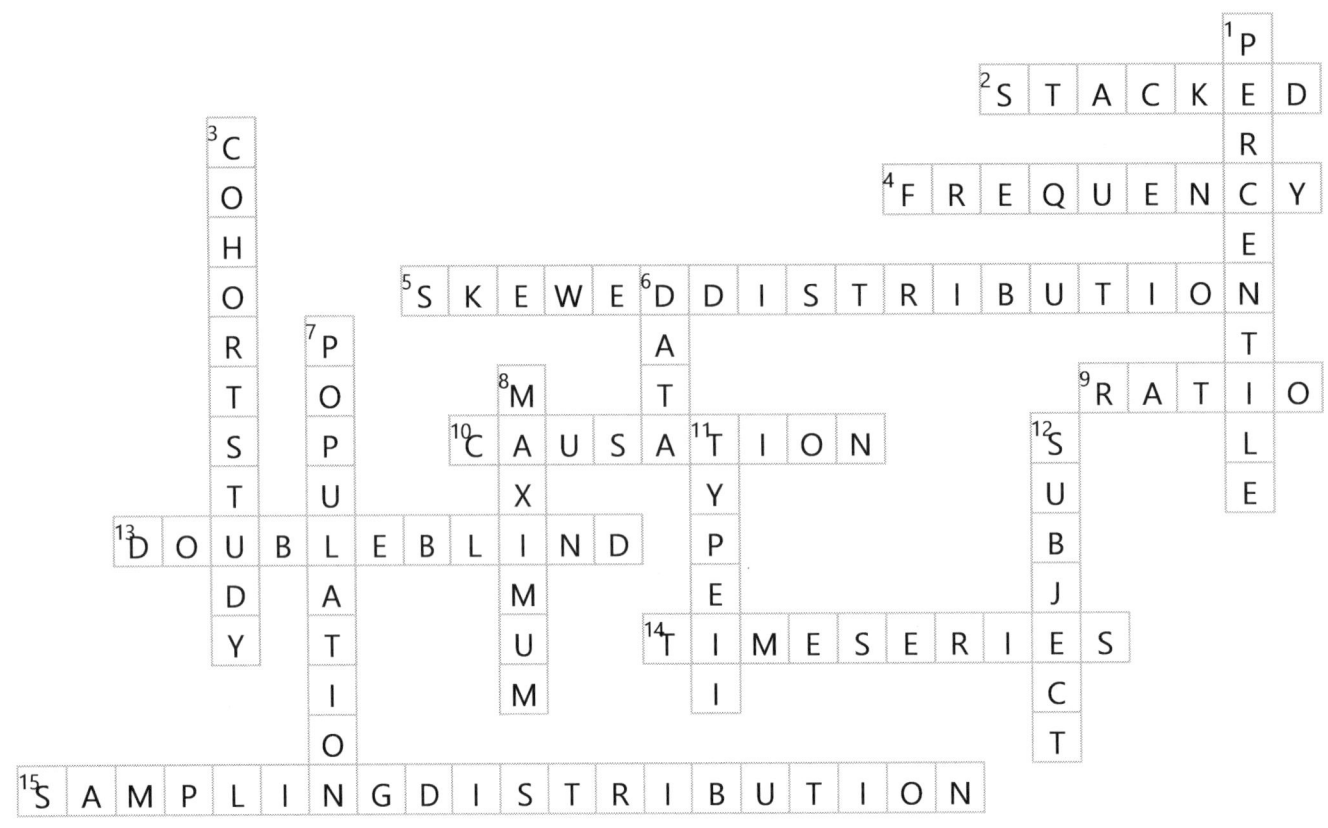

2. Bar graph that shows frequencies or relative frequencies in categories for more than one group frequencies within each category.
4. The number of times a variable occurs in a data set.
5. Distributions that are asymmetrical.
9. The quantitative relation between two amounts showing the number of times one value contains or is contained within the other.
10. The act of making something happen.
13. An experiment where neither the investigator nor the subjects know who has been assigned to which treatment.
14. A series of values of a variable at successive times.
15. The random variable is a statistic based on the results of more than one trial.

DOWN

1. Each of the 100 equal groups into which a population can be divided according to the distribution of values of a variable.
3. Group of subjects is studied to determine whether various factors of interest are associated with an outcome.
6. The values of the variables that we obtain.
7. The collection of all people, objects, or events having one or more specified characteristics.
8. As great, high, or intense as possible or permitted.
11. An error retaining a false null hypothesis.
12. When the experimental units are people.

- A. Double Blind
- B. Cohort Study
- C. Type II
- D. Population
- E. Sampling distribution
- F. Maximum
- G. Percentile
- H. Time series
- I. Ratio
- J. Subject
- K. Stacked
- L. Frequency
- M. Data
- N. Skewed distribution
- O. Causation

7.

			¹B	²O	X	P	L	O	T									
				P						³N	O	N	R	E	S	P	O	N	S	⁴E
				E															X
			⁵N	O	M	I	N	A	L	V	A	R	I	A	B	L	E	S	T
				E															R
				N			⁸S						⁶R	A	W	D	A	T	A
⁷P			D																P
⁹I	N	T	E	R	¹⁰Q	U	A	R	T	I	L	E	R	A	N	G	E	O
E			D			R													L
C			C			V			¹¹S										A
H			L			E			T										T
A			A	¹²S	Y	S	T	E	M	A	T	I	C	S	A	M	P	L	I	N	G
R			S						C										O
T		¹³Z	S	C	O	R	E			K			¹⁴F	R	E	Q	U	E	N	C	Y
			E						E										
¹⁵B	E	L	L	S	H	A	P	E	D										

ACROSS

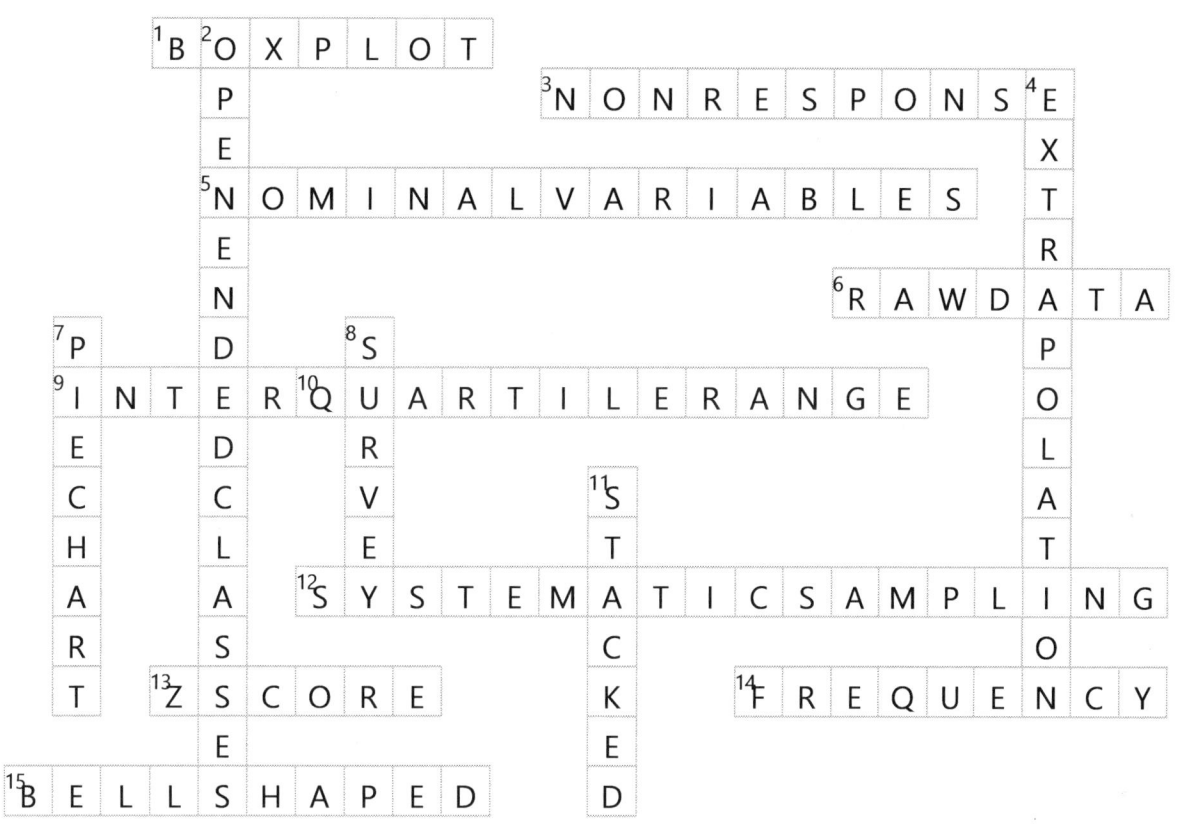

1. A graphic way to display the median, quartiles, and extremes of a data set on a number line to show the distribution of the data.
3. A response where the opinions of non-responders tend to differ from the opinions of those who do respond.
5. Type of qualitative variable. Have no natural ordering.
6. Actual measurements or observations collected from the sample.
9. Found by subtracting the 1st quartile from the 3rd quartile. One method for detecting outliers.
12. Items are ordered, and every nth item is chosen to be included in the sample.
13. Tells how many standard deviations that value is from its population mean.
14. The number of times a variable occurs in a data set.
15. Histogram with single mode the near center of the data and are approximately symmetric.

DOWN

2. When the first class has no lower limit, or the last class has no upper limit.
4. Calculating a value outside the range of known values.
7. A circular chart divided into triangular areas proportional to the percentages of the whole.
8. Make a detailed inspection of; for statistical purposes.
10. Semi interquartile range.
11. Bar graph that shows frequencies or relative frequencies in categories for more than one group frequencies within each category.

A. Pie chart
D. Extrapolation
G. Non response
J. Boxplot
M. Nominal Variables
B. Systematic Sampling
E. Bell Shaped
H. Stacked
K. Raw data
N. Open Ended Classes
C. Q
F. Interquartile Range
I. Z Score
L. Survey
O. Frequency

8.

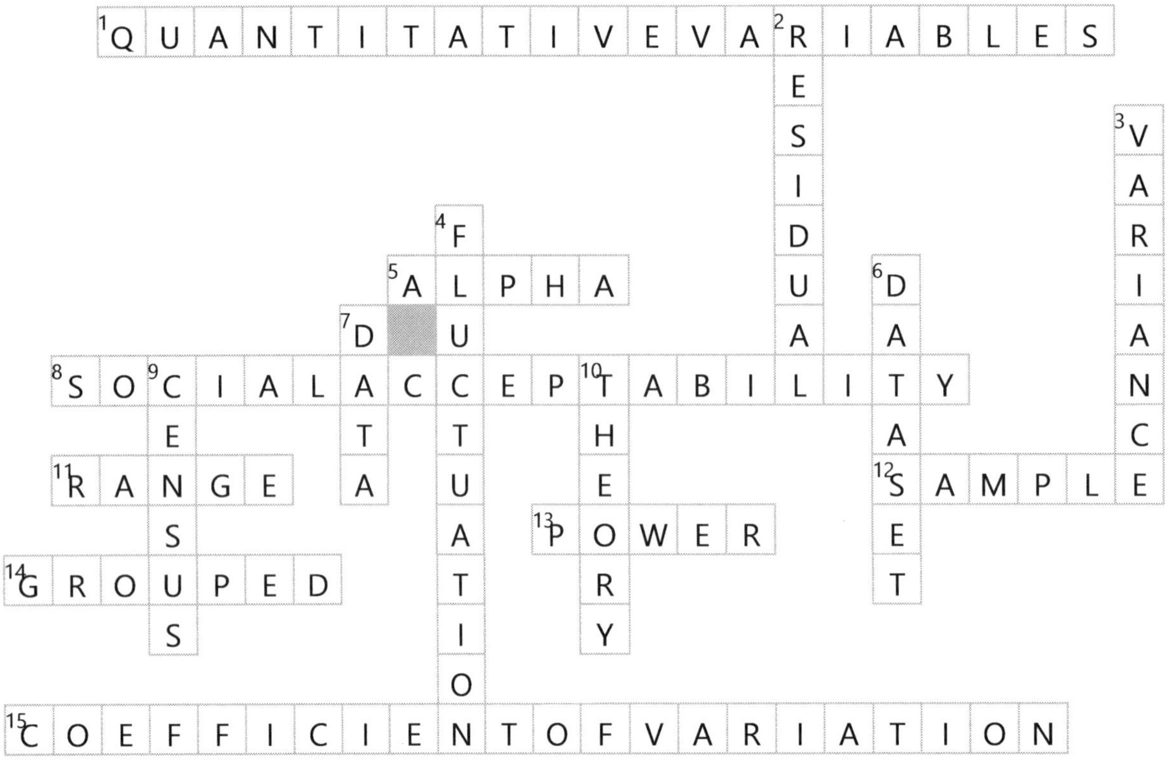

ACROSS

1. Tells how much or many of something there is.
5. Significance level; probability of a type I error.
8. A bias where people are reluctant to admit to behavior that may reflect negatively on them.
11. The difference between the largest and the smallest value.
12. A subset of a population.
13. The probability of correctly rejecting the null hypothesis.
14. Arranged into groups.
15. Tells how large the standard deviation is relative to the mean. It can be used to compare the spreads of data sets whose values have different units.

DOWN

1. Semi interquartile range.
2. The difference between actual score and predicted score.
3. A measure of how far the values in a data set are from the mean, on the average.
4. The quality of being unsteady and subject to changes.
6. All of the information collected.
7. The values of the variables that we obtain.
9. The collection of data from every member of the population.
10. Collection of propositions to illustrate the principles of a subject.

A. Residual
B. Quantitative Variables
C. Sample
D. Data
E. Alpha
F. Coefficient of Variation
G. Range
H. Variance
I. Census
J. Fluctuation
K. Grouped
L. Social Acceptability
M. Power
N. Q
O. Data Set
P. Theory

9.

```
        N           B
        O         3 D  I  S  T  R  I  B  U  T  I  O  N
        R           V
        M           A
        A       4 O B S E R V A T I O N A L S T U D Y
        L           I
        D           A
        I           T
      5 D E S C R I 6 P T I V E S T A T I S T I C S
        T           E                                   7 P   8 T
        R         9 O R D I N A L V A R I A B L E 10 S  O     I
        I       11 C   C                              T   P   M
        B        O    E                               R   U   E
        U        L    N         12 D E P E N D E N T S A M P L E S
        T        L    T                               T   A   E
        I        E  13 A L P H A                       U   T   R
        O        C    G                               M   I   I
        N      14 T R E A T M E N T S                     O   E
                                   15 C A U S A T I O N   S
```

ACROSS

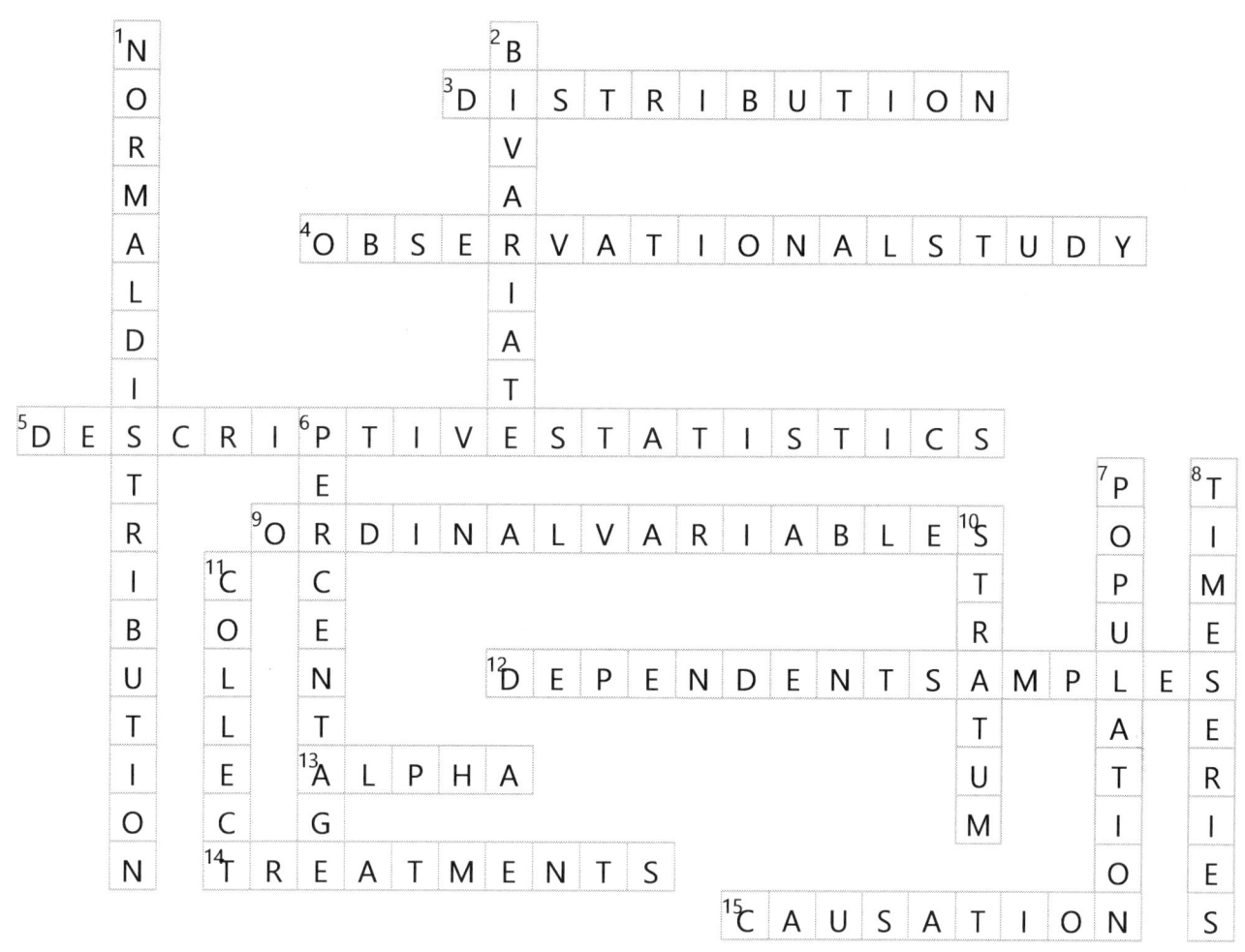

3. The way in which a variable's values are spread over all possible values.
4. The assignment to treatment groups is not made by the investigator.
5. Numerical and graphical summaries of data.
9. Type of qualitative variable. Have a natural ordering, but have no mathematically value.
12. The selection of participants in one sample is affected by the selection of participants in the other sample.
13. Significance level; probability of a type I error.
14. The procedures applied to each experimental unit.
15. The act of making something happen.

DOWN

1. A probability distribution that is unimodal and symmetrical.
2. Having two variables.
6. A proportion in relation to a whole.
7. The collection of all people, objects, or events having one or more specified characteristics.
8. A series of values of a variable at successive times.
10. People having the same social or economic status.
11. Come together and form a group or mass.

A. percentage
B. Population
C. Causation
D. Descriptive Statistics
E. Observational Study
F. Treatments
G. Normal distribution
H. Time series
I. Collect
J. Ordinal Variables
K. Bivariate
L. Distribution
M. Stratum
N. Dependent samples
O. Alpha

57

10.

ACROSS

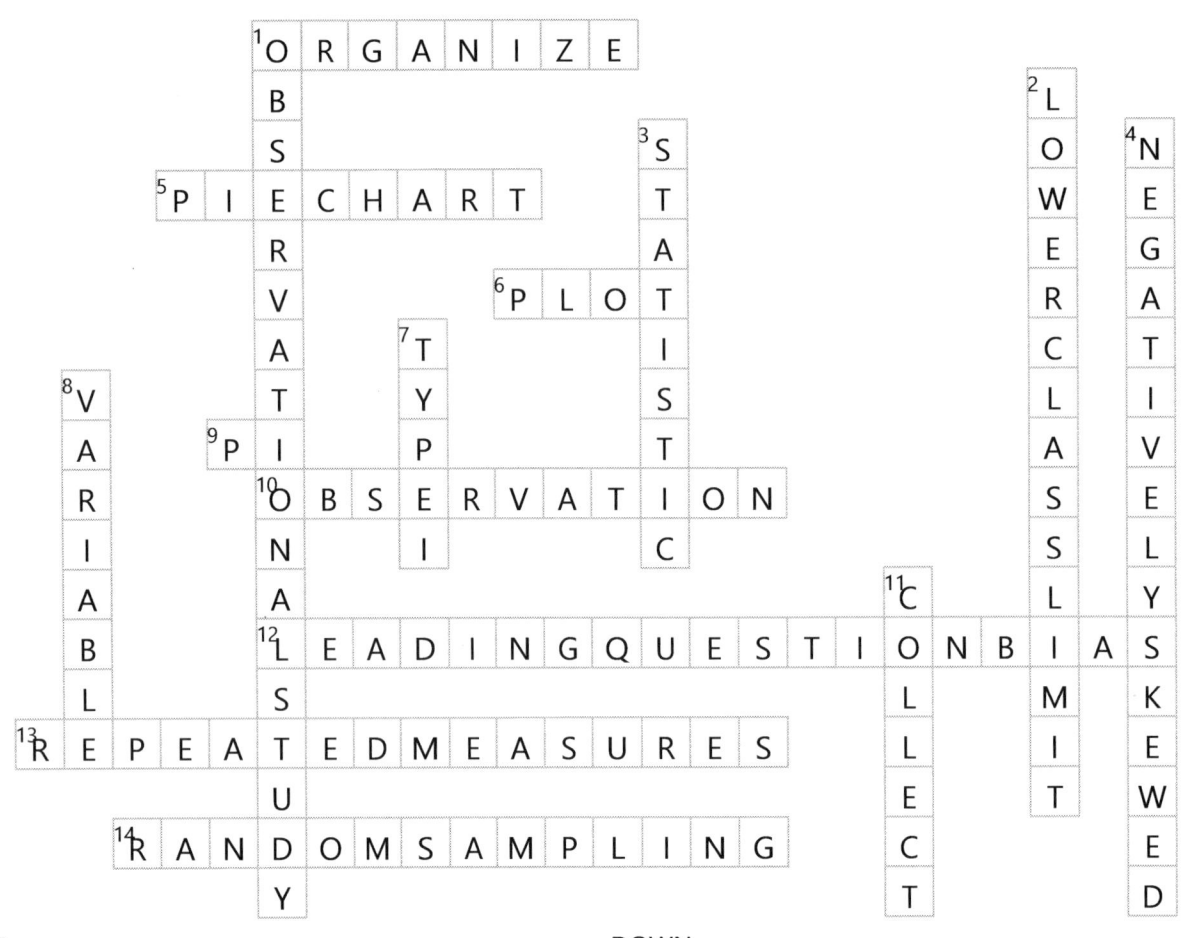

1. Arrange into a structured whole; order.
5. A circular chart divided into triangular areas proportional to the percentages of the whole.
6. Make a drawing that shows interactions among variables.
9. Ratio of a circle's circumference to its diameter, ≈ 3.1416
10. The act of making and recording a measurement.
12. Sometimes questions are worded in a way that suggest a particular response.
13. Observing the same participants under both the experimental and control conditions.
14. The selection of a random sample.

DOWN

1. The assignment to treatment groups is not made by the investigator.
2. The smallest value that can appear in that class.
3. Descriptive measure for a sample.
4. Longer tail extends to the left
7. An error rejecting a true null hypothesis.
8. A characteristic that differs from one subject to the next.
11. Come together and form a group or mass.

A. Pie chart
D. Statistic
G. Variable
J. Observation
M. Plot
B. Collect
E. Observational Study
H. Type I
K. random sampling
N. Lower Class Limit
C. Organize
F. Leading Question Bias
I. Pi
L. Repeated measures
O. Negatively skewed

11.

```
 ¹S T A T I ²S T I C S         ³P
         U           ⁴G R O U P       ⁵M
 ⁶D O U B L E  L I N D   S           E
         J           I      ⁷P  ⁸B    D
         ⁹C O E F F I C I E N T O F V A R I A T I O N
         C           I      R  M     A
         T           V      A  O     N
              ¹⁰G R O U P E D   M  D
                     L      E  A
              ¹¹M    Y      T  L
         ¹²P A R A L L E L   S      E
              X      K      ¹³T R E N D L I N E
              I      ¹⁴M E A N
              M      W
              U      E
         ¹⁵S A M P L I N G D I S T R I B U T I O N
```

ACROSS

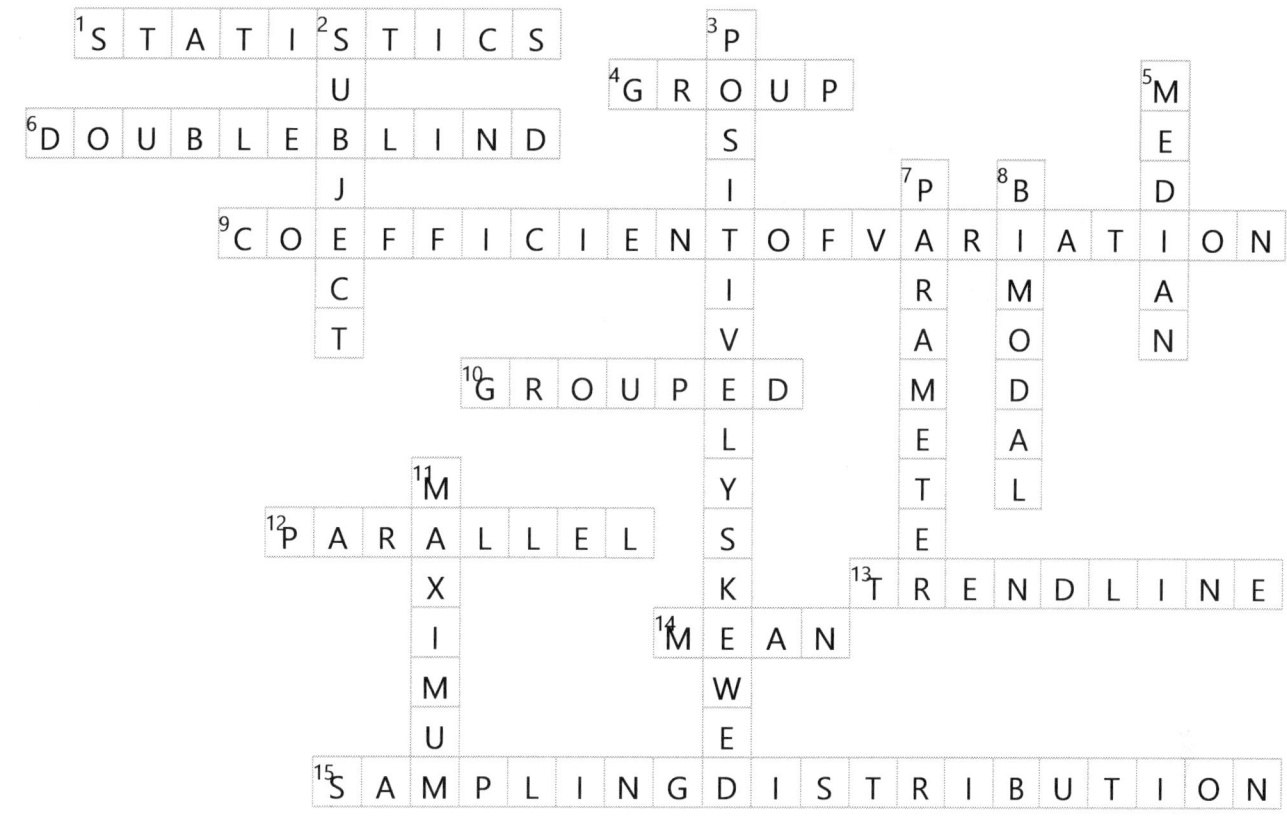

1. A branch of mathematics concerned with quantitative data.
3. probability of a success.
4. Any number of entities members considered as a unit.
6. An experiment where neither the investigator nor the subjects know who has been assigned to which treatment.
9. Tells how large the standard deviation is relative to the mean. It can be used to compare the spreads of data sets whose values have different units.
10. Arranged into groups.
12. Make or place alongside something.
13. A line on a graph indicating a statistical trend.
14. A measure of center in a data set.
15. The random variable is a statistic based on the results of more than one trial.

DOWN

2. When the experimental units are people.
3. Longer tail extends to the right
5. The middle value that divides the data into two equal groups.
7. Descriptive measure for a population represented by Greek letters.
8. Two clearly distinct modes.
11. As great, high, or intense as possible or permitted.

A. Maximum
B. Group
C. P
D. Trend line
E. Positively skewed
F. Subject
G. Sampling distribution
H. Parameter
I. Median
J. Mean
K. Statistics
L. Bimodal
M. parallel
N. Double Blind
O. Coefficient of Variation
P. Grouped

12.

```
            ¹C
  ²E X T R A P O L A T I O N
            U                    ³Q      ⁴I
    ⁵R A N D O M S A M P L I N G  U      N
      A         T                 E      T
    ⁶R A N G E  ⁷B E L L S H A P E D     E
      D         R                 T      R
      O         S                 I      V
  ⁸S I G M A  ⁹O R G A N I Z E  ¹⁰H I S T O G R A M
                M                 N      L
              ¹¹P A R A L L E L   N
                L                 A
              ¹²Q U A L I T A T I V E V A R I A B L E
                N                 R
              ¹³G R O U P       ¹⁴M E D I A N
```

ACROSS

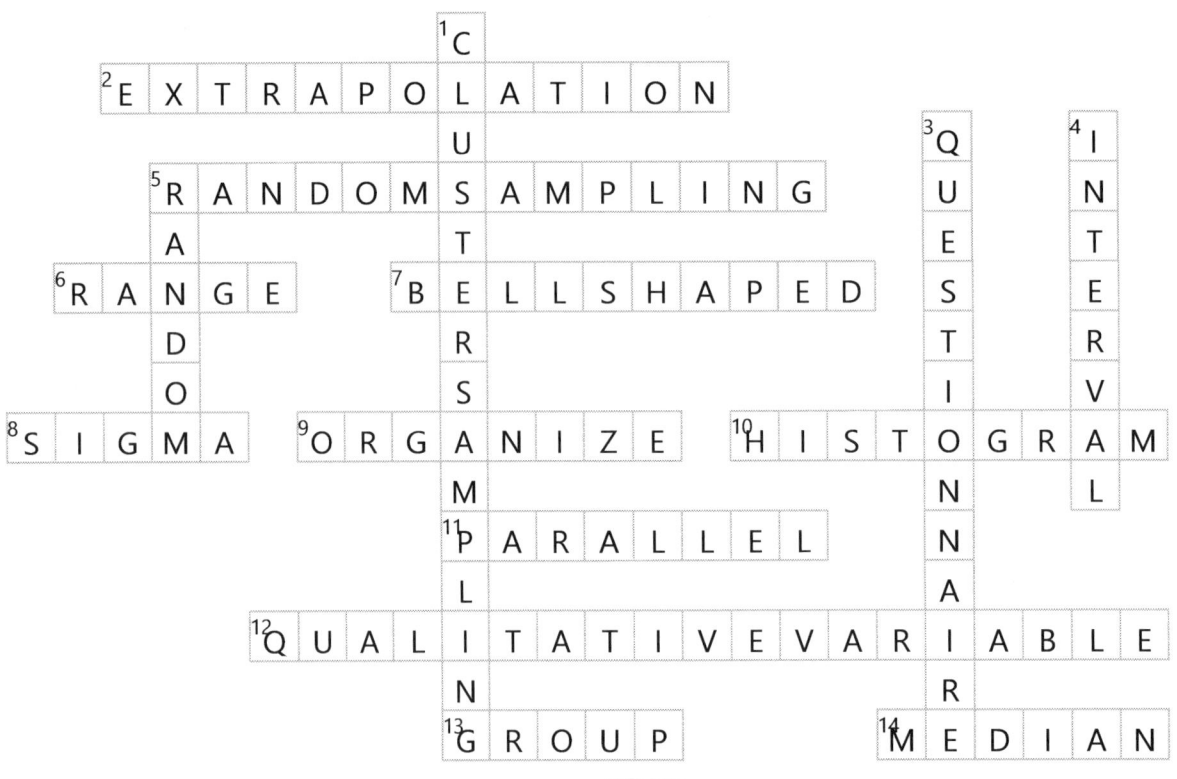

2. Calculating a value outside the range of known values.
3. Semi interquartile range.
5. Every possible sample of a size has an equal chance of being selected.
6. The difference between the largest and the smallest value.
7. Histogram with single mode the near center of the data and are approximately symmetric.
8. population standard deviation.
9. Arrange into a structured whole; order.
10. Graphical representation of frequency distribution for quantitative data. Rectangle for each class.
11. Make or place alongside something.
12. Classify individuals into categories.
13. Any number of entities members considered as a unit.
14. The middle value that divides the data into two equal groups.

DOWN

1. Population is divided into groups that are randomly sampled, and all the members of the selected from the sample.
3. A form with a set of queries to gain statistical information.
4. A set containing all points between two given endpoints.
5. Made, done, happening, or chosen without method or conscious decision.

A. Random sampling	B. Sigma	C. Median	D. Range
E. Interval	F. Group	G. Qualitative Variable	H. Extrapolation
I. Histogram	J. Q	K. Random	L. parallel
M. Organize	N. Bell Shaped	O. Questionnaire	P. Cluster Sampling

13.

ACROSS

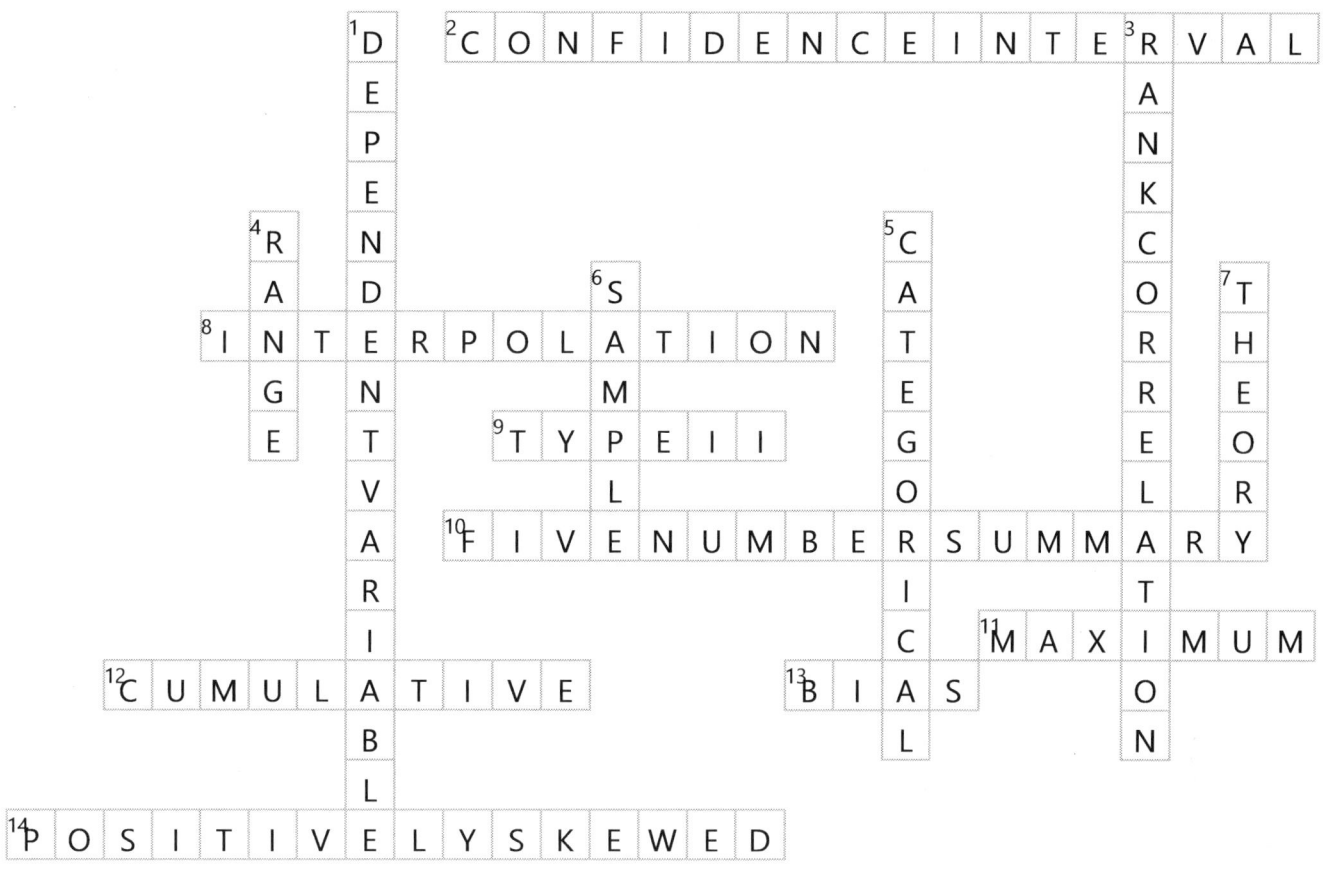

2. A range of values so defined that there is a specified probability that the value of a parameter lies within it.
8. Calculation of the value of a function between known values.
9. An error retaining a false null hypothesis.
10. Minimum, 1st Quartile, Median, 3rd Quartile, Maximum.
11. As great, high, or intense as possible or permitted.
12. Increasing by successive addition.
13. Any problem in the design or conduct of a statistical study that tends to favor certain results.
14. Longer tail extends to the right

DOWN

1. A quantity whose value depends on another quantity.
3. The relationship between rankings of different ordinal variables.
4. The difference between the largest and the smallest value.
5. Relating to or included in a class or classes.
6. A subset of a population.
7. Collection of propositions to illustrate the principles of a subject.

A. Categorical
B. Maximum
C. Bias
D. Sample
E. Theory
F. Type II
G. Confidence interval
H. Interpolation
I. Dependent variable
J. Range
K. Rank Correlation
L. Five Number Summary
M. Positively skewed
N. Cumulative

14.

```
 1L O W E 2R C L A S S L I M I T           3C
       A                                   O
      4T I M E S E 5R I E S       6P V A L U E
       I         A                         L
       O        7I N T E R Q U A R T I L E R A N G E
                 G                         C
              8P A R E 9T O C H A R T  10T H E O R Y
                       Y
                     11E X P E R I M E N T A L U N I T S
                       E
             12A N A L Y S I S O F V A 13R I A N C E
                                       H
                    14O B S E R V A T I O N A L S T U D Y
```

ACROSS

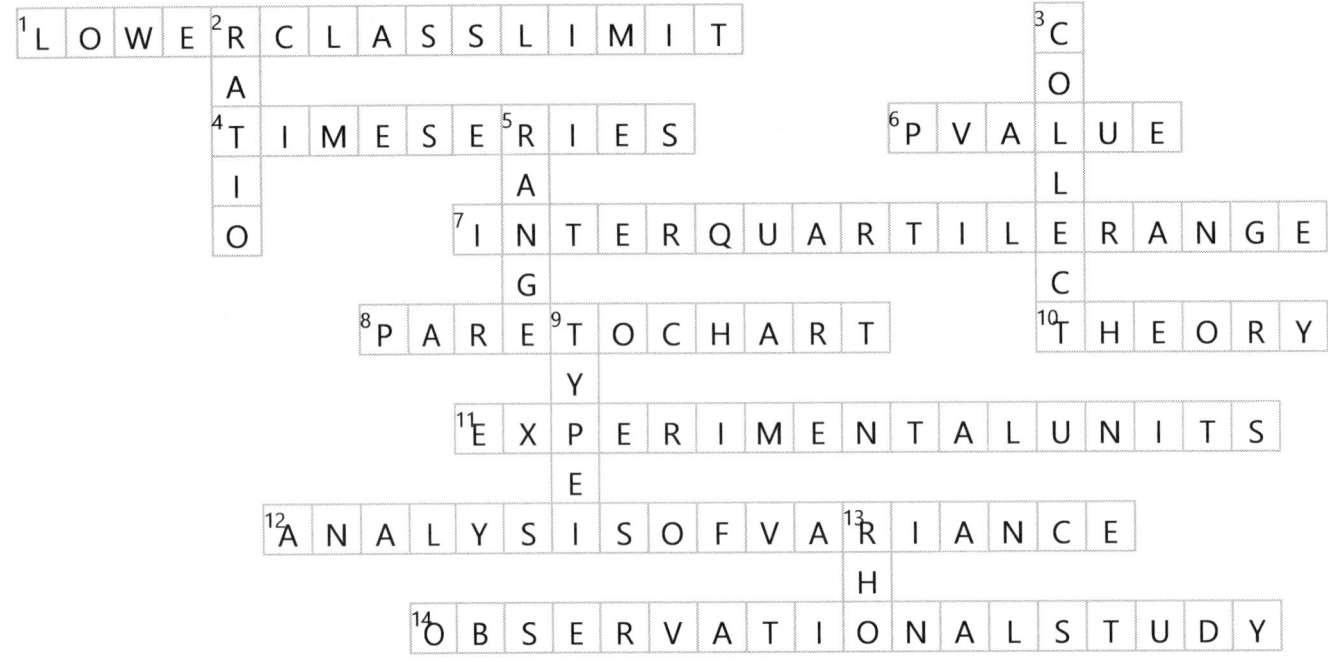

1. The smallest value that can appear in that class.
4. A series of values of a variable at successive times.
6. The probability of obtaining a value of the test statistic equal to or more extreme than that observed.
7. Found by subtracting the 1st quartile from the 3rd quartile. One method for detecting outliers.
8. Bar graph in which categories are represented in order of frequency.
10. Collection of propositions to illustrate the principles of a subject.
11. Things who are studied.
12. A procedure for determining how much of the variability among scores to attribute to a range of sources of variation.
14. The assignment to treatment groups is not made by the investigator.

DOWN

2. The quantitative relation between two amounts showing the number of times one value contains or is contained within the other.
3. Come together and form a group or mass.
5. The difference between the largest and the smallest value.
9. An error rejecting a true null hypothesis.
13. A non-parametric measure of rank correlation.

A. Theory
B. Rho
C. Time series
D. Type I
E. Experimental Units
F. Range
G. Collect
H. Lower Class Limit
I. Observational Study
J. Analysis of variance
K. Pareto Chart
L. P value
M. Interquartile Range
N. Ratio

15.

ACROSS

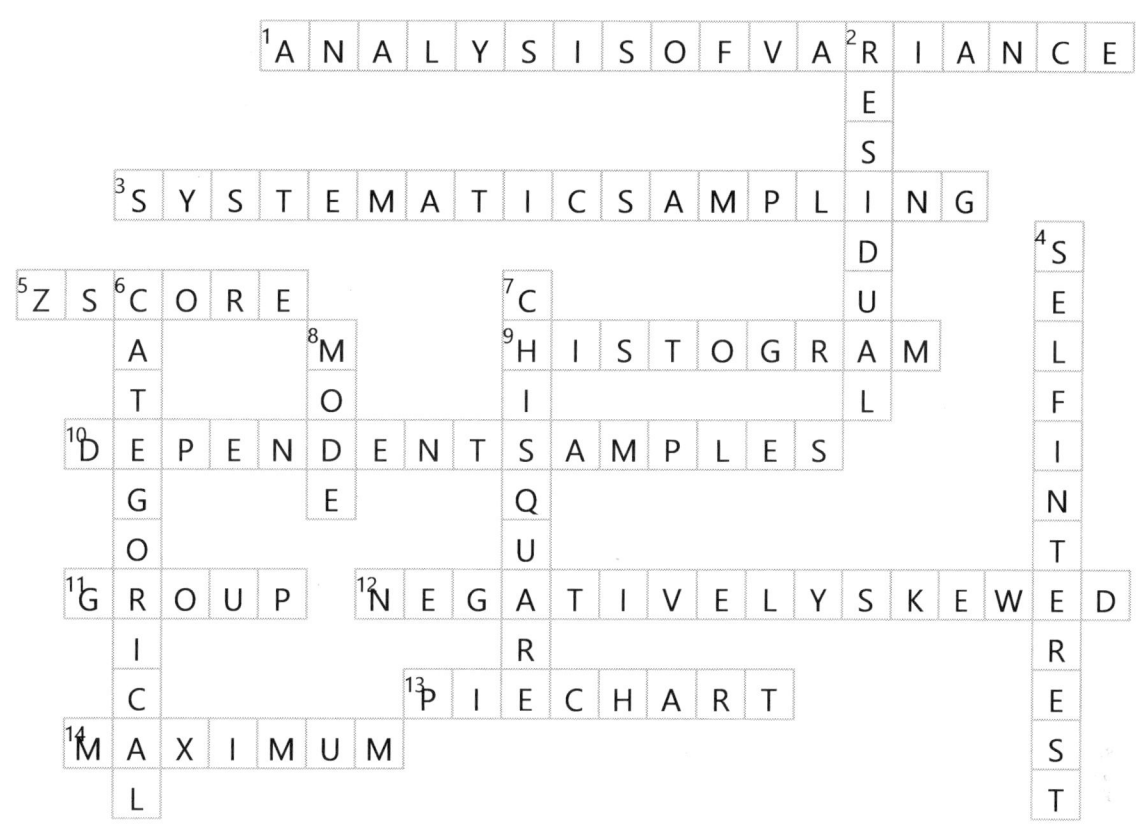

1. A procedure for determining how much of the variability among scores to attribute to a range of sources of variation.
3. Items are ordered, and every nth item is chosen to be included in the sample.
5. Tells how many standard deviations that value is from its population mean.
9. A bar graph used for quantitative variables.
10. The selection of participants in one sample is affected by the selection of participants in the other sample.
11. Any number of entities members considered as a unit.
12. Longer tail extends to the left
13. A circular chart divided into triangular areas proportional to the percentages of the whole.
14. As great, high, or intense as possible or permitted.

DOWN

2. The difference between actual score and predicted score.
4. A bias where people who have an interest in the outcome of an experiment have an incentive to use biased methods.
6. Relating to or included in a class or classes.
7. Relating to or denoting a statistical method assessing the goodness of fit between observed values and those expected theoretically.
8. The score or qualitative category that occurs with greatest frequency.

A. Chi square
B. Residual
C. Negatively skewed
D. Systematic Sampling
E. Self Interest
F. Mode
G. Z Score
H. Group
I. Analysis of variance
J. Pie chart
K. Categorical
L. Histogram
M. Maximum
N. Dependent samples

16.

Crossword solution grid:
- 3 Across: SURVEY
- 5 Across: RANDOM
- 6 Across: ORDINAL
- 8 Across: RHO
- 9 Across: POSITIVELY SKEWED
- 10 Across: STACKED
- 12 Across: DEPENDENT SAMPLES
- 13 Across: NOMINAL VARIABLES
- 14 Across: NEGATIVELY SKEWED
- 1 Down: MATCHED SAMPLES
- 2 Down: GROUPED
- 4 Down: RANGE
- 7 Down: PERCENTILE
- 11 Down: CENSUS

ACROSS

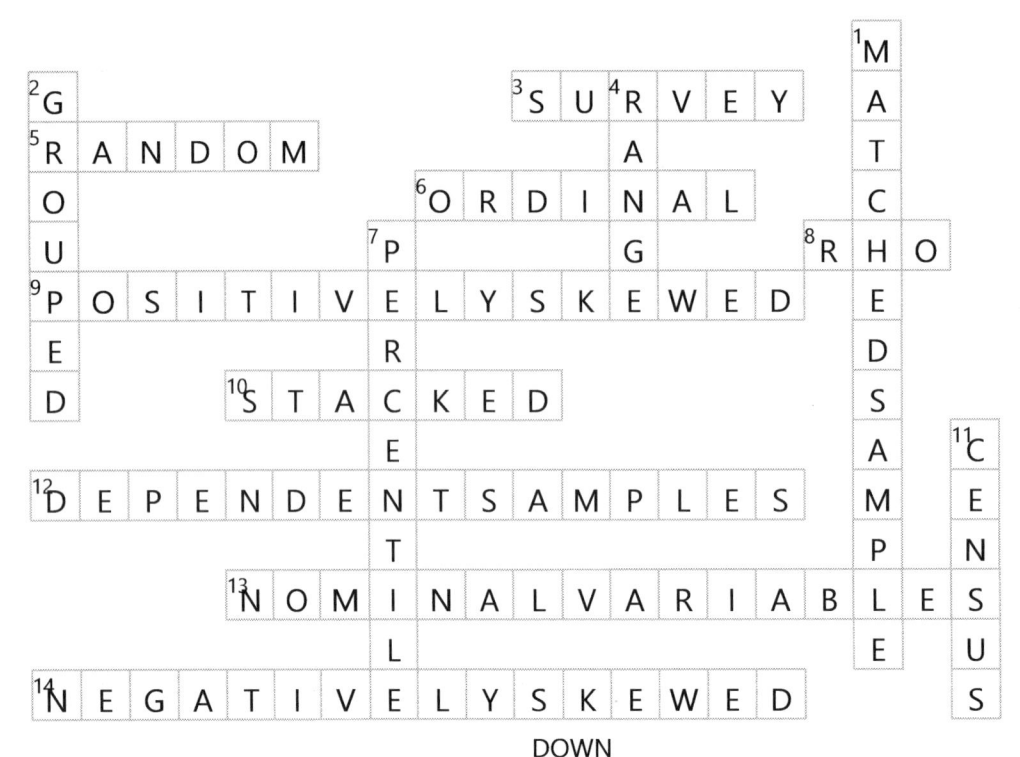

3. Make a detailed inspection of; for statistical purposes.
5. Made, done, happening, or chosen without method or conscious decision.
6. The number designating place in an ordered sequence.
8. A non-parametric measure of rank correlation.
9. Longer tail extends to the right
10. Bar graph that shows frequencies or relative frequencies in categories for more than one group frequencies within each category.
12. The selection of participants in one sample is affected by the selection of participants in the other sample.
13. Type of qualitative variable. Have no natural ordering.
14. Longer tail extends to the left

DOWN

1. Matching each participant in the experimental condition with a participant in the control condition.
2. Arranged into groups.
4. The difference between the largest and the smallest value.
7. Each of the 100 equal groups into which a population can be divided according to the distribution of values of a variable.
11. The collection of data from every member of the population.

A. Survey
B. Nominal Variables
C. Stacked
D. Grouped
E. ordinal
F. Dependent samples
G. Census
H. Percentile
I. Random
J. Negatively skewed
K. Positively skewed
L. Matched sample
M. Range
N. Rho

17.

ACROSS

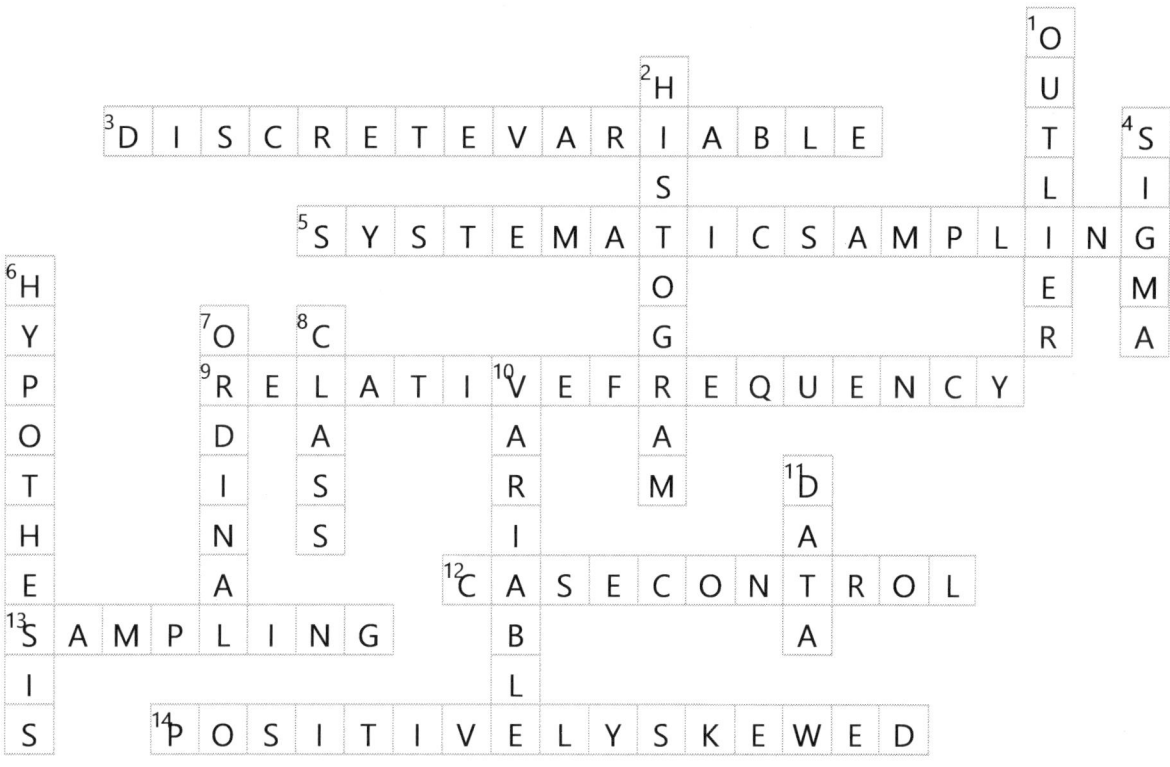

3. Type of quantitative variable whose possible values can be listed.
5. Items are ordered, and every nth item is chosen to be included in the sample.
9. A distribution that shows the proportion or percent frequency for each interval.
12. A type of study where two samples are drawn.
13. The selection of a suitable sample for study.
14. Longer tail extends to the right

DOWN

1. Scores that differ so markedly from the main body of data that their accuracy is questioned.
2. Graphical representation of frequency distribution for quantitative data. Rectangle for each class.
4. population standard deviation.
6. A supposition or proposed explanation based on limited evidence as a starting point for further investigation.
7. The number designating place in an ordered sequence.
8. Arrange or order by categories.
10. A characteristic that differs from one subject to the next.
11. The values of the variables that we obtain.

A. Sampling
B. Relative frequency
C. Data
D. Discrete Variable
E. Histogram
F. Case Control
G. Systematic Sampling
H. ordinal
I. Variable
J. Outlier
K. Sigma
L. Hypothesis
M. Positively skewed
N. Class

18.

Crossword Solution

											¹T	R	E	A	²T	M	E	N	T	S		³R
															R							A
			⁴Q												E							N
			U						⁵C						N							K
⁶I	N	D	E	P	E	N	D	E	N	T	S	A	M	P	L	E	S					C
			S						A						L							O
			T			⁷R	E	S	I	S	T	A	N	T	S	T	A	T	I	S	T	I	C	R
			I						S						N							R
	⁸C	O	H	O	R	T		⁹U	N	¹⁰B	I	A	S	E	D			¹¹R	A	N	G	E
	O								E						S							L
	N								T													A
	N			¹²C	O	R	R	E	L	A	¹³T	I	O	N	C	O	E	F	F	I	C	I	E	N	T
	A										Y											I
	I										P											O
	R										E											N
	E										I											
¹⁴F	R	E	Q	U	E	N	C	Y	D	I	S	T	R	I	B	U	T	I	O	N

ACROSS

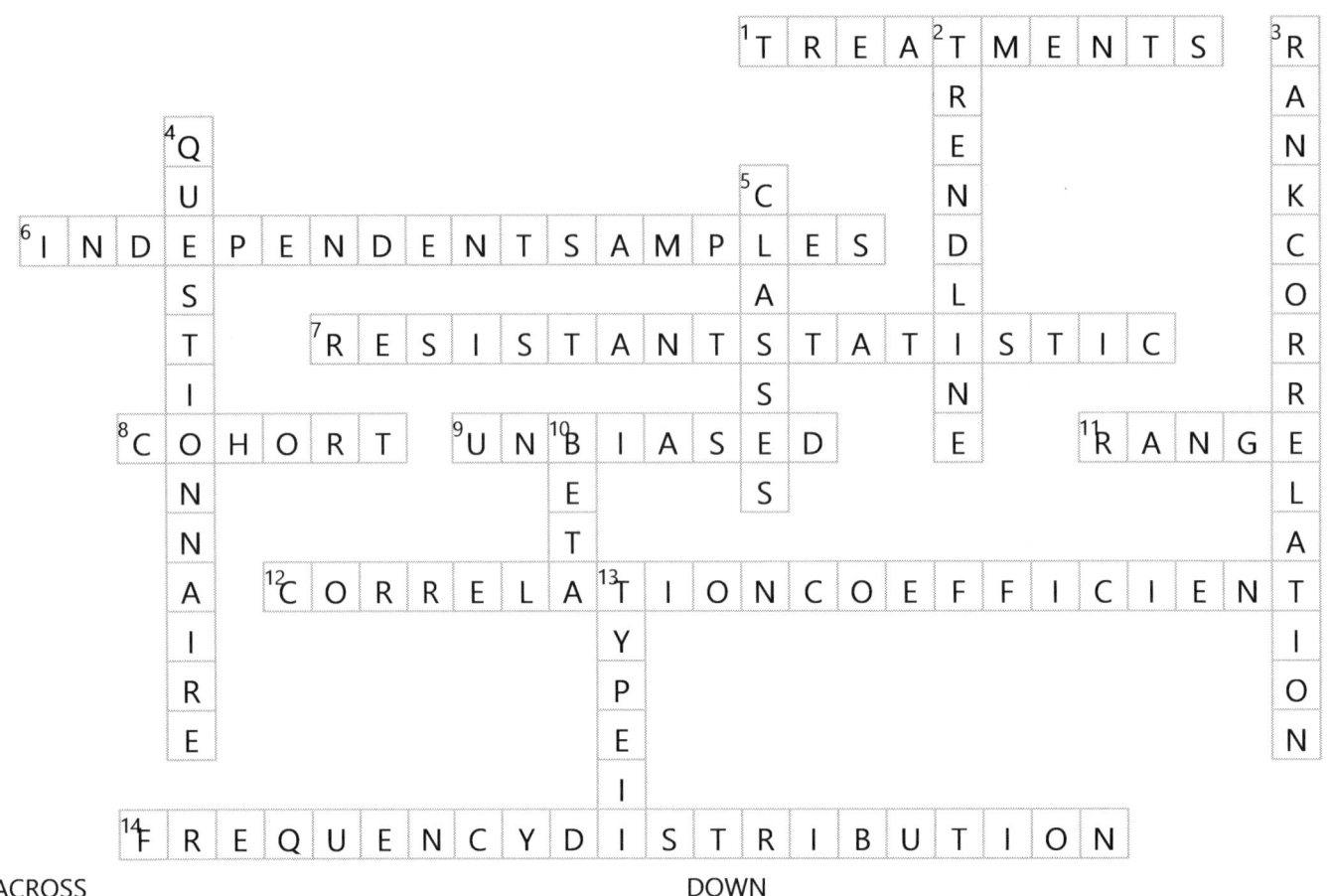

1. The procedures applied to each experimental unit.
6. The selection of participants in one sample is not affected by the selection of participants in the other sample.
7. Its value is not affected much by extreme values in the data set.
8. A group.
9. Studies conducted by a procedure that produces the correct result on average.
11. The difference between the largest and the smallest value.
12. A number that represents the degree of association or strength of relationship between two variables.
14. Presented in a table that gives the frequency for each category.

DOWN

2. A line on a graph indicating a statistical trend.
3. The relationship between rankings of different ordinal variables.
4. A form with a set of queries to gain statistical information.
5. Intervals of equal width that cover all values observed in the data set.
10. Probability of a type II error.
13. An error retaining a false null hypothesis.

A. Correlation coefficient
B. Classes
C. Independent samples
D. Cohort
E. Rank Correlation
F. Unbiased
G. Type II
H. Trend line
I. Questionnaire
J. Frequency Distribution
K. Range
L. Beta
M. Treatments
N. Resistant Statistic

19.

ACROSS

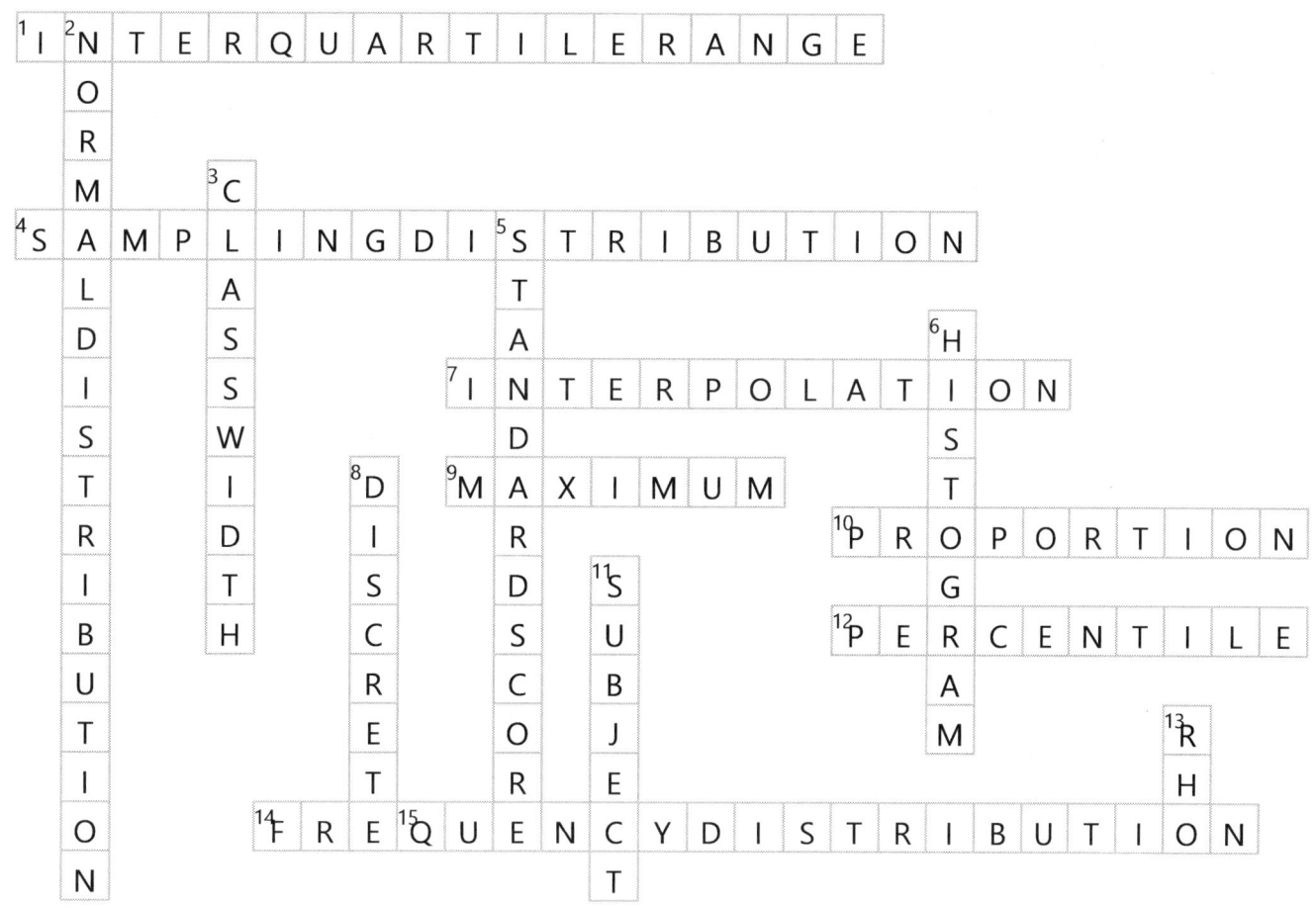

1. Found by subtracting the 1st quartile from the 3rd quartile. One method for detecting outliers.
4. The random variable is a statistic based on the results of more than one trial.
7. Calculation of the value of a function between known values.
9. As great, high, or intense as possible or permitted.
10. A part, share, or number considered in comparative relation to a whole.
12. Each of the 100 equal groups into which a population can be divided according to the distribution of values of a variable.
14. Presented in a table that gives the frequency for each category.

DOWN

2. A probability distribution that is unimodal and symmetrical.
3. The difference between consecutive lower class limits.
5. Expresses the value of a score relative to the mean and standard deviation of its distribution.
6. A bar graph used for quantitative variables.
8. Constituting a separate entity or part.
11. When the experimental units are people.
13. A non-parametric measure of rank correlation.
15. Semi interquartile range.

A. Standard score
B. Subject
C. Percentile
D. Proportion
E. Class Width
F. Maximum
G. Interquartile Range
H. Discrete
I. Frequency Distribution
J. Q
K. Histogram
L. Rho
M. Sampling distribution
N. Normal distribution
O. Interpolation

20.

```
                                          ¹R
                                           A
              ²R A N K C O R R E L A T I O N
                                           D
                                           O
                    ³U P P E R C L A S S L I M I T
                                           S
         ⁴C O N F I D E N C E I N T E R V A L
          H                                M
         ⁵I N ⁶D E ⁷P E N D E N T S A M P L E S   P
          S   A                                  L
          Q   T        ⁸T Y P E I      ⁹C         I
          U   A           H             O         N
          A  ¹⁰S Y S T E M A T I C S A M P L I N G
          R   E           O             L
          E   T        ¹¹P A R A L L E L ¹²F R E Q U E N C Y
                          Y             C
                       ¹³C U M U L A T I V E
```

ACROSS

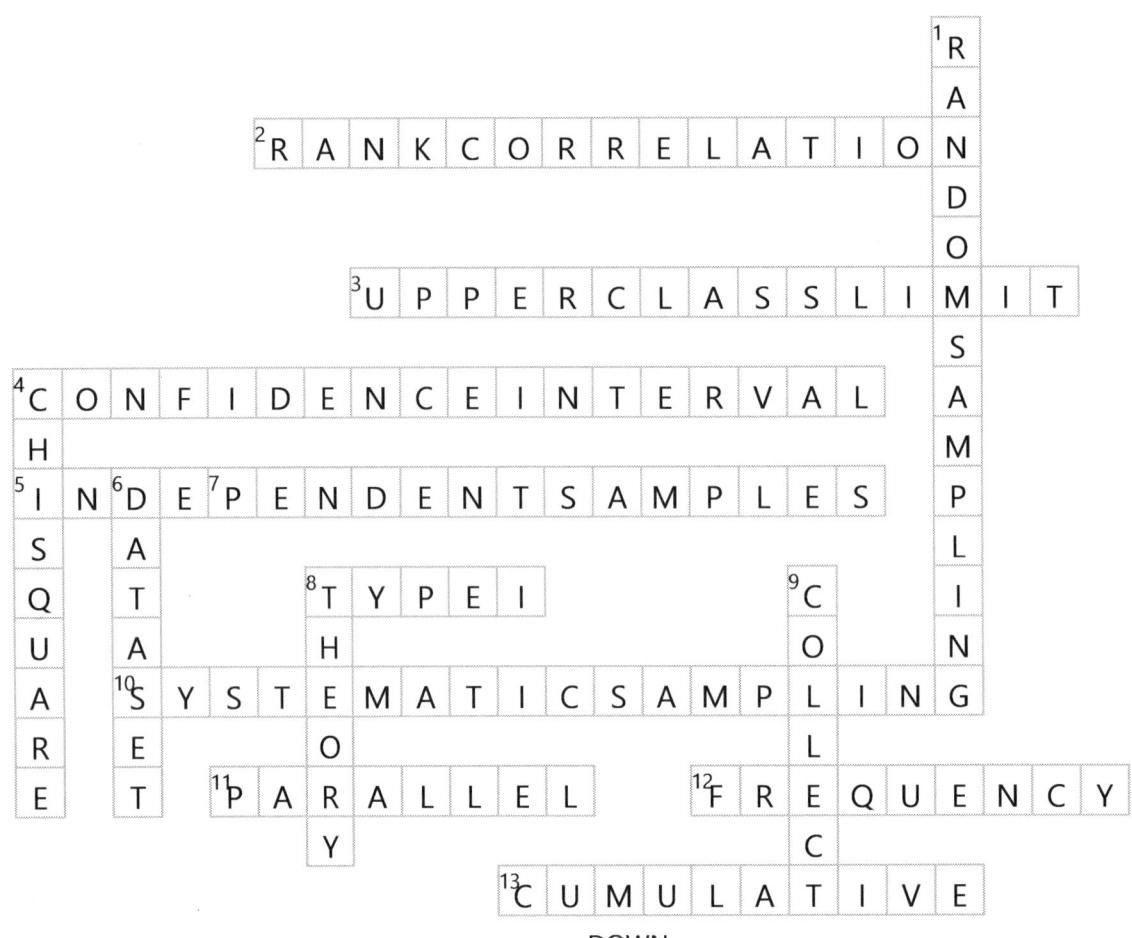

2. The relationship between rankings of different ordinal variables.
3. The largest value that can appear in that class.
4. A range of values so defined that there is a specified probability that the value of a parameter lies within it.
5. The selection of participants in one sample is not affected by the selection of participants in the other sample.
8. An error rejecting a true null hypothesis.
10. Items are ordered, and every nth item is chosen to be included in the sample.
11. Make or place alongside something.
12. The number of times a variable occurs in a data set.
13. Increasing by successive addition.

DOWN

1. The selection of a random sample.
4. Relating to or denoting a statistical method assessing the goodness of fit between observed values and those expected theoretically.
6. All of the information collected.
7. probability of a success.
8. Collection of propositions to illustrate the principles of a subject.
9. Come together and form a group or mass.

A. Cumulative
D. parallel
G. Type I
J. Collect
M. Systematic Sampling
B. Data Set
E. Rank Correlation
H. P
K. random sampling
N. Upper Class Limit
C. Confidence interval
F. Chi square
I. Independent samples
L. Frequency
O. Theory

21.

	C	L	U	S	T	E	R	S	A	M	P	L	I	N	G		M	A	X	I	M	U	M
	R																					P	
	O																					P	
	S			C	O	N	F	I	D	E	N	C	E	I	N	T	E	R	V	A	L	E	
	S				U				O													R	
	S				T				U													C	
	E				L			O	B	S	E	R	V	A	T	I	O	N				L	
	C				I				L								Y					A	
	T				E		T	R	E	A	T	M	E	N	T	S	P					S	
	I				R				B					C			E					S	
T	H	E	O	R	Y		Q	U	A	L	I	T	A	T	I	V	E	V	A	R	I	A	B	L	E

ACROSS

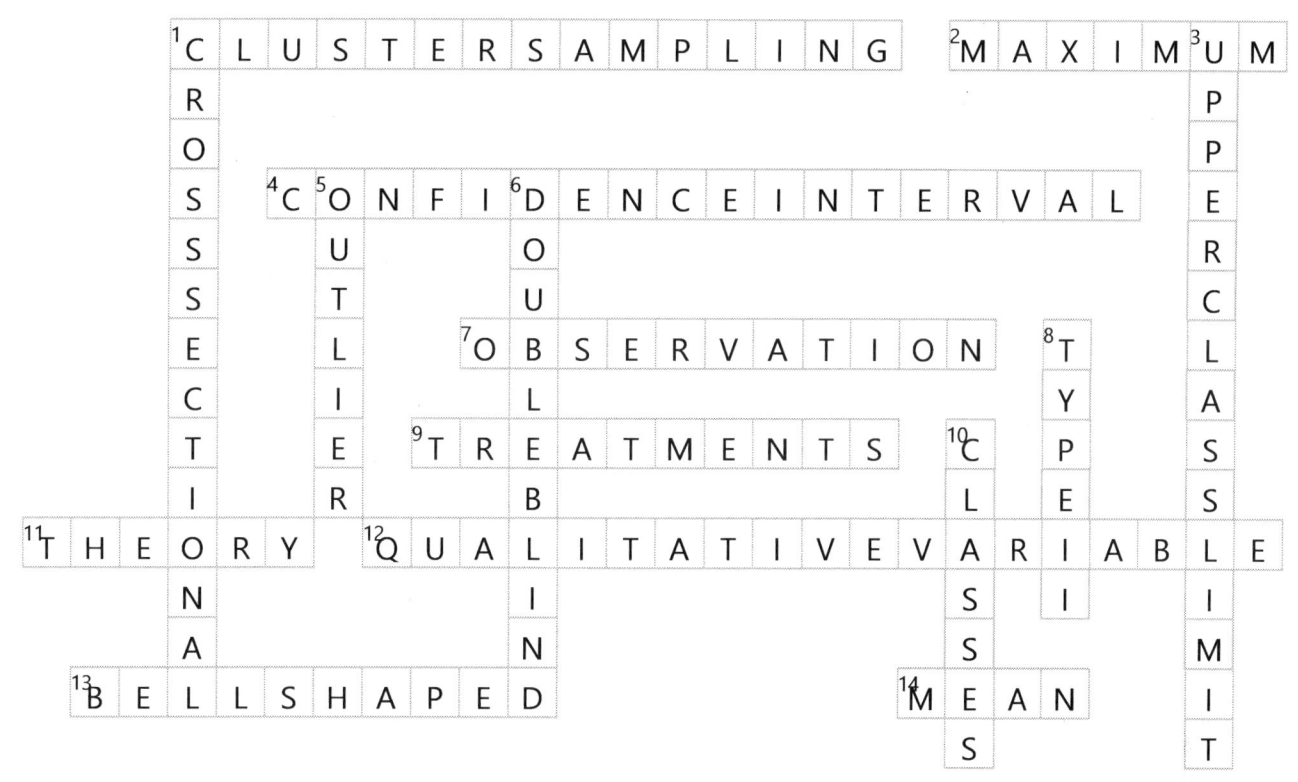

1. Population is divided into groups that are randomly sampled, and all the members of the selected from the sample.
2. As great, high, or intense as possible or permitted.
4. A range of values so defined that there is a specified probability that the value of a parameter lies within it.
7. The act of making and recording a measurement.
9. The procedures applied to each experimental unit.
11. Collection of propositions to illustrate the principles of a subject.
12. Classify individuals into categories.
13. Histogram with single mode the near center of the data and are approximately symmetric.
14. A measure of center in a data set.

DOWN

1. Type of cohort where measurements are taken at one point in time.
3. The largest value that can appear in that class.
5. Scores that differ so markedly from the main body of data that their accuracy is questioned.
6. An experiment where neither the investigator nor the subjects know who has been assigned to which treatment.
8. An error retaining a false null hypothesis.
10. Intervals of equal width that cover all values observed in the data set.

A. Theory
B. Cluster Sampling
C. Mean
D. Maximum
E. Confidence interval
F. Bell Shaped
G. Treatments
H. Cross Sectional
I. Double Blind
J. Upper Class Limit
K. Outlier
L. Type II
M. Observation
N. Qualitative Variable
O. Classes

22.

ACROSS

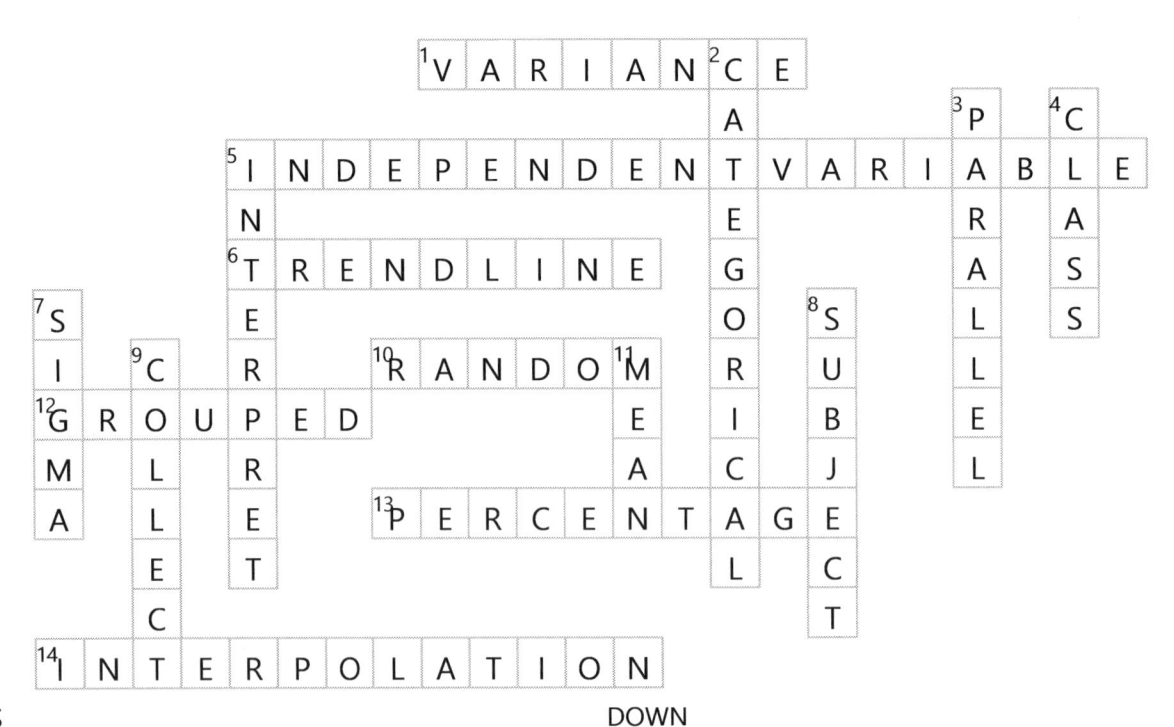

1. A measure of how far the values in a data set are from the mean, on the average.
5. A value that does not depend on changes in other values.
6. A line on a graph indicating a statistical trend.
10. Made, done, happening, or chosen without method or conscious decision.
12. Arranged into groups.
13. A proportion in relation to a whole.
14. Calculation of the value of a function between known values.

DOWN

2. Relating to or included in a class or classes.
3. Make or place alongside something.
4. Arrange or order by categories.
5. Explain the meaning of information, words, or actions.
7. population standard deviation.
8. When the experimental units are people.
9. Come together and form a group or mass.
11. A measure of center in a data set.

A. Collect
B. Independent variable
C. Categorical
D. Grouped
E. Interpolation
F. Subject
G. Sigma
H. percentage
I. Random
J. Trend line
K. Variance
L. Mean
M. Class
N. parallel
O. Interpret

23.

```
                    ¹R
                     A              ²S I M P L E R A N D O M S A M ³P L E
                     N                                             V
                    ⁴D E P E ⁵N D E N T S A M P L E S              A
                     O       O                         ⁶S          L
                    ⁷M U  ⁸A N A L Y S I S O F V A R I A N C E     U
                     S     R                            M
                     A  ⁹U  E            ¹⁰C L A S S   ¹¹P
                     M   N  S         ¹²R H O           I
                     P   I  P            H              E
                     L   M  O         ¹³G R O U P E D   C
                     I   O  N            R              H
                     N  ¹⁴D E S C R I P T I V E S T A T I S T I C S
                     G   A  E                           R
                         L                              T
```

ACROSS

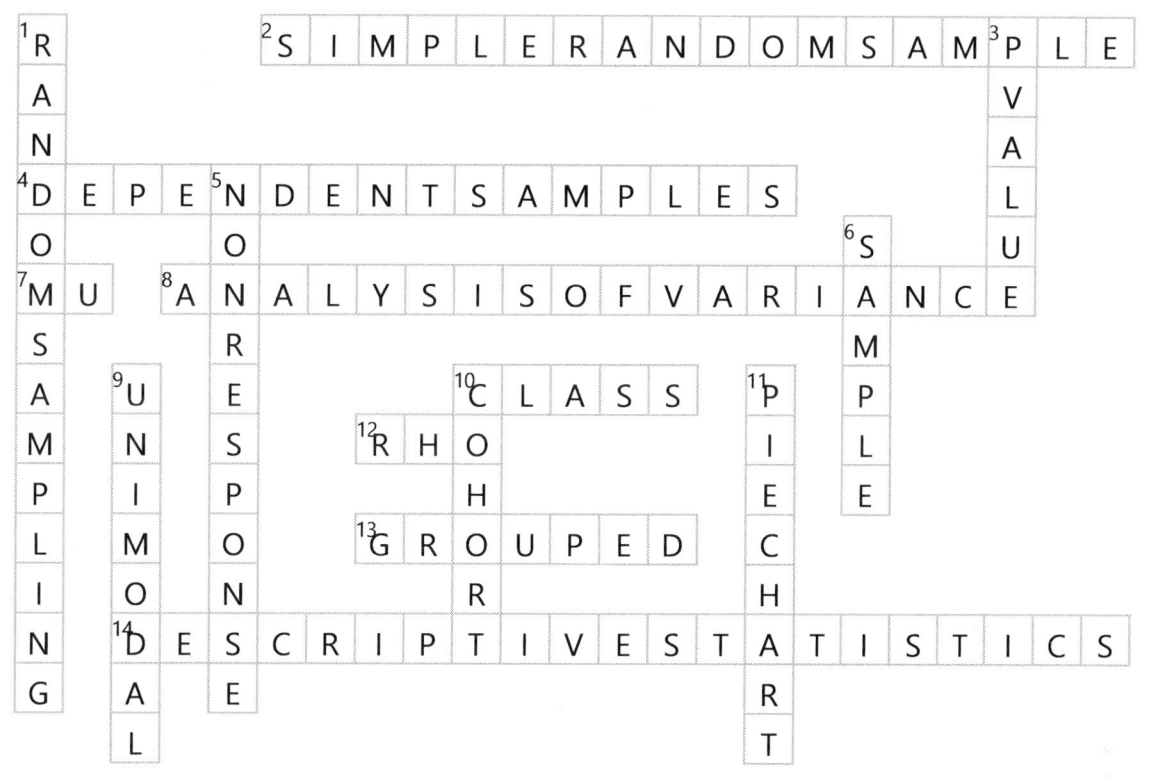

2. A sample is chosen by a method such that every member of the population is equally likely to be selected.
4. The selection of participants in one sample is affected by the selection of participants in the other sample.
7. Population mean.
8. A procedure for determining how much of the variability among scores to attribute to a range of sources of variation.
10. Arrange or order by categories.
12. A non-parametric measure of rank correlation.
13. Arranged into groups.
14. Numerical and graphical summaries of data.

DOWN

1. The selection of a random sample.
3. The probability of obtaining a value of the test statistic equal to or more extreme than that observed.
5. A response where the opinions of non-responders tend to differ from the opinions of those who do respond.
6. A subset of a population.
9. Only one mode.
10. A group.
11. A circular chart divided into triangular areas proportional to the percentages of the whole.

A. Rho
B. Unimodal
C. Class
D. Pie chart
E. Grouped
F. Dependent samples
G. Sample
H. Cohort
I. Simple Random Sample
J. Non response
K. random sampling
L. Analysis of variance
M. P value
N. Mu
O. Descriptive Statistics

24.

```
                              ¹S
       ²A                     K
        N    ³Q U A L I T A T I V E V A R I A B L E
        A                                       W
        L    ⁴C O R R E L A T I O N C O E F F I C I E N T
        Y   ⁵C                                  D
       ⁶S T A N D A R D S ⁷C O R E              D
        I    T             L                    I
        S    E    ⁸R       A    ⁹C O L L E ¹⁰C T S
        O    G    A        S       O      O     T
        F    O    W       ¹¹S A M P L E    N     R
        V    R    D        E       O      T     I
        A    I    A        S       U      I     B
        R    C    T                U      N     U
        I    A   ¹²S A ¹³M P L I N G      U     T
        A    L           U          D     O     I
        N               ¹⁴S T R A T I F I E D S A M P L I N G
        C
        E
```

ACROSS

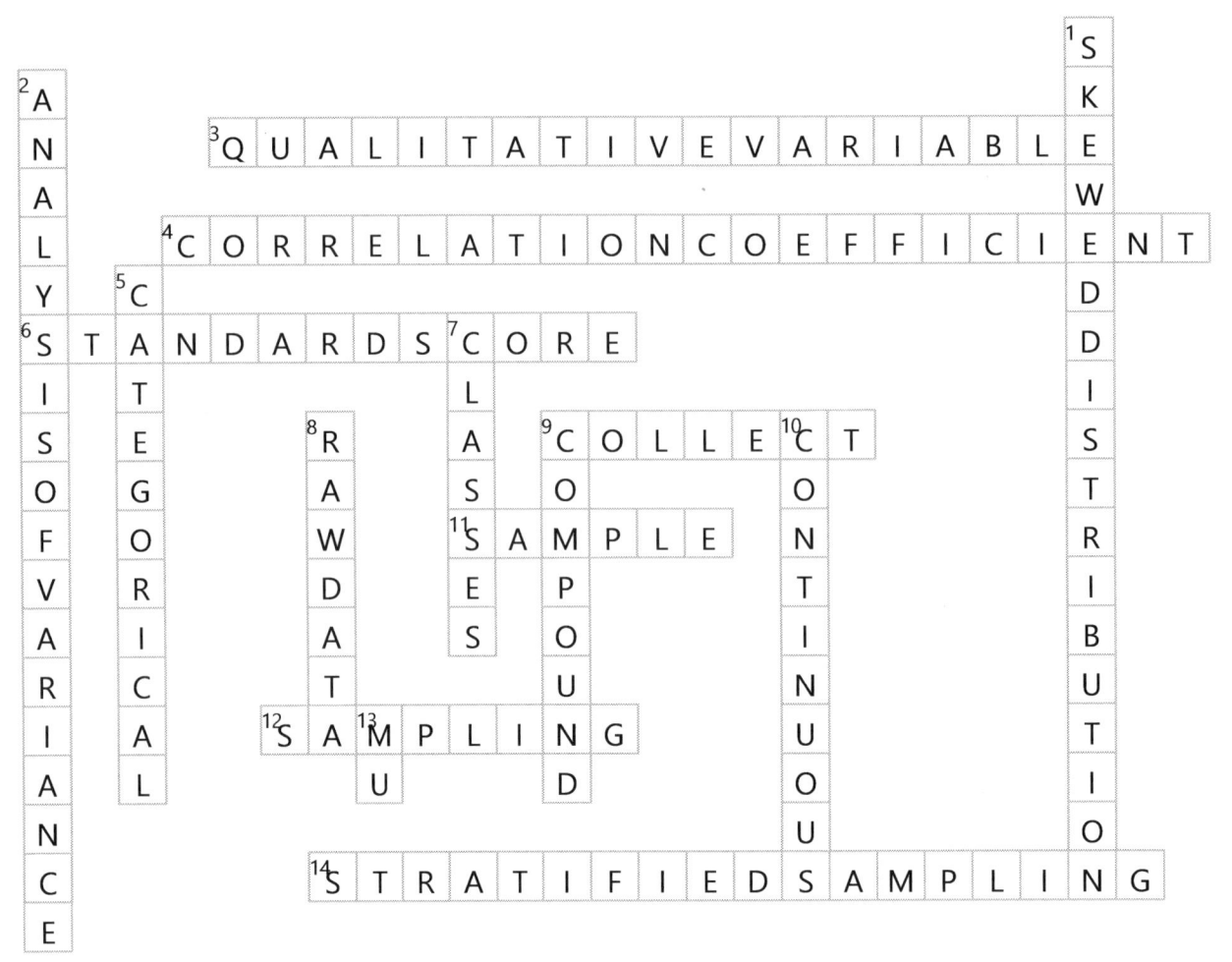

3. Classify individuals into categories.
4. A number that represents the degree of association or strength of relationship between two variables.
6. Expresses the value of a score relative to the mean and standard deviation of its distribution.
9. Come together and form a group or mass.
11. A subset of a population.
12. The selection of a suitable sample for study.
14. The population is divided into subpopulations and random samples are taken of each stratum.

DOWN

1. Distributions that are asymmetrical.
2. A procedure for determining how much of the variability among scores to attribute to a range of sources of variation.
5. Relating to or included in a class or classes.
7. Intervals of equal width that cover all values observed in the data set.
8. Actual measurements or observations collected from the sample.
9. Put or add together.
10. Extending without break or irregularity.
13. Population mean.

A. Correlation coefficient
B. Classes
C. Collect
D. Sample
E. Analysis of variance
F. Standard score
G. Stratified sampling
H. Raw data
I. Skewed distribution
J. Qualitative Variable
K. Sampling
L. Continuous
M. Mu
N. Categorical
O. Compound

25.

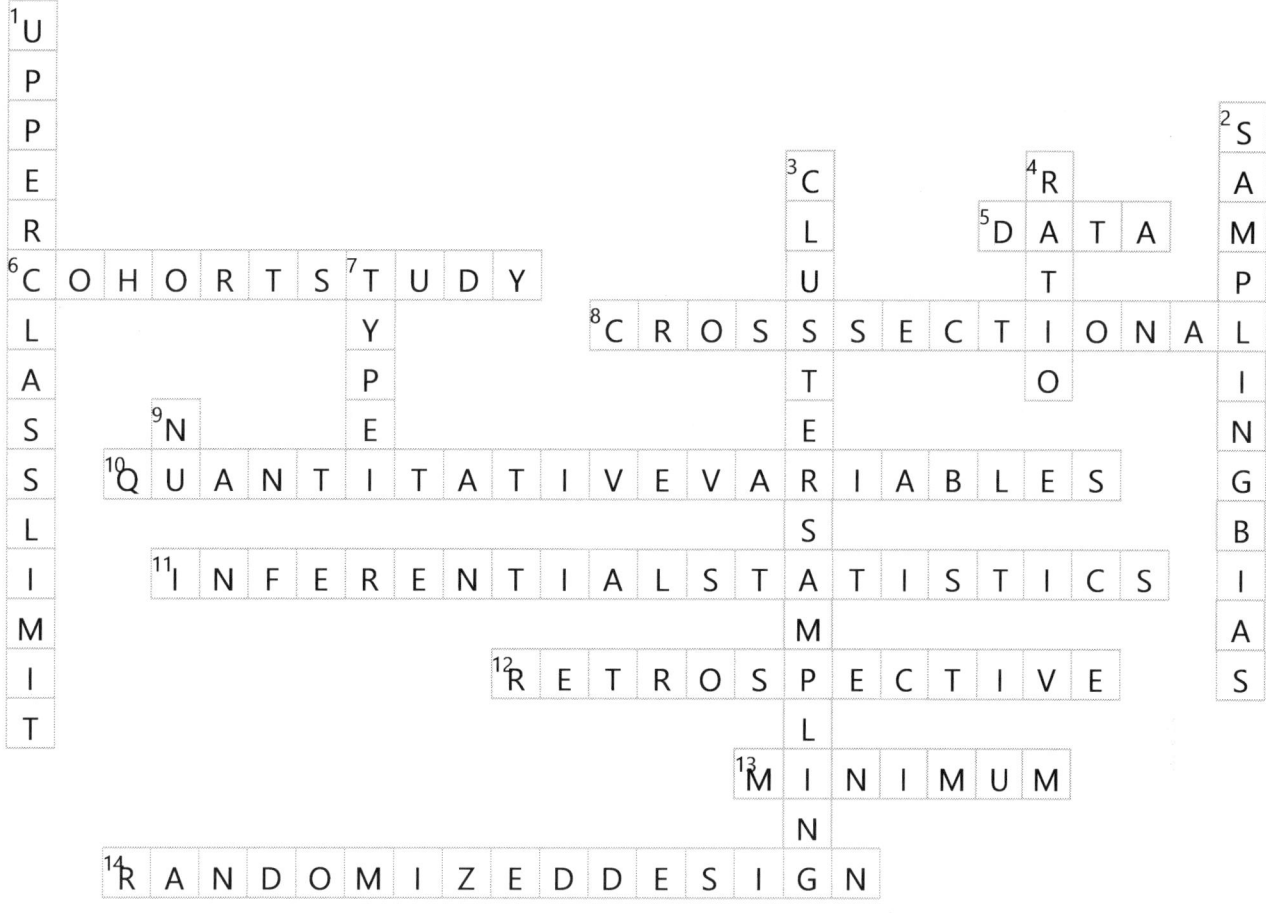

ACROSS
5. The values of the variables that we obtain.
6. Group of subjects is studied to determine whether various factors of interest are associated with an outcome.
8. Type of cohort where measurements are taken at one point in time.
10. Tells how much or many of something there is.
11. Drawing inferences from sample data to a population.
12. Type of cohort study where subjects are sampled after the outcome has occurred.
13. The least or smallest amount or quantity possible, attainable, or required.
14. A study in which the assignment of participants to treatment levels is completely random.

DOWN
1. The largest value that can appear in that class.
2. Occurs when some members in the population are more likely to be included in the sample than others.
3. Population is divided into groups that are randomly sampled, and all the members of the selected from the sample.
4. The quantitative relation between two amounts showing the number of times one value contains or is contained within the other.
7. An error rejecting a true null hypothesis.
9. Degrees of freedom.
10. Semi interquartile range.

A. Minimum
B. Sampling Bias
C. Inferential Statistics
D. Cohort Study
E. Ratio
F. Q
G. Cross Sectional
H. Quantitative Variables
I. Upper Class Limit
J. Retrospective
K. Nu
L. Type I
M. Randomized design
N. Cluster Sampling
O. Data

Multiple Choice

From the words provided for each clue, provide the letter of the word which best matches the clue.

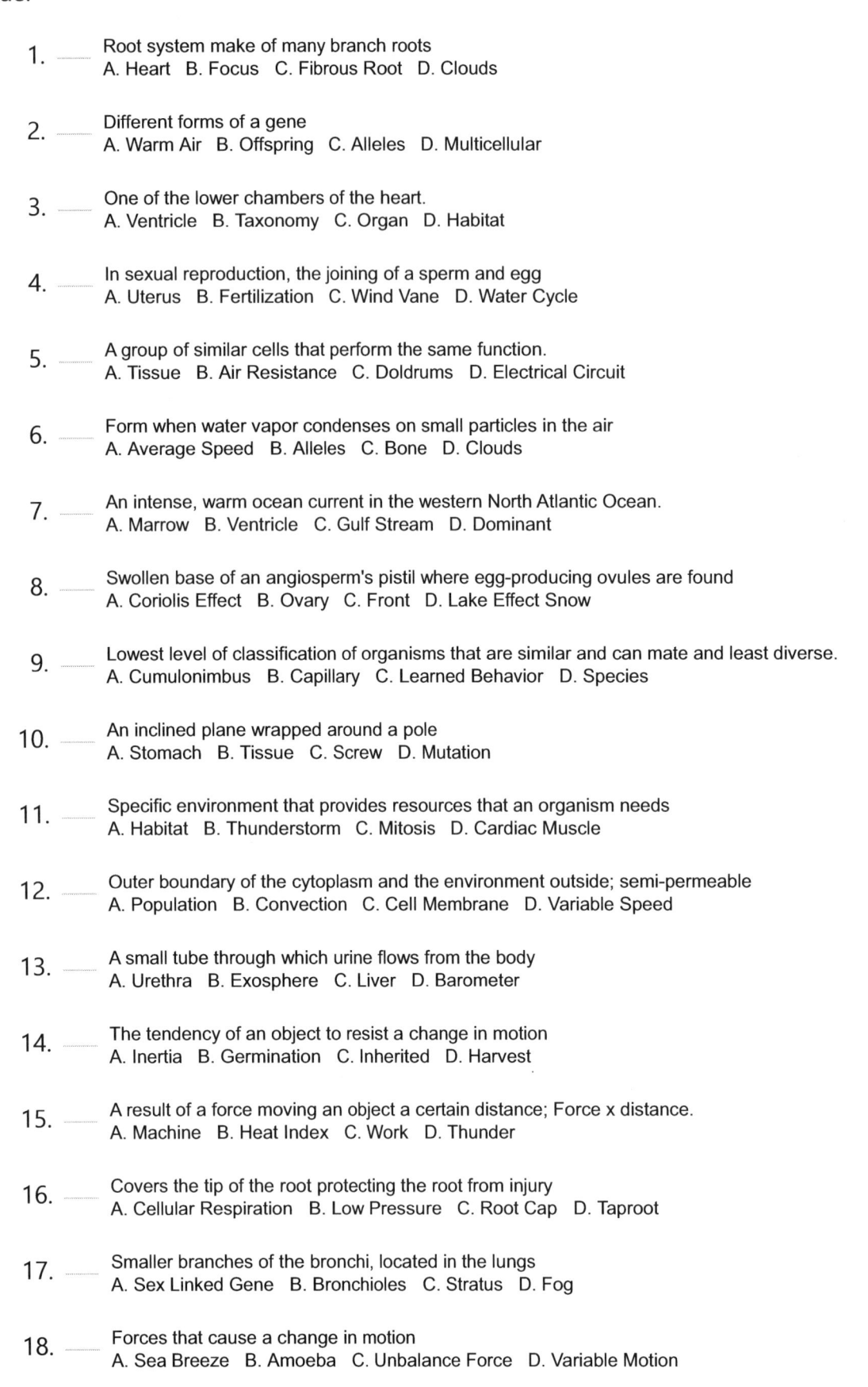

1. _____ Root system make of many branch roots
   A. Heart   B. Focus   C. Fibrous Root   D. Clouds

2. _____ Different forms of a gene
   A. Warm Air   B. Offspring   C. Alleles   D. Multicellular

3. _____ One of the lower chambers of the heart.
   A. Ventricle   B. Taxonomy   C. Organ   D. Habitat

4. _____ In sexual reproduction, the joining of a sperm and egg
   A. Uterus   B. Fertilization   C. Wind Vane   D. Water Cycle

5. _____ A group of similar cells that perform the same function.
   A. Tissue   B. Air Resistance   C. Doldrums   D. Electrical Circuit

6. _____ Form when water vapor condenses on small particles in the air
   A. Average Speed   B. Alleles   C. Bone   D. Clouds

7. _____ An intense, warm ocean current in the western North Atlantic Ocean.
   A. Marrow   B. Ventricle   C. Gulf Stream   D. Dominant

8. _____ Swollen base of an angiosperm's pistil where egg-producing ovules are found
   A. Coriolis Effect   B. Ovary   C. Front   D. Lake Effect Snow

9. _____ Lowest level of classification of organisms that are similar and can mate and least diverse.
   A. Cumulonimbus   B. Capillary   C. Learned Behavior   D. Species

10. _____ An inclined plane wrapped around a pole
    A. Stomach   B. Tissue   C. Screw   D. Mutation

11. _____ Specific environment that provides resources that an organism needs
    A. Habitat   B. Thunderstorm   C. Mitosis   D. Cardiac Muscle

12. _____ Outer boundary of the cytoplasm and the environment outside; semi-permeable
    A. Population   B. Convection   C. Cell Membrane   D. Variable Speed

13. _____ A small tube through which urine flows from the body
    A. Urethra   B. Exosphere   C. Liver   D. Barometer

14. _____ The tendency of an object to resist a change in motion
    A. Inertia   B. Germination   C. Inherited   D. Harvest

15. _____ A result of a force moving an object a certain distance; Force x distance.
    A. Machine   B. Heat Index   C. Work   D. Thunder

16. _____ Covers the tip of the root protecting the root from injury
    A. Cellular Respiration   B. Low Pressure   C. Root Cap   D. Taproot

17. _____ Smaller branches of the bronchi, located in the lungs
    A. Sex Linked Gene   B. Bronchioles   C. Stratus   D. Fog

18. _____ Forces that cause a change in motion
    A. Sea Breeze   B. Amoeba   C. Unbalance Force   D. Variable Motion

19. _____ A tiny blood vessel where substances are exchanged between the blood and the body cells.
A. Power B. Heredity C. Variable D. Capillary

20. _____ The combination of all forces acting on an object
A. Plant Cell B. Particulate Matter C. Net Force D. Peristalsis

21. _____ A muscular organ that mixes food and passes it to the small intestine- uses hydrochloric acid
A. Output Force B. Stomach C. Smooth Muscle D. Mesosphere

22. _____ Study of the classification of organisms
A. Taxonomy B. Sperm Cell C. Biotic Factor D. Stratosphere

23. _____ Electrical storm
A. Rock Cycle B. Digestion C. Ingestion D. Thunderstorm

24. _____ The ability to live
A. Unbalance Force B. Eye Spot C. Acceleration D. Viability

25. _____ The force in which air molecules push on a surface.
A. Lever B. Air Pressure C. Thermal Energy D. Species

26. _____ Separates the nucleus from the cytoplasm
A. Cold Front B. Community C. Dominant Allele D. Nuclear Membrane

27. _____ Describes an organism with two alleles that are the same for a trait
A. Brain B. Homozygous C. Rectum D. Response

28. _____ The effect of earth's rotation on the direction of winds and currents.
A. Urethra B. Fibrous Root C. Instinct D. Coriolis Effect

29. _____ Hair-like projections that extend from the plasma membrane and are used for locomotion
A. Carnivore B. Cilia C. Nimbus D. Water Vapor

30. _____ Second layer of the atmosphere that contains the ozone layer.
A. Cell Membrane B. Stratosphere C. Circulatory System D. Telophase

31. _____ Sprouting of the embryo from a seed; when first leaves are seen
A. Transformed B. Weather Front C. Chemical Digestion D. Germination

32. _____ A complete, closed path that electricity flows through.
A. Atmosphere B. Anaphase C. Electrical Circuit D. Acquired Trait

33. _____ A living part of an organism's habitat
A. Ureter B. Biotic Factor C. Ovary D. Nutrients

34. _____ The group that is exposed to changes in the independent variable
A. Local Wind B. Experimental Group C. Ecosystem D. Budding

35. _____ Haploid sex cell formed in the male reproductive organs
A. Asthenosphere B. Sperm C. Trial D. Volvox

36. _____ Filters waste from the blood like urea, water, salt and proteins.
A. Net Force B. Kidney C. Polar Easterlies D. Homozygous

37. _____ Sex cell
A. Alto B. Experimental Group C. Gamete D. Cirrus

38. Increased cooling you feel as a result of the wind
    A. Lithosphere   B. Wind Chill   C. Neurons   D. Embryo

39. Involuntary muscle found in many internal organs
    A. Viability   B. Hypothesis   C. Smooth Muscle   D. Small Intestine

40. Accomplishment of completing a job with minimum use of time and effort.
    A. Nucleus   B. Parallel Circuit   C. Efficiency   D. Troposphere

41. Each repetition of an experiment
    A. Closed Circuit   B. Force   C. Animal Cell   D. Trial

42. Water changes from liquid to gas.
    A. Weather   B. Evaporation   C. Stimulus   D. Wheel And Axle

43. Elevation or height above sea level
    A. Smog   B. Organic   C. Altitude   D. Transpiration

44. An alternative form of a gene.
    A. Alveoli   B. Lightning   C. Allele   D. Altitude

45. A form of asexual reproduction, forms by budding off the parent and forming an exact copy
    A. Root Hair   B. Radiation   C. Screw   D. Budding

46. Cloud that causes thunderstorms.
    A. Digestive System   B. Kidney   C. Warm Front   D. Cumulonimbus

47. Passed down from parent to offspring
    A. Gamete   B. Inherited   C. Inertia   D. Bladder

48. Movement of air from sea to land during the day.
    A. Sea Breeze   B. Wind Chill   C. Efficiency   D. Behavior

49. Water in the form of a gas
    A. Bronchioles   B. Cell Wall   C. Water Vapor   D. Evaporation

50. A mass of rising warm air that usually bring wet, stormy weather.
    A. Low Pressure   B. Work   C. Global Warming   D. Jet Stream

51. New diploid cell formed when a sperm fertilizes an egg.
    A. Organ System   B. Esophagus   C. Zygote   D. Cold Air

52. Substances that provide raw material and energy for organisms
    A. Nutrients   B. Groundwater   C. Wedge   D. Vein

53. A mixture of extremely small particles and liquid droplets suspended in the air
    A. Organism   B. Tornado   C. Particulate Matter   D. Testicles

54. A complete electric circuit that allows electricity to flow in a complete circle.
    A. Nuclear Membrane   B. Closed Circuit   C. Pseudopod   D. Speed

55. Cell process in which the nucleus divides to form two nuclei identical to each other.
    A. Zygote   B. Mitosis   C. DNA   D. Oxygen

56. A rigid structure that surrounds the cell membrane and provides support to the cell
    A. Genotype   B. Cell Wall   C. Chloroplast   D. Maritime Polar

57. _____ The new organisms produced by one or two parent organisms
A. Cilia   B. Offspring   C. Herbivore   D. Diaphragm

58. _____ Breaking down food into nutrients.
A. Root Cap   B. Digestion   C. Inclined Plane   D. Rain Gauge

59. _____ Organ where water is absorbed from the food and taken into the blood stream.
A. Tornado Alley   B. Large Intestines   C. Genetics   D. Punnet Square

60. _____ Speed that is not uniform and changes.
A. Variable Speed   B. Fertilization   C. Dependent Variable   D. Energy

61. _____ The ability to do work or to cause a change.
A. Energy   B. Urinary System   C. Gulf Stream   D. Composting

62. _____ Clouds that form in flat layers and often cover much of the sky.
A. Allele   B. Chlorophyll   C. Stratus   D. Trade Winds

63. _____ A device that is thick at one end and tapers to a thin edge at the other end.
A. Sex Cell   B. Sperm   C. Wedge   D. Molecule

64. _____ Removing seedlings to make room for one to grow better
A. Dew Point   B. Large Intestines   C. Slope   D. Thinning

65. _____ The end of the large intestine where waste material is compressed into a solid.
A. Rectum   B. Autotroph   C. Conclusion   D. Air Pressure

66. _____ A living thing
A. Ventricle   B. Organism   C. Runoff   D. Thinning

67. _____ Blood vessel carrying blood towards the heart
A. Multicellular   B. Nuclear Membrane   C. Vein   D. Warm Air

68. _____ Behavior based on practice or experience in the environment
A. Peristalsis   B. Learned Behavior   C. Average Speed   D. Stratus

69. _____ Possible explanation for a set of observation or answer to a scientific question; must be testable
A. Liver   B. Hypothesis   C. Front   D. Taproot

70. _____ The pre-fix for mid-level clouds
A. Organism   B. Root Hair   C. Alto   D. Kidney

71. _____ A group of organs that work together to pump and move blood throughout the body
A. Circulatory System   B. Unbalance Force   C. Chloroplast   D. Mutation

72. _____ Simple machine that consists of two circular objects of different sizes
A. Cardiac Muscle   B. Digestive System   C. Wheel And Axle   D. Polar Easterlies

73. _____ Step 3 in mitosis.
A. Stratosphere   B. Anaphase   C. Warm Front   D. Homozygous

74. _____ A muscular tube that connects the mouth to the stomach.
A. Esophagus   B. Cold Air   C. Jet Stream   D. Alleles

75. _____ The layer that fades to outer space.
A. Amoeba   B. Exosphere   C. Variable   D. Nutrients

76. _____ Produce sperm
A. Stomach B. Testicles C. Output Force D. Cold Front

77. _____ Genes that carry the x and y chromosomes
A. Ingestion B. Sex Linked Gene C. Focus D. Alto

78. _____ From living organisms
A. Organic B. Global Warming C. Fertilization D. Organ

79. _____ The plastic like layer of the earth on which the lithospheric plates float and move around
A. Sex Linked Gene B. Cellular Respiration C. Inertia D. Asthenosphere

80. _____ Rigid layer of earth about 100 km thick, made of the crust and a part of the upper mantle
A. Acquired Trait B. Root Cap C. Lithosphere D. Marrow

81. _____ A cell in a plant
A. Plant Cell B. Oxygen C. Embryo D. Thinning

82. _____ A collection of tissues that carry out a specialized function of the body
A. Sea Breeze B. Mesosphere C. Organ D. Population

83. _____ Gradual warming of the earth that may be caused in part by pollution and the greenhouse gas effect
A. Efficiency B. Global Warming C. Barometer D. Stimulus

84. _____ Able to hold less water vapor
A. Chemical Digestion B. Thunder C. Cold Air D. Viability

85. _____ Cold winds that blow from the east to the west near the North Pole and South Pole.
A. Polar Easterlies B. Urethra C. Dominant Allele D. Coriolis Effect

86. _____ Measures wind direction
A. Habitat B. Wind Vane C. Fibrous Root D. Evaporation

87. _____ Bottom layer in the atmosphere-where all the weather occurs
A. Work B. Troposphere C. Acceleration D. Smooth Muscle

88. _____ The male reproductive cell
A. Variable Speed B. Sperm Cell C. Transpiration D. Ecosystem

89. _____ Describes a trait that covers over, or dominates another form of that trait.
A. Wind Vane B. Dominant C. Low Pressure D. Sperm Cell

90. _____ Substance in center of bones that makes blood cells
A. Marrow B. Germination C. Maritime Polar D. Machine

91. _____ Found at 0°-30° latitude
A. Net Force B. Cell Wall C. Trade Winds D. Large Intestines

92. _____ Community of organisms that live in a particular area.
A. Smog B. Exosphere C. Ecosystem D. Heredity

93. _____ Any change made to DNA.
A. Mutation B. Genetics C. Telophase D. Air Resistance

94. _____ Layers of air surrounding the earth.
A. Asthenosphere B. Power C. Atmosphere D. Pseudopod

95. ___ Scientific study of heredity
   A. Genetics B. Runoff C. Animal Cell D. Dominant

96. ___ Organ system that produces, stores, and eliminates urine
   A. Screw B. Anaphase C. Altitude D. Urinary System

97. ___ Heterotroph that eats only animals
   A. Tornado B. Slope C. Carnivore D. Capillary

98. ___ Distance
   A. Speed B. Parallel Circuit C. Weather Front D. Instinct

99. ___ The condition of earth's atmosphere at a particular time and place
   A. Nucleus B. Organic C. Weather D. Urinary System

100. ___ Air sacs in the lungs where gas exchange happens
   A. Vein B. Alveoli C. Bone D. Clouds

From the words provided for each clue, provide the letter of the word which best matches the clue.

101. ___ Moving a plant and replanting it to help it grow
   A. Reference Point B. Transplant C. Ecology D. Nimbus

102. ___ Different forms of a gene
   A. Air Pressure B. Herbaceous C. Rectum D. Alleles

103. ___ The amount of water vapor in the air
   A. Urinary System B. Humidity C. Root Cap D. Testicles

104. ___ Passed down from parent to offspring
   A. Thunderstorm B. Gamete C. Genes D. Inherited

105. ___ Area of the female reproductive system where the fetus develops
   A. Acquired Trait B. Uterus C. Meteorology D. Maritime Tropical

106. ___ Heat energy; occurs due to friction.
   A. Density B. Autotroph C. Thermal Energy D. Skeletal Muscle

107. ___ A system for specifying the precise location of objects in space and time
   A. Herbivore B. Fertilization C. Frame Of Reference D. Polar Easterlies

108. ___ Winds that blow steadily from specific directions over long distances
   A. Hypothesis B. Thermosphere C. Recessive Trait D. Global Winds

109. ___ The rate of change of position in which the same distance is traveled each second
   A. Input Force B. Constant Speed C. Smooth Muscle D. Telophase

110. ___ Study of how organisms interact with their environment.
   A. Uterus B. Ecology C. Global Warming D. Global Wind

111. ___ Made of many cells
   A. Nuclear Membrane B. Inertia C. Multicellular D. Potential Energy

112. ___ Snow created when cold air flows over relatively warm water then over cold land
   A. Multicellular B. Photosynthesis C. Lake Effect Snow D. Radiation

113. Describes a trait that covers over, or dominates another form of that trait.
A. Bronchioles B. Pseudopod C. Dominant D. Fallopian Tubes

114. Each repetition of an experiment
A. Germination B. Flagella C. Series Circuit D. Trial

115. A rigid bar that is free to move around a fixed point
A. Dominant B. Lever C. Lightning D. Parallel Circuit

116. The new organisms produced by one or two parent organisms
A. Lithosphere B. Thermal Energy C. Offspring D. Output Force

117. Both alleles for a trait are the same and dominant.
A. Instinct B. Ecosystem C. Genotype D. Homozygous Dominant

118. A simple device without moving parts that changes the magnitude or direction of a force
A. Simple Machine B. Alleles C. Sex Cell D. Vector

119. Air sacs in the lungs where gas exchange happens
A. Dominant Allele B. Alveoli C. Marrow D. Variable Motion

120. Scientific study of heredity
A. Nitrogen B. Animal Cell C. Exosphere D. Genetics

121. Uses the brain, nerve cells, spinal cord to sense and respond to the environment
A. Paramecium B. Displacement C. Sperm Cell D. Nervous System

122. A line on a weather map that joins places that have the same air pressure
A. Isobar B. Epiglottis C. Thunder D. Plant Cell

123. Organ system that produces, stores, and eliminates urine
A. Urinary System B. Amoeba C. Cold Air D. Weather Front

124. A narrow belt of strong winds that blow in the upper troposphere
A. Jet Stream B. Ionosphere C. Particulate Matter D. Bladder

125. A front where cold air moves in under a warm air mass.
A. Cold Front B. Biotic Factor C. Binary Fission D. Ingestion

126. A physical characteristic coded by a gene
A. Small Intestine B. Ovary C. Taxonomy D. Trait

127. Measures wind direction
A. Sex Chromosomes B. Habitat C. Wind Vane D. Transpiration

128. Helps make proteins for the cell
A. Metaphase B. Ribosomes C. Constant Speed D. Lever

129. The position of a place in relation to another place
A. Tornado Alley B. Nucleus C. Relative Location D. Eukaryote

130. A diagram that shows the occurrence of a genetic trait in several generations of a family.
A. Life Science B. Pedigree C. Homeostasis D. Genetics

131. In sexual reproduction, the joining of a sperm and egg
A. Nutrients B. Wind Chill C. Fertilization D. Gulf Stream

132. Swollen base of an angiosperm's pistil where egg-producing ovules are found
A. Ovary   B. Stratosphere   C. Peristalsis   D. Phenotype

133. Brings fair skies and clear, nice weather; moves clockwise
A. Receptors   B. Vein   C. High Pressure   D. Composting

134. The thick vertical root with root hairs
A. Taproot   B. Trial   C. Organs   D. Heterozygous

135. Increased cooling you feel as a result of the wind
A. Dew Point   B. Volvox   C. Relative Location   D. Wind Chill

136. The pair of chromosomes that determine the sex of an organism
A. Cytoplasm   B. Wheel And Axle   C. Sex Chromosomes   D. Heat Index

137. Diagram that shows the slow, continuous process of rocks changing from one type to another
A. Respiratory System   B. Rock Cycle   C. Viability   D. Pedigree

138. Simple machine that consists of two circular objects of different sizes
A. Asthenosphere   B. Territory   C. Humidity   D. Wheel And Axle

139. Organic material worked on by decomposers to breaking it down
A. Carnivore   B. Composting   C. Conduction   D. Wind Vane

140. Brain of the cell, contains DNA.
A. Inherited   B. Nucleus   C. Organ   D. Ribosomes

141. Violently swirling winds that are sometimes visible as a funnel-shaped cloud
A. Tornado   B. Fulcrum   C. Diaphragm   D. Atmosphere

142. The lower part of the thermosphere
A. Ionosphere   B. Cellular Respiration   C. Niche   D. Water Vapor

143. A collection of tissues that carry out a specialized function of the body
A. Force   B. Anaphase   C. Punnet Square   D. Organ

144. Specific environment that provides resources that an organism needs
A. Budding   B. Prophase   C. Convection   D. Habitat

145. Distance
A. Electrical Circuit   B. Simple Machine   C. Large Intestines   D. Speed

146. A front where warm air moves over cold air weather.
A. Response   B. Warm Front   C. Harvest   D. High Pressure

147. Taking food into the body
A. Compound Machine   B. Ingestion   C. Allele   D. Screw

148. Separates the nucleus from the cytoplasm
A. Nuclear Membrane   B. Taproot   C. Transplant   D. Population Density

149. A cell that has half the number of chromosomes found in the organism's body cells.
A. Isobar   B. Warm Air   C. Sex Cell   D. Neurons

150. A blood vessel that carries blood away from the heart
A. Warm Front   B. Cell   C. Nervous System   D. Artery

151. Organ where water is absorbed from the food and taken into the blood stream.
A. Large Intestines   B. Oxygen   C. Equilibrium   D. Recessive Allele

152. An organism's physical appearance, or visible traits.
A. Procedure   B. Capillary   C. Phenotype   D. Chlorophyll

153. Able to hold less water vapor
A. Cumulus Clouds   B. Cold Air   C. Fibrous Root   D. Frame Of Reference

154. A place or object used for comparison to determine if an object is in motion
A. Esophagus   B. Condensation   C. Reference Point   D. Molecule

155. The condition of earth's atmosphere at a particular time and place
A. Homozygous Dominant   B. Weather   C. Air Quality Index   D. Circulatory System

156. The study of the entire atmosphere, including the weather
A. Experiment   B. Trait   C. Troposphere   D. Meteorology

157. Plant process of using water, carbon dioxide and sunshine to make food
A. Offspring   B. Stationary Front   C. Speed   D. Photosynthesis

158. Typical weather pattern in an area over a long period of time
A. Artery   B. Climate   C. Jet Stream   D. Continental Polar

159. Occurs when opposite charges attract, between two clouds or between a cloud and the ground
A. Learned Behavior   B. Lake Effect Snow   C. Homozygous   D. Lightning

160. Heterotroph that eats only plants
A. Cold Front   B. Open Circuit   C. Climate   D. Herbivore

161. The force in which air molecules push on a surface.
A. Bronchi   B. Air Pressure   C. Alveoli   D. Heart

162. A muscular tube that connects the mouth to the stomach.
A. Polar Air Masses   B. Esophagus   C. Mutation   D. Sexual Reproduction

163. Layers of air surrounding the earth.
A. Runoff   B. Atmosphere   C. Rock Cycle   D. Global Winds

164. The male reproductive cell
A. Dew   B. Organelle   C. Sperm Cell   D. Closed Circuit

165. A machine that is made up of two or more simple machines
A. Weather   B. Compound Machine   C. Responding Variable   D. Friction

166. Energy that is stored and held in readiness.
A. Urethra   B. Potential Energy   C. Cell Wall   D. Power

167. Possible explanation for a set of observation or answer to a scientific question; must be testable
A. Paramecium   B. Vector   C. Hypothesis   D. Ecology

168. A force that opposes motion between two surfaces that are in contact
A. Cellular Respiration   B. Life Science   C. Screw   D. Friction

169. A tiny cell structure that carries out a specific function within the cell
A. Learned Behavior   B. Ecosystem   C. Organelle   D. Metaphase

170. Produce sperm
A. Open Circuit   B. Fulcrum   C. Testicles   D. Thunderstorm

171. Occurs when the air is heated, it rapidly expands.
A. Genotype   B. Thunder   C. Lightning   D. Urethra

172. Able to hold more water vapor
A. Genes   B. Weather   C. Water Vapor   D. Warm Air

173. A cell in a plant
A. Ovary   B. Punnet Square   C. Plant Cell   D. Eukaryote

174. Behavior based on practice or experience in the environment
A. Learned Behavior   B. Receptors   C. Asthenosphere   D. Mutation

175. Evaporation of water from the leaves of a plant
A. Nervous System   B. Transpiration   C. Thermal Energy   D. Flagella

176. Stem that is soft and green
A. Herbaceous   B. Recessive Trait   C. Genetics   D. Dew

177. Occurs when molecules of one substance are spread evenly throughout another substance.
A. Equilibrium   B. Continental Polar   C. Atmosphere   D. Humidity

178. Number of individuals in a given area.
A. Cytoplasm   B. Conduction   C. Sperm Cell   D. Population Density

179. Action that changes; is caused by a stimulus; a reaction
A. Response   B. Runoff   C. Composting   D. Meteorology

180. Community of organisms that live in a particular area.
A. Series Circuit   B. Ecosystem   C. Diaphragm   D. Amoeba

181. The increased temperature you feel as a result of relative humidity
A. Variable Motion   B. Acquired Trait   C. Heat Index   D. Inherited

182. Structure, such as the heart, made up of different types of tissues that all work together
A. Stratosphere   B. Organ   C. Cumulus Clouds   D. Nucleus

183. A flap of tissue that prevents food from entering the trachea, or windpipe, during swallowing.
A. Output Force   B. Epiglottis   C. Oxygen   D. Photosynthesis

184. Area in North America where tornadoes occur most often
A. Response   B. Tornado Alley   C. Cold Front   D. Allele

185. A large dome shaped muscle that plays an important role in breathing.
A. Heterozygous   B. Diaphragm   C. Niche   D. Pedigree

186. The plastic like layer of the earth on which the lithospheric plates float and move around
A. Asthenosphere   B. Respiratory System   C. Ingestion   D. Tornado

187. The transfer of heat energy from one substance to another through direct contact
A. Maritime Tropical   B. Conduction   C. Nitrogen   D. Reference Point

188. A group of organs that work together to pump and move blood throughout the body
A. Circulatory System   B. Hypothesis   C. Biotic Factor   D. Transpiration

189. _____ A long, whip-like filament that helps in cell motility.
A. Power   B. Flagella   C. Rectum   D. Habitat

190. _____ A form of asexual reproduction in which one cell divides to form two identical cells.
A. Lever   B. Binary Fission   C. Procedure   D. Air Quality Index

191. _____ A push or a pull
A. Tornado Alley   B. Nuclear Membrane   C. Force   D. Alleles

192. _____ The tendency of an object to resist a change in motion
A. Organ   B. Budding   C. Jet Stream   D. Inertia

193. _____ A complete electric circuit that allows electricity to flow in a complete circle.
A. Alveoli   B. Global Wind   C. Closed Circuit   D. Multicellular

194. _____ The rate at which work is done.
A. Power   B. Thunder   C. Epiglottis   D. Trait

195. _____ Type of heat transfer the sun's energy travels to the earth's surface
A. Skeletal Muscle   B. Weather Front   C. Radiation   D. Closed Circuit

196. _____ A circuit that contains more than one path for current flow.
A. Ionosphere   B. Parallel Circuit   C. Heart   D. Displacement

197. _____ A type of Protista characterized by great flexibility and the presence of pseudopodia.
A. Fibrous Root   B. Cell   C. Experiment   D. Amoeba

198. _____ A muscle that is attached to the bones of the skeleton and provides the force that moves the bones
A. Exosphere   B. Telophase   C. Speed   D. Skeletal Muscle

199. _____ Sex cell
A. Circulatory System   B. Gamete   C. Binary Fission   D. Animal Cell

200. _____ A colorless, odorless, tasteless nonflammable gas; 21% of atmosphere
A. Oxygen   B. Population Density   C. Thermosphere   D. Gulf Stream

From the words provided for each clue, provide the letter of the word which best matches the clue.

201. _____ Occurs when molecules of one substance are spread evenly throughout another substance.
A. Experiment   B. Electrical Circuit   C. Bronchi   D. Equilibrium

202. _____ Action that changes; is caused by a stimulus; a reaction
A. Response   B. Habitat   C. Polar Air Masses   D. Multicellular

203. _____ Snow created when cold air flows over relatively warm water then over cold land
A. Conduction   B. Lake Effect Snow   C. Meiosis   D. Frame Of Reference

204. _____ Organ system that produces, stores, and eliminates urine
A. Average Speed   B. Fibrous Root   C. Response   D. Urinary System

205. _____ Equal forces acting on an object in opposite directions
A. DNA   B. Balanced Force   C. Stationary Front   D. Allele

206. _____ Uses the brain, nerve cells, spinal cord to sense and respond to the environment
A. Organ System   B. Fog   C. Nervous System   D. Esophagus

207. The outermost layer of earth's atmosphere.
A. Thermosphere   B. Transformed   C. Chlorophyll   D. Binary Fission

208. Distance
A. Responding Variable   B. Input Force   C. Speed   D. Recessive Allele

209. Water in the form of a gas
A. Water Vapor   B. Instinct   C. Homeostasis   D. Hurricane

210. Temperature at which the air becomes saturated or full of water vapor.
A. Digestion   B. Organelle   C. Dew Point   D. Closed Circuit

211. A single strand of DNA tightly coiled around special proteins
A. Amoeba   B. Variable   C. Urinary System   D. Chromosome

212. Produces bile
A. Liver   B. Model   C. Cell Wall   D. Eukaryote

213. A front where warm air moves over cold air weather.
A. Digestive System   B. Skeletal Muscle   C. Warm Front   D. Heart

214. A place or object used for comparison to determine if an object is in motion
A. Slope   B. Land Breeze   C. Reference Point   D. Motion

215. The plastic like layer of the earth on which the lithospheric plates float and move around
A. Food Chain   B. Asthenosphere   C. Lake Effect Snow   D. Gulf Stream

216. Speed and direction of a moving body; velocity equals the displacement divided by the time
A. Ionosphere   B. Velocity   C. High Pressure   D. Heterozygous

217. Sugar that is major source of energy for cells
A. Equilibrium   B. Glucose   C. Taproot   D. Nervous System

218. Basic unit of structure and function in all living things or organisms
A. Trait   B. Dew Point   C. Cell   D. Ovary

219. Made of many cells
A. Multicellular   B. Experimental Group   C. Predator   D. Mitosis

220. Area in North America where tornadoes occur most often
A. Bone   B. Lysosome   C. Occluded Front   D. Tornado Alley

221. Green pigment in chloroplasts of plants and algae needed for photosynthesis
A. Deceleration   B. Chlorophyll   C. Thunderstorm   D. Respiratory System

222. Cell division that produces gametes
A. Stomach   B. Meiosis   C. Condensation   D. Viability

223. Any factor that can affect the results of an experiment.
A. Unicellular   B. Variable   C. Sperm   D. Egg

224. Absorbs water and forms feces
A. Large Intestine   B. Rain Gauge   C. Herbivore   D. Chloroplast

225. A scale that ranks levels of ozone and other air pollutants
A. Air Quality Index   B. Peristalsis   C. Cumulonimbus   D. Stratus

226. Root system make of many branch roots
A. Air Quality Index   B. Data   C. Large Intestine   D. Fibrous Root

227. Cell process in which the nucleus divides to form two nuclei identical to each other.
A. Mitosis   B. Alleles   C. Screw   D. Inertia

228. Each repetition of an experiment
A. Population Density   B. Prokaryote   C. Trial   D. Evaporation

229. A front where cold air moves in under a warm air mass.
A. Velocity   B. Balanced Force   C. Cold Front   D. Speed

230. The ability to live
A. Viability   B. Mitochondria   C. Particulate Matter   D. Focus

231. An organism's genetic makeup, or allele combinations.
A. Genotype   B. Tornado   C. Ecology   D. Flagella

232. An organelle found in plant and algae cells where photosynthesis occurs
A. Machine   B. Photosynthesis   C. Chloroplast   D. Plasma

233. Area occupied and protected by an animal or group
A. Recessive Trait   B. Sea Breeze   C. Territory   D. Marrow

234. A single cell organism that lives in pond water and uses cilia to move
A. Circulatory System   B. Urethra   C. Mechanical Energy   D. Paramecium

235. Brain of the cell, contains DNA.
A. Nucleus   B. Open Circuit   C. Cold Front   D. Atrium

236. Violently swirling winds that are sometimes visible as a funnel-shaped cloud
A. Exact Location   B. Tornado   C. Genotype   D. Liver

237. A decrease in speed; negative acceleration.
A. Capillary   B. Species   C. Deceleration   D. Rock Cycle

238. A group of organs that work together to perform a major function
A. Organ System   B. Epiglottis   C. Ecosystem   D. Sexual Reproduction

239. Plant process of using water, carbon dioxide and sunshine to make food
A. Territory   B. Exosphere   C. Photosynthesis   D. Bladder

240. The increased temperature you feel as a result of relative humidity
A. Heat Index   B. Density   C. Brain   D. Organic

241. Factor in experiment that changes in response to another factor; dependent variable.
A. Receptors   B. Responding Variable   C. Lightning   D. Groundwater

242. Haploid sex cell formed in the female reproductive organs.
A. Gamete   B. White Blood Cell   C. Egg   D. Warm Air

243. A temporary, "false foot" of cytoplasm that helps a Protista move and eat.
A. Climate   B. Nucleus   C. Series Circuit   D. Pseudopod

244. Forces that cause a change in motion
A. Unbalance Force   B. Transplant   C. Excretion   D. Troposphere

245. Process by which a gas changes to a liquid
A. Organ   B. Ventricle   C. Cell   D. Condensation

246. Swollen base of an angiosperm's pistil where egg-producing ovules are found
A. Continental Polar   B. Distance   C. Golgi Body   D. Ovary

247. From living organisms
A. Compound Machine   B. Oxygen   C. Isobar   D. Organic

248. Location of a place using longitude and latitude.
A. Inherited   B. Exact Location   C. Kidney   D. Volvox

249. Covers the tip of the root protecting the root from injury
A. Cirrus   B. Root Cap   C. Tornado Alley   D. Mutation

250. Point deep inside earth where energy is released, causing an earthquake
A. Efficiency   B. Pedigree   C. Heat Index   D. Focus

251. Break down food and release energy to the cell
A. Mitochondria   B. Scientific Method   C. Cardiac Muscle   D. Parallel Circuit

252. Made of a single cell
A. Unicellular   B. Taxonomy   C. Dominant Trait   D. Sex Chromosomes

253. The transfer of heat energy from one substance to another through direct contact
A. Fertilization   B. Nimbus   C. Lungs   D. Conduction

254. A controlled procedure designed to answer a scientific question.
A. Doldrums   B. Experiment   C. Constant Speed   D. Zygote

255. Different distances traveled in equal times.
A. Unbalance Force   B. Variable Motion   C. Reference Point   D. Warm Front

256. A measure of how far an object moves in relation to a reference point.
A. Cumulus   B. Autotroph   C. Distance   D. Tissue

257. A small tube through which urine flows from the body
A. Meteorology   B. Urethra   C. Coriolis Effect   D. Large Intestines

258. A series of steps that a scientist follows in order to solve a problem or answer a question
A. Thermal Energy   B. Conclusion   C. Rectum   D. Scientific Method

259. Describes an organism with two alleles that are the same for a trait
A. Homozygous   B. Root Cap   C. Pollution   D. Behavior

260. The mass of nerve tissue that is the main control center of the nervous system
A. Organs   B. Glucose   C. Sperm Cell   D. Brain

261. An alternative form of a gene.
A. Chromosome   B. Science   C. Sex Linked Gene   D. Allele

262. A colorless, odorless, tasteless nonflammable gas; 21% of atmosphere
A. Trial   B. Pseudopod   C. Oxygen   D. Paramecium

263. Involuntary muscle tissue found only in the heart
A. Dominant   B. Animal Cell   C. Cardiac Muscle   D. Thermosphere

264. The rate of change of position in which the same distance is traveled each second
A. Genetics   B. Constant Speed   C. Potential Energy   D. Runoff

265. A type of Protista characterized by great flexibility and the presence of pseudopodia.
A. Asthenosphere   B. Relative Location   C. Trachea   D. Amoeba

266. A muscular tube that connects the mouth to the stomach.
A. Taproot   B. Esophagus   C. Water Vapor   D. Cytoplasm

267. Electrical storm
A. Thunderstorm   B. Allele   C. Inertia   D. Continental Polar

268. Passed down from parent to offspring
A. Stratus   B. Deceleration   C. Chloroplast   D. Inherited

269. Contains digestive enzymes that destroy damaged organelles and invaders
A. Organs   B. Habitat   C. Lysosome   D. Rectum

270. A long, whip-like filament that helps in cell motility.
A. Transformed   B. Groundwater   C. Flagella   D. Bronchi

271. The position of a place in relation to another place
A. Mutation   B. Relative Location   C. Air Quality Index   D. Stationary Front

272. An intense, warm ocean current in the western North Atlantic Ocean.
A. Parallel Circuit   B. Relative Location   C. Gulf Stream   D. Liver

273. A colonial form of live green algae, round in shape.
A. Volvox   B. Herbivore   C. Capillary   D. Responding Variable

274. The male reproductive cell
A. Cold Front   B. Sperm Cell   C. Peristalsis   D. Model

275. Heterotroph that eats only plants
A. Asthenosphere   B. Cell Wall   C. Particulate Matter   D. Herbivore

276. Unicellular only - no nucleus or organelles with dna that are not organized into chromosomes.
A. High Pressure   B. Volvox   C. Prokaryote   D. Lysosome

277. A line on a weather map that joins places that have the same air pressure
A. Isobar   B. Unbalance Force   C. Occluded Front   D. Exosphere

278. Organ where water is absorbed from the food and taken into the blood stream.
A. Large Intestines   B. Digestive System   C. Mechanical Energy   D. Homozygous

279. The organism that feeds off another.
A. Predator   B. Thermosphere   C. Condensation   D. Heterozygous

280. How tightly packed the matter in a substance is.
A. Large Intestine   B. Density   C. Alleles   D. Meiosis

281. Moving a plant and replanting it to help it grow
A. Excretion   B. Transplant   C. Stomach   D. Constant Speed

282. A complex molecule containing the genetic information that makes up the chromosomes.
A. Esophagus   B. Oxygen   C. Chromosome   D. DNA

283. Elastic, hollow, muscular organ that provides temporary storage for urine
A. Frame Of Reference   B. Ovary   C. Trait   D. Bladder

284. The lower part of the thermosphere
A. Warm Air   B. Urethra   C. Ionosphere   D. Doldrums

285. Cells from two parents unite to form the first cell of a new organism
A. Nimbus   B. Sexual Reproduction   C. Input Force   D. Isobar

286. Located in colder regions of the world
A. Lungs   B. Gamete   C. Screw   D. Polar Air Masses

287. Community of organisms that live in a particular area.
A. Motion   B. Ecosystem   C. Closed Circuit   D. Sexual Reproduction

288. Diagram that shows the slow, continuous process of rocks changing from one type to another
A. Transplant   B. Chlorophyll   C. Plasma   D. Rock Cycle

289. A device that makes work easier by changing the size or direction of a force
A. Troposphere   B. Prokaryote   C. Machine   D. Slope

290. Able to hold more water vapor
A. Territory   B. Cytoplasm   C. Genetics   D. Warm Air

291. Accomplishment of completing a job with minimum use of time and effort.
A. Heart   B. Efficiency   C. Cumulus   D. Runoff

292. Wispy, feathery clouds made mostly of ice crystals that form at high levels
A. Lake Effect Snow   B. Cirrus   C. Variable   D. Sex Linked Gene

293. Movement of air from land to sea at night.
A. Mitosis   B. Land Breeze   C. Food Chain   D. Marrow

294. A muscular organ that mixes food and passes it to the small intestine- uses hydrochloric acid
A. Brain   B. Open Circuit   C. Stomach   D. Organelle

295. A rigid structure that surrounds the cell membrane and provides support to the cell
A. Predator   B. Cell Wall   C. Scientific Method   D. Land Breeze

296. A group of organs that work together to pump and move blood throughout the body
A. Cirrus   B. Exact Location   C. Circulatory System   D. Paramecium

297. The end of the large intestine where waste material is compressed into a solid.
A. Thunderstorm   B. Tornado Alley   C. Rectum   D. Skeletal Muscle

298. Heat energy; occurs due to friction.
A. Thermal Energy   B. Fog   C. Climate   D. Hurricane

299. Process where wastes are removed from the body or cell.
A. Egg   B. Nervous System   C. Series Circuit   D. Excretion

300. Liquid part of blood
A. Plasma   B. Multicellular   C. Homeostasis   D. Velocity

From the words provided for each clue, provide the letter of the word which best matches the clue.

301. Scientific study of heredity
A. Sex Cell   B. Doldrums   C. Volvox   D. Genetics

302. Smaller branches of the bronchi, located in the lungs
A. Bronchioles   B. Force   C. Community   D. Maritime Polar

303. The new organisms produced by one or two parent organisms
A. Dew Point   B. Offspring   C. Gamete   D. Genotype

304. Sprouting of the embryo from a seed; when first leaves are seen
A. Germination   B. Polar Air Masses   C. Kinetic Energy   D. Scientific Method

305. Process by which a gas changes to a liquid
A. Excretion   B. Condensation   C. Egg   D. Relative Location

306. Describes a trait that covers over, or dominates another form of that trait.
A. Gene   B. Biotic Factor   C. Dominant   D. Dominant Allele

307. Equal forces acting on an object in opposite directions
A. Rectum   B. Ecology   C. Balanced Force   D. Ribosomes

308. A group of similar cells that perform the same function.
A. Constant Speed   B. Isobar   C. Fulcrum   D. Tissue

309. Diagram that shows the slow, continuous process of rocks changing from one type to another
A. Distance   B. Golgi Body   C. Rock Cycle   D. Carnivore

310. Organism that makes its own food (generally plants).
A. Oxygen   B. High Pressure   C. Receptors   D. Autotroph

311. Brings fair skies and clear, nice weather; moves clockwise
A. Lake Effect Snow   B. Precipitation   C. Dominant   D. High Pressure

312. The rate of change of position in which the same distance is traveled each second
A. Cardiac Muscle   B. Viability   C. Stratus   D. Constant Speed

313. Community of organisms that live in a particular area.
A. Barometer   B. Ecosystem   C. Thunder   D. Chemical Digestion

314. Any change made to DNA.
A. Genetics   B. Hybrid   C. Rain Gauge   D. Mutation

315. Protista that moves by a flagellum.
A. Open Circuit   B. Balanced Force   C. Euglena   D. Predator

316. Separates the nucleus from the cytoplasm
A. Trachea   B. Artery   C. Nuclear Membrane   D. Ovary

317. A temporary, "false foot" of cytoplasm that helps a Protista move and eat.
A. Liver   B. Pseudopod   C. Inherited   D. Trait

318. Loosening soil around plants to allow moisture in and roots to grow.
A. Local Wind   B. Offspring   C. Habitat   D. Cultivate

319. Measures air pressure
A. Barometer   B. Fibrous Root   C. Conservation   D. Skeletal Muscle

320. Point deep inside earth where energy is released, causing an earthquake
A. Variable Motion   B. Atmosphere   C. Focus   D. Dominant Trait

321. Heterotroph that eats only animals
A. Bronchi   B. Carnivore   C. Chloroplast   D. Multicellular

322. An offspring that was given different genetic information for a trait from each parent
A. Hybrid   B. Friction   C. Kidney   D. Marrow

323. A blood vessel that carries blood away from the heart
A. Heat Index   B. Artery   C. Taxonomy   D. Deceleration

324. The energy of motion
A. Bronchioles   B. Stratosphere   C. Kinetic Energy   D. Red Blood Cell

325. The increased temperature you feel as a result of relative humidity
A. Germination   B. Hurricane   C. Oral Cavity   D. Heat Index

326. A type of Protista characterized by great flexibility and the presence of pseudopodia.
A. Plant Cell   B. Peristalsis   C. Tornado   D. Amoeba

327. A violently rotating column of air stretching from a cloud to the ground-turns counterclockwise
A. Tornado   B. Dependent Variable   C. Jet Stream   D. Autotroph

328. Breaks down food into smaller molecules.
A. Warm Air   B. Sexual Reproduction   C. Flagella   D. Digestive System

329. A colonial form of live green algae, round in shape.
A. Volvox   B. Learned Behavior   C. Molecule   D. Pulley

330. A physical characteristic coded by a gene
A. Uterus   B. Vein   C. Wedge   D. Trait

331. Snow created when cold air flows over relatively warm water then over cold land
A. Lake Effect Snow   B. Smog   C. Meteorology   D. Sperm Cell

332. An organelle found in plant and algae cells where photosynthesis occurs
A. Clouds   B. Chloroplast   C. Brain   D. Diaphragm

333. Two or more atoms combine.
A. Large Intestines   B. Molecule   C. Condensation   D. Instinct

334. A muscular tube that connects the mouth to the stomach.
A. Altitude   B. Energy   C. Esophagus   D. Heterozygous

335. Enzymes are used to break foods into their smaller chemical building blocks
A. Weather Front   B. Bladder   C. Chemical Digestion   D. Food Chain

336. Layer above the troposphere where meteors burn up
A. Displacement   B. Mesosphere   C. Transformed   D. Cold Air

337. Thin hair like roots on the outer layer of the tap root, absorb water and anchor plant
A. Wheel And Axle   B. Root Hair   C. Nimbus   D. Taproot

338. Measures wind speed
A. Nuclear Membrane   B. Plasma   C. Anemometer   D. Fog

339. The fixed point about which a lever pivots
A. Fulcrum   B. Cilia   C. Nucleus   D. Telophase

340. An organism's genetic makeup, or allele combinations.
A. Ionosphere   B. Cultivate   C. Vacuole   D. Genotype

341. Elevation or height above sea level
A. Mesosphere   B. Euglena   C. Altitude   D. Digestion

342. A segment of DNA on a chromosome that codes for a specific trait
A. Ecosystem   B. Loam   C. Thinning   D. Gene

343. Sex cell
A. Cold Front   B. Esophagus   C. Focus   D. Gamete

344. Cells from two parents unite to form the first cell of a new organism
A. Exosphere   B. Chromosome   C. Sexual Reproduction   D. Epiglottis

345. Haploid sex cell formed in the female reproductive organs.
A. Stationary Front   B. Velocity   C. Efficiency   D. Egg

346. A series of events in which one organism eats another to obtain energy
A. Procedure   B. Ovule   C. Homeostasis   D. Food Chain

347. Second layer of the atmosphere that contains the ozone layer.
A. Stratosphere   B. Power   C. Cumulus Clouds   D. Rock Cycle

348. Made of a single cell
A. Organs   B. Unicellular   C. Photosynthesis   D. Anemometer

349. The rate at which work is done.
A. Wind Chill   B. Power   C. Cell Membrane   D. Chlorophyll

350. The pre-fix for mid-level clouds
A. Air Quality   B. Mutation   C. Alto   D. Work

351. Brain of the cell, contains DNA.
A. Tissue   B. Vector   C. Nucleus   D. Anaphase

352. An intense, warm ocean current in the western North Atlantic Ocean.
A. Gulf Stream   B. Population Density   C. Animal Cell   D. Air Mass

353. Both alleles for a trait are the same and dominant.
A. Radiation   B. Sea Breeze   C. Cellular Respiration   D. Homozygous Dominant

354. A cell that has half the number of chromosomes found in the organism's body cells.
A. Polar Easterlies   B. Skeletal System   C. Sex Cell   D. Digestive System

355. The highest atmosphere layer leading to outer space.
A. Smooth Muscle   B. Exosphere   C. Alveoli   D. Humidity

356. Involuntary muscle found in many internal organs
A. Weather   B. Organ   C. Smooth Muscle   D. Exact Location

357. A single strand of DNA tightly coiled around special proteins
A. Pseudopod   B. Organic   C. Nitrogen   D. Chromosome

358. Protecting the environment by not over using or replacing resources
A. Mitosis   B. Air Resistance   C. Amoeba   D. Conservation

359. All members of one species in a particular area.
A. Water Vapor   B. Population   C. Motion   D. Ingestion

360. Force that opposes the motion of objects that move through the air
A. Composting   B. Air Resistance   C. Recessive Trait   D. Homozygous Dominant

361. An organism that has two different alleles for a trait
A. Climate   B. Alto   C. Heterozygous   D. Unicellular

362. Organic material worked on by decomposers to breaking it down
A. Composting   B. Heredity   C. Gulf Stream   D. Thermosphere

363. Swollen base of an angiosperm's pistil where egg-producing ovules are found
A. DNA   B. Population   C. Ovary   D. Cumulonimbus

364. The mass of nerve tissue that is the main control center of the nervous system
A. Brain   B. Asthenosphere   C. Meiosis   D. Series Circuit

365. Plant process of using water, carbon dioxide and sunshine to make food
A. Photosynthesis   B. Neurons   C. Root Hair   D. Maritime Tropical

366. Hair-like projections that extend from the plasma membrane and are used for locomotion
A. Organ System   B. Eye Spot   C. Cilia   D. Cytoplasm

367. Layers of air surrounding the earth.
A. Dew Point   B. Warm Air   C. Precipitation   D. Atmosphere

368. Blood cells that carry oxygen from the lungs to the body cells.
A. Diaphragm   B. Dependent Variable   C. Energy   D. Red Blood Cell

369. A collection of tissues that carry out a specialized function of the body
A. Red Blood Cell   B. Organ   C. Cold Front   D. Uterus

370. Green pigment in chloroplasts of plants and algae needed for photosynthesis
A. Marrow   B. Chlorophyll   C. Deceleration   D. Liver

371. Wavelike contractions of smooth muscles in the organs of the digestive tract.
A. Force   B. Rock Cycle   C. Peristalsis   D. High Pressure

372. The measurable effect, outcome, or response in which the research is interested.
A. Maritime Polar   B. Instinct   C. Dependent Variable   D. Velocity

373. Simple machine that consists of two circular objects of different sizes
A. Hybrid   B. Lake Effect Snow   C. Homozygous Dominant   D. Wheel And Axle

374. Made of many cells
A. Unicellular   B. Organic   C. Heredity   D. Multicellular

375. Taking food into the body
A. Oral Cavity   B. Ingestion   C. Peristalsis   D. Stratosphere

376. Filters waste from the blood like urea, water, salt and proteins.
A. Kidney   B. Oxygen   C. Thinning   D. Weather Front

377. The ability to live
A. Viability   B. Dominant Trait   C. Barometer   D. Stratus

378. A complex molecule containing the genetic information that makes up the chromosomes.
A. DNA   B. Ovary   C. Polar Easterlies   D. Viability

379. A cell in an animal
A. Bronchi   B. Organ System   C. Nimbus   D. Animal Cell

380. A boundary between air masses that don't move possibly causing rain for several days
A. Air Quality   B. Esophagus   C. Stationary Front   D. Meiosis

381. A muscle that is attached to the bones of the skeleton and provides the force that moves the bones
A. Skeletal Muscle   B. Chromosome   C. Population Density   D. Air Resistance

382. Allele whose trait always shows.
A. Dominant Allele   B. Biotic Factor   C. Habitat   D. Taxonomy

383. Area of low atmospheric pressure and calm westerly winds located at the equator.
A. Nucleus   B. Doldrums   C. Meteorology   D. Asthenosphere

384. To change in appearance or character
A. Rectum   B. Transformed   C. Thermosphere   D. Vacuole

385. Outer boundary of the cytoplasm and the environment outside; semi-permeable
A. Anaphase   B. Open Circuit   C. Chloroplast   D. Cell Membrane

386. The amount of water vapor in the air
A. Humidity   B. Cold Air   C. Wind Chill   D. Anemometer

387. Substance in center of bones that makes blood cells
A. Distance   B. Vein   C. Marrow   D. Ecosystem

388. Violently swirling winds that are sometimes visible as a funnel-shaped cloud
A. Tornado   B. Sperm Cell   C. Alto   D. Transformed

389. A large body of air that has about the same temperature and moisture throughout.
A. Motion   B. Climate   C. Ionosphere   D. Air Mass

390. Involuntary muscle tissue found only in the heart
A. Sexual Reproduction   B. Cardiac Muscle   C. Kinetic Energy   D. Ribosomes

391. The condition of earth's atmosphere at a particular time and place
A. Vector   B. Telophase   C. Recessive Trait   D. Weather

392. All the different populations that live together in an area
A. Bronchioles   B. Cardiac Muscle   C. Hurricane   D. Community

393. Cell division that produces gametes
A. Scientific Method   B. Meiosis   C. Air Mass   D. Epiglottis

394. A dark cloud whose name means rain.
A. Skeletal System   B. Nimbus   C. Root Hair   D. Egg

395. Fluid in a cell that holds all the organelles in place.
A. Cytoplasm   B. Inherited   C. Offspring   D. Organs

396. Air sacs in the lungs where gas exchange happens
A. Molecule   B. Trait   C. Tornado   D. Alveoli

397. Speed and direction of a moving body; velocity equals the displacement divided by the time
A. Radiation   B. Photosynthesis   C. Velocity   D. Local Wind

398. A form of pollution that is brownish haze resembling fog
A. Receptors   B. Exosphere   C. Smog   D. Kidney

399. Increased cooling you feel as a result of the wind
A. Wind Chill   B. Volvox   C. Mutation   D. Chlorophyll

400. Clouds that look like fluffy, rounded piles of cotton and usually mean fair weather.
A. Composting   B. Digestive System   C. Skeletal Muscle   D. Cumulus Clouds

From the words provided for each clue, provide the letter of the word which best matches the clue.

1. __C__ Root system make of many branch roots
   A. Heart   B. Focus   C. Fibrous Root   D. Clouds

2. __C__ Different forms of a gene
   A. Warm Air   B. Offspring   C. Alleles   D. Multicellular

3. __A__ One of the lower chambers of the heart.
   A. Ventricle   B. Taxonomy   C. Organ   D. Habitat

4. __B__ In sexual reproduction, the joining of a sperm and egg
   A. Uterus   B. Fertilization   C. Wind Vane   D. Water Cycle

5. __A__ A group of similar cells that perform the same function.
   A. Tissue   B. Air Resistance   C. Doldrums   D. Electrical Circuit

6. __D__ Form when water vapor condenses on small particles in the air
   A. Average Speed   B. Alleles   C. Bone   D. Clouds

7. __C__ An intense, warm ocean current in the western North Atlantic Ocean.
   A. Marrow   B. Ventricle   C. Gulf Stream   D. Dominant

8. __B__ Swollen base of an angiosperm's pistil where egg-producing ovules are found
   A. Coriolis Effect   B. Ovary   C. Front   D. Lake Effect Snow

9. __D__ Lowest level of classification of organisms that are similar and can mate and least diverse.
   A. Cumulonimbus   B. Capillary   C. Learned Behavior   D. Species

10. __C__ An inclined plane wrapped around a pole
    A. Stomach   B. Tissue   C. Screw   D. Mutation

11. __A__ Specific environment that provides resources that an organism needs
    A. Habitat   B. Thunderstorm   C. Mitosis   D. Cardiac Muscle

12. __C__ Outer boundary of the cytoplasm and the environment outside; semi-permeable
    A. Population   B. Convection   C. Cell Membrane   D. Variable Speed

13. __A__ A small tube through which urine flows from the body
    A. Urethra   B. Exosphere   C. Liver   D. Barometer

14. __A__ The tendency of an object to resist a change in motion
    A. Inertia   B. Germination   C. Inherited   D. Harvest

15. __C__ A result of a force moving an object a certain distance; Force x distance.
    A. Machine   B. Heat Index   C. Work   D. Thunder

16. __C__ Covers the tip of the root protecting the root from injury
    A. Cellular Respiration   B. Low Pressure   C. Root Cap   D. Taproot

17. __B__ Smaller branches of the bronchi, located in the lungs
    A. Sex Linked Gene   B. Bronchioles   C. Stratus   D. Fog

18. __C__ Forces that cause a change in motion
    A. Sea Breeze   B. Amoeba   C. Unbalance Force   D. Variable Motion

19. D A tiny blood vessel where substances are exchanged between the blood and the body cells.
    A. Power B. Heredity C. Variable D. Capillary

20. C The combination of all forces acting on an object
    A. Plant Cell B. Particulate Matter C. Net Force D. Peristalsis

21. B A muscular organ that mixes food and passes it to the small intestine- uses hydrochloric acid
    A. Output Force B. Stomach C. Smooth Muscle D. Mesosphere

22. A Study of the classification of organisms
    A. Taxonomy B. Sperm Cell C. Biotic Factor D. Stratosphere

23. D Electrical storm
    A. Rock Cycle B. Digestion C. Ingestion D. Thunderstorm

24. D The ability to live
    A. Unbalance Force B. Eye Spot C. Acceleration D. Viability

25. B The force in which air molecules push on a surface.
    A. Lever B. Air Pressure C. Thermal Energy D. Species

26. D Separates the nucleus from the cytoplasm
    A. Cold Front B. Community C. Dominant Allele D. Nuclear Membrane

27. B Describes an organism with two alleles that are the same for a trait
    A. Brain B. Homozygous C. Rectum D. Response

28. D The effect of earth's rotation on the direction of winds and currents.
    A. Urethra B. Fibrous Root C. Instinct D. Coriolis Effect

29. B Hair-like projections that extend from the plasma membrane and are used for locomotion
    A. Carnivore B. Cilia C. Nimbus D. Water Vapor

30. B Second layer of the atmosphere that contains the ozone layer.
    A. Cell Membrane B. Stratosphere C. Circulatory System D. Telophase

31. D Sprouting of the embryo from a seed; when first leaves are seen
    A. Transformed B. Weather Front C. Chemical Digestion D. Germination

32. C A complete, closed path that electricity flows through.
    A. Atmosphere B. Anaphase C. Electrical Circuit D. Acquired Trait

33. B A living part of an organism's habitat
    A. Ureter B. Biotic Factor C. Ovary D. Nutrients

34. B The group that is exposed to changes in the independent variable
    A. Local Wind B. Experimental Group C. Ecosystem D. Budding

35. B Haploid sex cell formed in the male reproductive organs
    A. Asthenosphere B. Sperm C. Trial D. Volvox

36. B Filters waste from the blood like urea, water, salt and proteins.
    A. Net Force B. Kidney C. Polar Easterlies D. Homozygous

37. C Sex cell
    A. Alto B. Experimental Group C. Gamete D. Cirrus

38. __B__ Increased cooling you feel as a result of the wind
   A. Lithosphere   B. Wind Chill   C. Neurons   D. Embryo

39. __C__ Involuntary muscle found in many internal organs
   A. Viability   B. Hypothesis   C. Smooth Muscle   D. Small Intestine

40. __C__ Accomplishment of completing a job with minimum use of time and effort.
   A. Nucleus   B. Parallel Circuit   C. Efficiency   D. Troposphere

41. __D__ Each repetition of an experiment
   A. Closed Circuit   B. Force   C. Animal Cell   D. Trial

42. __B__ Water changes from liquid to gas.
   A. Weather   B. Evaporation   C. Stimulus   D. Wheel And Axle

43. __C__ Elevation or height above sea level
   A. Smog   B. Organic   C. Altitude   D. Transpiration

44. __C__ An alternative form of a gene.
   A. Alveoli   B. Lightning   C. Allele   D. Altitude

45. __D__ A form of asexual reproduction, forms by budding off the parent and forming an exact copy
   A. Root Hair   B. Radiation   C. Screw   D. Budding

46. __D__ Cloud that causes thunderstorms.
   A. Digestive System   B. Kidney   C. Warm Front   D. Cumulonimbus

47. __B__ Passed down from parent to offspring
   A. Gamete   B. Inherited   C. Inertia   D. Bladder

48. __A__ Movement of air from sea to land during the day.
   A. Sea Breeze   B. Wind Chill   C. Efficiency   D. Behavior

49. __C__ Water in the form of a gas
   A. Bronchioles   B. Cell Wall   C. Water Vapor   D. Evaporation

50. __A__ A mass of rising warm air that usually bring wet, stormy weather.
   A. Low Pressure   B. Work   C. Global Warming   D. Jet Stream

51. __C__ New diploid cell formed when a sperm fertilizes an egg.
   A. Organ System   B. Esophagus   C. Zygote   D. Cold Air

52. __A__ Substances that provide raw material and energy for organisms
   A. Nutrients   B. Groundwater   C. Wedge   D. Vein

53. __C__ A mixture of extremely small particles and liquid droplets suspended in the air
   A. Organism   B. Tornado   C. Particulate Matter   D. Testicles

54. __B__ A complete electric circuit that allows electricity to flow in a complete circle.
   A. Nuclear Membrane   B. Closed Circuit   C. Pseudopod   D. Speed

55. __B__ Cell process in which the nucleus divides to form two nuclei identical to each other.
   A. Zygote   B. Mitosis   C. DNA   D. Oxygen

56. __B__ A rigid structure that surrounds the cell membrane and provides support to the cell
   A. Genotype   B. Cell Wall   C. Chloroplast   D. Maritime Polar

57. __B__ The new organisms produced by one or two parent organisms
A. Cilia B. Offspring C. Herbivore D. Diaphragm

58. __B__ Breaking down food into nutrients.
A. Root Cap B. Digestion C. Inclined Plane D. Rain Gauge

59. __B__ Organ where water is absorbed from the food and taken into the blood stream.
A. Tornado Alley B. Large Intestines C. Genetics D. Punnet Square

60. __A__ Speed that is not uniform and changes.
A. Variable Speed B. Fertilization C. Dependent Variable D. Energy

61. __A__ The ability to do work or to cause a change.
A. Energy B. Urinary System C. Gulf Stream D. Composting

62. __C__ Clouds that form in flat layers and often cover much of the sky.
A. Allele B. Chlorophyll C. Stratus D. Trade Winds

63. __C__ A device that is thick at one end and tapers to a thin edge at the other end.
A. Sex Cell B. Sperm C. Wedge D. Molecule

64. __D__ Removing seedlings to make room for one to grow better
A. Dew Point B. Large Intestines C. Slope D. Thinning

65. __A__ The end of the large intestine where waste material is compressed into a solid.
A. Rectum B. Autotroph C. Conclusion D. Air Pressure

66. __B__ A living thing
A. Ventricle B. Organism C. Runoff D. Thinning

67. __C__ Blood vessel carrying blood towards the heart
A. Multicellular B. Nuclear Membrane C. Vein D. Warm Air

68. __B__ Behavior based on practice or experience in the environment
A. Peristalsis B. Learned Behavior C. Average Speed D. Stratus

69. __B__ Possible explanation for a set of observation or answer to a scientific question; must be testable
A. Liver B. Hypothesis C. Front D. Taproot

70. __C__ The pre-fix for mid-level clouds
A. Organism B. Root Hair C. Alto D. Kidney

71. __A__ A group of organs that work together to pump and move blood throughout the body
A. Circulatory System B. Unbalance Force C. Chloroplast D. Mutation

72. __C__ Simple machine that consists of two circular objects of different sizes
A. Cardiac Muscle B. Digestive System C. Wheel And Axle D. Polar Easterlies

73. __B__ Step 3 in mitosis.
A. Stratosphere B. Anaphase C. Warm Front D. Homozygous

74. __A__ A muscular tube that connects the mouth to the stomach.
A. Esophagus B. Cold Air C. Jet Stream D. Alleles

75. __B__ The layer that fades to outer space.
A. Amoeba B. Exosphere C. Variable D. Nutrients

76. __B__ Produce sperm
   A. Stomach   B. Testicles   C. Output Force   D. Cold Front

77. __B__ Genes that carry the x and y chromosomes
   A. Ingestion   B. Sex Linked Gene   C. Focus   D. Alto

78. __A__ From living organisms
   A. Organic   B. Global Warming   C. Fertilization   D. Organ

79. __D__ The plastic like layer of the earth on which the lithospheric plates float and move around
   A. Sex Linked Gene   B. Cellular Respiration   C. Inertia   D. Asthenosphere

80. __C__ Rigid layer of earth about 100 km thick, made of the crust and a part of the upper mantle
   A. Acquired Trait   B. Root Cap   C. Lithosphere   D. Marrow

81. __A__ A cell in a plant
   A. Plant Cell   B. Oxygen   C. Embryo   D. Thinning

82. __C__ A collection of tissues that carry out a specialized function of the body
   A. Sea Breeze   B. Mesosphere   C. Organ   D. Population

83. __B__ Gradual warming of the earth that may be caused in part by pollution and the greenhouse gas effect
   A. Efficiency   B. Global Warming   C. Barometer   D. Stimulus

84. __C__ Able to hold less water vapor
   A. Chemical Digestion   B. Thunder   C. Cold Air   D. Viability

85. __A__ Cold winds that blow from the east to the west near the North Pole and South Pole.
   A. Polar Easterlies   B. Urethra   C. Dominant Allele   D. Coriolis Effect

86. __B__ Measures wind direction
   A. Habitat   B. Wind Vane   C. Fibrous Root   D. Evaporation

87. __B__ Bottom layer in the atmosphere-where all the weather occurs
   A. Work   B. Troposphere   C. Acceleration   D. Smooth Muscle

88. __B__ The male reproductive cell
   A. Variable Speed   B. Sperm Cell   C. Transpiration   D. Ecosystem

89. __B__ Describes a trait that covers over, or dominates another form of that trait.
   A. Wind Vane   B. Dominant   C. Low Pressure   D. Sperm Cell

90. __A__ Substance in center of bones that makes blood cells
   A. Marrow   B. Germination   C. Maritime Polar   D. Machine

91. __C__ Found at 0°-30° latitude
   A. Net Force   B. Cell Wall   C. Trade Winds   D. Large Intestines

92. __C__ Community of organisms that live in a particular area.
   A. Smog   B. Exosphere   C. Ecosystem   D. Heredity

93. __A__ Any change made to DNA.
   A. Mutation   B. Genetics   C. Telophase   D. Air Resistance

94. __C__ Layers of air surrounding the earth.
   A. Asthenosphere   B. Power   C. Atmosphere   D. Pseudopod

95. __A__ Scientific study of heredity
   A. Genetics   B. Runoff   C. Animal Cell   D. Dominant

96. __D__ Organ system that produces, stores, and eliminates urine
   A. Screw   B. Anaphase   C. Altitude   D. Urinary System

97. __C__ Heterotroph that eats only animals
   A. Tornado   B. Slope   C. Carnivore   D. Capillary

98. __A__ Distance
   A. Speed   B. Parallel Circuit   C. Weather Front   D. Instinct

99. __C__ The condition of earth's atmosphere at a particular time and place
   A. Nucleus   B. Organic   C. Weather   D. Urinary System

100. __B__ Air sacs in the lungs where gas exchange happens
   A. Vein   B. Alveoli   C. Bone   D. Clouds

From the words provided for each clue, provide the letter of the word which best matches the clue.

101. __B__ Moving a plant and replanting it to help it grow
   A. Reference Point   B. Transplant   C. Ecology   D. Nimbus

102. __D__ Different forms of a gene
   A. Air Pressure   B. Herbaceous   C. Rectum   D. Alleles

103. __B__ The amount of water vapor in the air
   A. Urinary System   B. Humidity   C. Root Cap   D. Testicles

104. __D__ Passed down from parent to offspring
   A. Thunderstorm   B. Gamete   C. Genes   D. Inherited

105. __B__ Area of the female reproductive system where the fetus develops
   A. Acquired Trait   B. Uterus   C. Meteorology   D. Maritime Tropical

106. __C__ Heat energy; occurs due to friction.
   A. Density   B. Autotroph   C. Thermal Energy   D. Skeletal Muscle

107. __C__ A system for specifying the precise location of objects in space and time
   A. Herbivore   B. Fertilization   C. Frame Of Reference   D. Polar Easterlies

108. __D__ Winds that blow steadily from specific directions over long distances
   A. Hypothesis   B. Thermosphere   C. Recessive Trait   D. Global Winds

109. __B__ The rate of change of position in which the same distance is traveled each second
   A. Input Force   B. Constant Speed   C. Smooth Muscle   D. Telophase

110. __B__ Study of how organisms interact with their environment.
   A. Uterus   B. Ecology   C. Global Warming   D. Global Wind

111. __C__ Made of many cells
   A. Nuclear Membrane   B. Inertia   C. Multicellular   D. Potential Energy

112. __C__ Snow created when cold air flows over relatively warm water then over cold land
   A. Multicellular   B. Photosynthesis   C. Lake Effect Snow   D. Radiation

113. C Describes a trait that covers over, or dominates another form of that trait.
    A. Bronchioles B. Pseudopod C. Dominant D. Fallopian Tubes

114. D Each repetition of an experiment
    A. Germination B. Flagella C. Series Circuit D. Trial

115. B A rigid bar that is free to move around a fixed point
    A. Dominant B. Lever C. Lightning D. Parallel Circuit

116. C The new organisms produced by one or two parent organisms
    A. Lithosphere B. Thermal Energy C. Offspring D. Output Force

117. D Both alleles for a trait are the same and dominant.
    A. Instinct B. Ecosystem C. Genotype D. Homozygous Dominant

118. A A simple device without moving parts that changes the magnitude or direction of a force
    A. Simple Machine B. Alleles C. Sex Cell D. Vector

119. B Air sacs in the lungs where gas exchange happens
    A. Dominant Allele B. Alveoli C. Marrow D. Variable Motion

120. D Scientific study of heredity
    A. Nitrogen B. Animal Cell C. Exosphere D. Genetics

121. D Uses the brain, nerve cells, spinal cord to sense and respond to the environment
    A. Paramecium B. Displacement C. Sperm Cell D. Nervous System

122. A A line on a weather map that joins places that have the same air pressure
    A. Isobar B. Epiglottis C. Thunder D. Plant Cell

123. A Organ system that produces, stores, and eliminates urine
    A. Urinary System B. Amoeba C. Cold Air D. Weather Front

124. A A narrow belt of strong winds that blow in the upper troposphere
    A. Jet Stream B. Ionosphere C. Particulate Matter D. Bladder

125. A A front where cold air moves in under a warm air mass.
    A. Cold Front B. Biotic Factor C. Binary Fission D. Ingestion

126. D A physical characteristic coded by a gene
    A. Small Intestine B. Ovary C. Taxonomy D. Trait

127. C Measures wind direction
    A. Sex Chromosomes B. Habitat C. Wind Vane D. Transpiration

128. B Helps make proteins for the cell
    A. Metaphase B. Ribosomes C. Constant Speed D. Lever

129. C The position of a place in relation to another place
    A. Tornado Alley B. Nucleus C. Relative Location D. Eukaryote

130. B A diagram that shows the occurrence of a genetic trait in several generations of a family.
    A. Life Science B. Pedigree C. Homeostasis D. Genetics

131. C In sexual reproduction, the joining of a sperm and egg
    A. Nutrients B. Wind Chill C. Fertilization D. Gulf Stream

132. **A** Swollen base of an angiosperm's pistil where egg-producing ovules are found
A. Ovary   B. Stratosphere   C. Peristalsis   D. Phenotype

133. **C** Brings fair skies and clear, nice weather; moves clockwise
A. Receptors   B. Vein   C. High Pressure   D. Composting

134. **A** The thick vertical root with root hairs
A. Taproot   B. Trial   C. Organs   D. Heterozygous

135. **D** Increased cooling you feel as a result of the wind
A. Dew Point   B. Volvox   C. Relative Location   D. Wind Chill

136. **C** The pair of chromosomes that determine the sex of an organism
A. Cytoplasm   B. Wheel And Axle   C. Sex Chromosomes   D. Heat Index

137. **B** Diagram that shows the slow, continuous process of rocks changing from one type to another
A. Respiratory System   B. Rock Cycle   C. Viability   D. Pedigree

138. **D** Simple machine that consists of two circular objects of different sizes
A. Asthenosphere   B. Territory   C. Humidity   D. Wheel And Axle

139. **B** Organic material worked on by decomposers to breaking it down
A. Carnivore   B. Composting   C. Conduction   D. Wind Vane

140. **B** Brain of the cell, contains DNA.
A. Inherited   B. Nucleus   C. Organ   D. Ribosomes

141. **A** Violently swirling winds that are sometimes visible as a funnel-shaped cloud
A. Tornado   B. Fulcrum   C. Diaphragm   D. Atmosphere

142. **A** The lower part of the thermosphere
A. Ionosphere   B. Cellular Respiration   C. Niche   D. Water Vapor

143. **D** A collection of tissues that carry out a specialized function of the body
A. Force   B. Anaphase   C. Punnet Square   D. Organ

144. **D** Specific environment that provides resources that an organism needs
A. Budding   B. Prophase   C. Convection   D. Habitat

145. **D** Distance
A. Electrical Circuit   B. Simple Machine   C. Large Intestines   D. Speed

146. **B** A front where warm air moves over cold air weather.
A. Response   B. Warm Front   C. Harvest   D. High Pressure

147. **B** Taking food into the body
A. Compound Machine   B. Ingestion   C. Allele   D. Screw

148. **A** Separates the nucleus from the cytoplasm
A. Nuclear Membrane   B. Taproot   C. Transplant   D. Population Density

149. **C** A cell that has half the number of chromosomes found in the organism's body cells.
A. Isobar   B. Warm Air   C. Sex Cell   D. Neurons

150. **D** A blood vessel that carries blood away from the heart
A. Warm Front   B. Cell   C. Nervous System   D. Artery

151. __A__ Organ where water is absorbed from the food and taken into the blood stream.
A. Large Intestines B. Oxygen C. Equilibrium D. Recessive Allele

152. __C__ An organism's physical appearance, or visible traits.
A. Procedure B. Capillary C. Phenotype D. Chlorophyll

153. __B__ Able to hold less water vapor
A. Cumulus Clouds B. Cold Air C. Fibrous Root D. Frame Of Reference

154. __C__ A place or object used for comparison to determine if an object is in motion
A. Esophagus B. Condensation C. Reference Point D. Molecule

155. __B__ The condition of earth's atmosphere at a particular time and place
A. Homozygous Dominant B. Weather C. Air Quality Index D. Circulatory System

156. __D__ The study of the entire atmosphere, including the weather
A. Experiment B. Trait C. Troposphere D. Meteorology

157. __D__ Plant process of using water, carbon dioxide and sunshine to make food
A. Offspring B. Stationary Front C. Speed D. Photosynthesis

158. __B__ Typical weather pattern in an area over a long period of time
A. Artery B. Climate C. Jet Stream D. Continental Polar

159. __D__ Occurs when opposite charges attract, between two clouds or between a cloud and the ground
A. Learned Behavior B. Lake Effect Snow C. Homozygous D. Lightning

160. __D__ Heterotroph that eats only plants
A. Cold Front B. Open Circuit C. Climate D. Herbivore

161. __B__ The force in which air molecules push on a surface.
A. Bronchi B. Air Pressure C. Alveoli D. Heart

162. __B__ A muscular tube that connects the mouth to the stomach.
A. Polar Air Masses B. Esophagus C. Mutation D. Sexual Reproduction

163. __B__ Layers of air surrounding the earth.
A. Runoff B. Atmosphere C. Rock Cycle D. Global Winds

164. __C__ The male reproductive cell
A. Dew B. Organelle C. Sperm Cell D. Closed Circuit

165. __B__ A machine that is made up of two or more simple machines
A. Weather B. Compound Machine C. Responding Variable D. Friction

166. __B__ Energy that is stored and held in readiness.
A. Urethra B. Potential Energy C. Cell Wall D. Power

167. __C__ Possible explanation for a set of observation or answer to a scientific question; must be testable
A. Paramecium B. Vector C. Hypothesis D. Ecology

168. __D__ A force that opposes motion between two surfaces that are in contact
A. Cellular Respiration B. Life Science C. Screw D. Friction

169. __C__ A tiny cell structure that carries out a specific function within the cell
A. Learned Behavior B. Ecosystem C. Organelle D. Metaphase

170. __C__ Produce sperm
A. Open Circuit B. Fulcrum C. Testicles D. Thunderstorm

171. __B__ Occurs when the air is heated, it rapidly expands.
A. Genotype B. Thunder C. Lightning D. Urethra

172. __D__ Able to hold more water vapor
A. Genes B. Weather C. Water Vapor D. Warm Air

173. __C__ A cell in a plant
A. Ovary B. Punnet Square C. Plant Cell D. Eukaryote

174. __A__ Behavior based on practice or experience in the environment
A. Learned Behavior B. Receptors C. Asthenosphere D. Mutation

175. __B__ Evaporation of water from the leaves of a plant
A. Nervous System B. Transpiration C. Thermal Energy D. Flagella

176. __A__ Stem that is soft and green
A. Herbaceous B. Recessive Trait C. Genetics D. Dew

177. __A__ Occurs when molecules of one substance are spread evenly throughout another substance.
A. Equilibrium B. Continental Polar C. Atmosphere D. Humidity

178. __D__ Number of individuals in a given area.
A. Cytoplasm B. Conduction C. Sperm Cell D. Population Density

179. __A__ Action that changes; is caused by a stimulus; a reaction
A. Response B. Runoff C. Composting D. Meteorology

180. __B__ Community of organisms that live in a particular area.
A. Series Circuit B. Ecosystem C. Diaphragm D. Amoeba

181. __C__ The increased temperature you feel as a result of relative humidity
A. Variable Motion B. Acquired Trait C. Heat Index D. Inherited

182. __B__ Structure, such as the heart, made up of different types of tissues that all work together
A. Stratosphere B. Organ C. Cumulus Clouds D. Nucleus

183. __B__ A flap of tissue that prevents food from entering the trachea, or windpipe, during swallowing.
A. Output Force B. Epiglottis C. Oxygen D. Photosynthesis

184. __B__ Area in North America where tornadoes occur most often
A. Response B. Tornado Alley C. Cold Front D. Allele

185. __B__ A large dome shaped muscle that plays an important role in breathing.
A. Heterozygous B. Diaphragm C. Niche D. Pedigree

186. __A__ The plastic like layer of the earth on which the lithospheric plates float and move around
A. Asthenosphere B. Respiratory System C. Ingestion D. Tornado

187. __B__ The transfer of heat energy from one substance to another through direct contact
A. Maritime Tropical B. Conduction C. Nitrogen D. Reference Point

188. __A__ A group of organs that work together to pump and move blood throughout the body
A. Circulatory System B. Hypothesis C. Biotic Factor D. Transpiration

189. B A long, whip-like filament that helps in cell motility.
A. Power B. Flagella C. Rectum D. Habitat

190. B A form of asexual reproduction in which one cell divides to form two identical cells.
A. Lever B. Binary Fission C. Procedure D. Air Quality Index

191. C A push or a pull
A. Tornado Alley B. Nuclear Membrane C. Force D. Alleles

192. D The tendency of an object to resist a change in motion
A. Organ B. Budding C. Jet Stream D. Inertia

193. C A complete electric circuit that allows electricity to flow in a complete circle.
A. Alveoli B. Global Wind C. Closed Circuit D. Multicellular

194. A The rate at which work is done.
A. Power B. Thunder C. Epiglottis D. Trait

195. C Type of heat transfer the sun's energy travels to the earth's surface
A. Skeletal Muscle B. Weather Front C. Radiation D. Closed Circuit

196. B A circuit that contains more than one path for current flow.
A. Ionosphere B. Parallel Circuit C. Heart D. Displacement

197. D A type of Protista characterized by great flexibility and the presence of pseudopodia.
A. Fibrous Root B. Cell C. Experiment D. Amoeba

198. D A muscle that is attached to the bones of the skeleton and provides the force that moves the bones
A. Exosphere B. Telophase C. Speed D. Skeletal Muscle

199. B Sex cell
A. Circulatory System B. Gamete C. Binary Fission D. Animal Cell

200. A A colorless, odorless, tasteless nonflammable gas; 21% of atmosphere
A. Oxygen B. Population Density C. Thermosphere D. Gulf Stream

From the words provided for each clue, provide the letter of the word which best matches the clue.

201. D Occurs when molecules of one substance are spread evenly throughout another substance.
A. Experiment B. Electrical Circuit C. Bronchi D. Equilibrium

202. A Action that changes; is caused by a stimulus; a reaction
A. Response B. Habitat C. Polar Air Masses D. Multicellular

203. B Snow created when cold air flows over relatively warm water then over cold land
A. Conduction B. Lake Effect Snow C. Meiosis D. Frame Of Reference

204. D Organ system that produces, stores, and eliminates urine
A. Average Speed B. Fibrous Root C. Response D. Urinary System

205. B Equal forces acting on an object in opposite directions
A. DNA B. Balanced Force C. Stationary Front D. Allele

206. C Uses the brain, nerve cells, spinal cord to sense and respond to the environment
A. Organ System B. Fog C. Nervous System D. Esophagus

207. A The outermost layer of earth's atmosphere.
    A. Thermosphere   B. Transformed   C. Chlorophyll   D. Binary Fission

208. C Distance
    A. Responding Variable   B. Input Force   C. Speed   D. Recessive Allele

209. A Water in the form of a gas
    A. Water Vapor   B. Instinct   C. Homeostasis   D. Hurricane

210. C Temperature at which the air becomes saturated or full of water vapor.
    A. Digestion   B. Organelle   C. Dew Point   D. Closed Circuit

211. D A single strand of DNA tightly coiled around special proteins
    A. Amoeba   B. Variable   C. Urinary System   D. Chromosome

212. A Produces bile
    A. Liver   B. Model   C. Cell Wall   D. Eukaryote

213. C A front where warm air moves over cold air weather.
    A. Digestive System   B. Skeletal Muscle   C. Warm Front   D. Heart

214. C A place or object used for comparison to determine if an object is in motion
    A. Slope   B. Land Breeze   C. Reference Point   D. Motion

215. B The plastic like layer of the earth on which the lithospheric plates float and move around
    A. Food Chain   B. Asthenosphere   C. Lake Effect Snow   D. Gulf Stream

216. B Speed and direction of a moving body; velocity equals the displacement divided by the time
    A. Ionosphere   B. Velocity   C. High Pressure   D. Heterozygous

217. B Sugar that is major source of energy for cells
    A. Equilibrium   B. Glucose   C. Taproot   D. Nervous System

218. C Basic unit of structure and function in all living things or organisms
    A. Trait   B. Dew Point   C. Cell   D. Ovary

219. A Made of many cells
    A. Multicellular   B. Experimental Group   C. Predator   D. Mitosis

220. D Area in North America where tornadoes occur most often
    A. Bone   B. Lysosome   C. Occluded Front   D. Tornado Alley

221. B Green pigment in chloroplasts of plants and algae needed for photosynthesis
    A. Deceleration   B. Chlorophyll   C. Thunderstorm   D. Respiratory System

222. B Cell division that produces gametes
    A. Stomach   B. Meiosis   C. Condensation   D. Viability

223. B Any factor that can affect the results of an experiment.
    A. Unicellular   B. Variable   C. Sperm   D. Egg

224. A Absorbs water and forms feces
    A. Large Intestine   B. Rain Gauge   C. Herbivore   D. Chloroplast

225. A A scale that ranks levels of ozone and other air pollutants
    A. Air Quality Index   B. Peristalsis   C. Cumulonimbus   D. Stratus

226. D Root system make of many branch roots
    A. Air Quality Index   B. Data   C. Large Intestine   D. Fibrous Root

227. A Cell process in which the nucleus divides to form two nuclei identical to each other.
    A. Mitosis   B. Alleles   C. Screw   D. Inertia

228. C Each repetition of an experiment
    A. Population Density   B. Prokaryote   C. Trial   D. Evaporation

229. C A front where cold air moves in under a warm air mass.
    A. Velocity   B. Balanced Force   C. Cold Front   D. Speed

230. A The ability to live
    A. Viability   B. Mitochondria   C. Particulate Matter   D. Focus

231. A An organism's genetic makeup, or allele combinations.
    A. Genotype   B. Tornado   C. Ecology   D. Flagella

232. C An organelle found in plant and algae cells where photosynthesis occurs
    A. Machine   B. Photosynthesis   C. Chloroplast   D. Plasma

233. C Area occupied and protected by an animal or group
    A. Recessive Trait   B. Sea Breeze   C. Territory   D. Marrow

234. D A single cell organism that lives in pond water and uses cilia to move
    A. Circulatory System   B. Urethra   C. Mechanical Energy   D. Paramecium

235. A Brain of the cell, contains DNA.
    A. Nucleus   B. Open Circuit   C. Cold Front   D. Atrium

236. B Violently swirling winds that are sometimes visible as a funnel-shaped cloud
    A. Exact Location   B. Tornado   C. Genotype   D. Liver

237. C A decrease in speed; negative acceleration.
    A. Capillary   B. Species   C. Deceleration   D. Rock Cycle

238. A A group of organs that work together to perform a major function
    A. Organ System   B. Epiglottis   C. Ecosystem   D. Sexual Reproduction

239. C Plant process of using water, carbon dioxide and sunshine to make food
    A. Territory   B. Exosphere   C. Photosynthesis   D. Bladder

240. A The increased temperature you feel as a result of relative humidity
    A. Heat Index   B. Density   C. Brain   D. Organic

241. B Factor in experiment that changes in response to another factor; dependent variable.
    A. Receptors   B. Responding Variable   C. Lightning   D. Groundwater

242. C Haploid sex cell formed in the female reproductive organs.
    A. Gamete   B. White Blood Cell   C. Egg   D. Warm Air

243. D A temporary, "false foot" of cytoplasm that helps a Protista move and eat.
    A. Climate   B. Nucleus   C. Series Circuit   D. Pseudopod

244. A Forces that cause a change in motion
    A. Unbalance Force   B. Transplant   C. Excretion   D. Troposphere

245. D Process by which a gas changes to a liquid
    A. Organ   B. Ventricle   C. Cell   D. Condensation

246. D Swollen base of an angiosperm's pistil where egg-producing ovules are found
    A. Continental Polar   B. Distance   C. Golgi Body   D. Ovary

247. D From living organisms
    A. Compound Machine   B. Oxygen   C. Isobar   D. Organic

248. B Location of a place using longitude and latitude.
    A. Inherited   B. Exact Location   C. Kidney   D. Volvox

249. B Covers the tip of the root protecting the root from injury
    A. Cirrus   B. Root Cap   C. Tornado Alley   D. Mutation

250. D Point deep inside earth where energy is released, causing an earthquake
    A. Efficiency   B. Pedigree   C. Heat Index   D. Focus

251. A Break down food and release energy to the cell
    A. Mitochondria   B. Scientific Method   C. Cardiac Muscle   D. Parallel Circuit

252. A Made of a single cell
    A. Unicellular   B. Taxonomy   C. Dominant Trait   D. Sex Chromosomes

253. D The transfer of heat energy from one substance to another through direct contact
    A. Fertilization   B. Nimbus   C. Lungs   D. Conduction

254. B A controlled procedure designed to answer a scientific question.
    A. Doldrums   B. Experiment   C. Constant Speed   D. Zygote

255. B Different distances traveled in equal times.
    A. Unbalance Force   B. Variable Motion   C. Reference Point   D. Warm Front

256. C A measure of how far an object moves in relation to a reference point.
    A. Cumulus   B. Autotroph   C. Distance   D. Tissue

257. B A small tube through which urine flows from the body
    A. Meteorology   B. Urethra   C. Coriolis Effect   D. Large Intestines

258. D A series of steps that a scientist follows in order to solve a problem or answer a question
    A. Thermal Energy   B. Conclusion   C. Rectum   D. Scientific Method

259. A Describes an organism with two alleles that are the same for a trait
    A. Homozygous   B. Root Cap   C. Pollution   D. Behavior

260. D The mass of nerve tissue that is the main control center of the nervous system
    A. Organs   B. Glucose   C. Sperm Cell   D. Brain

261. D An alternative form of a gene.
    A. Chromosome   B. Science   C. Sex Linked Gene   D. Allele

262. C A colorless, odorless, tasteless nonflammable gas; 21% of atmosphere
    A. Trial   B. Pseudopod   C. Oxygen   D. Paramecium

263. C Involuntary muscle tissue found only in the heart
    A. Dominant   B. Animal Cell   C. Cardiac Muscle   D. Thermosphere

264. B The rate of change of position in which the same distance is traveled each second
   A. Genetics   B. Constant Speed   C. Potential Energy   D. Runoff

265. D A type of Protista characterized by great flexibility and the presence of pseudopodia.
   A. Asthenosphere   B. Relative Location   C. Trachea   D. Amoeba

266. B A muscular tube that connects the mouth to the stomach.
   A. Taproot   B. Esophagus   C. Water Vapor   D. Cytoplasm

267. A Electrical storm
   A. Thunderstorm   B. Allele   C. Inertia   D. Continental Polar

268. D Passed down from parent to offspring
   A. Stratus   B. Deceleration   C. Chloroplast   D. Inherited

269. C Contains digestive enzymes that destroy damaged organelles and invaders
   A. Organs   B. Habitat   C. Lysosome   D. Rectum

270. C A long, whip-like filament that helps in cell motility.
   A. Transformed   B. Groundwater   C. Flagella   D. Bronchi

271. B The position of a place in relation to another place
   A. Mutation   B. Relative Location   C. Air Quality Index   D. Stationary Front

272. C An intense, warm ocean current in the western North Atlantic Ocean.
   A. Parallel Circuit   B. Relative Location   C. Gulf Stream   D. Liver

273. A A colonial form of live green algae, round in shape.
   A. Volvox   B. Herbivore   C. Capillary   D. Responding Variable

274. B The male reproductive cell
   A. Cold Front   B. Sperm Cell   C. Peristalsis   D. Model

275. D Heterotroph that eats only plants
   A. Asthenosphere   B. Cell Wall   C. Particulate Matter   D. Herbivore

276. C Unicellular only - no nucleus or organelles with dna that are not organized into chromosomes.
   A. High Pressure   B. Volvox   C. Prokaryote   D. Lysosome

277. A A line on a weather map that joins places that have the same air pressure
   A. Isobar   B. Unbalance Force   C. Occluded Front   D. Exosphere

278. A Organ where water is absorbed from the food and taken into the blood stream.
   A. Large Intestines   B. Digestive System   C. Mechanical Energy   D. Homozygous

279. A The organism that feeds off another.
   A. Predator   B. Thermosphere   C. Condensation   D. Heterozygous

280. B How tightly packed the matter in a substance is.
   A. Large Intestine   B. Density   C. Alleles   D. Meiosis

281. B Moving a plant and replanting it to help it grow
   A. Excretion   B. Transplant   C. Stomach   D. Constant Speed

282. D A complex molecule containing the genetic information that makes up the chromosomes.
   A. Esophagus   B. Oxygen   C. Chromosome   D. DNA

283. __D__ Elastic, hollow, muscular organ that provides temporary storage for urine
A. Frame Of Reference   B. Ovary   C. Trait   D. Bladder

284. __C__ The lower part of the thermosphere
A. Warm Air   B. Urethra   C. Ionosphere   D. Doldrums

285. __B__ Cells from two parents unite to form the first cell of a new organism
A. Nimbus   B. Sexual Reproduction   C. Input Force   D. Isobar

286. __D__ Located in colder regions of the world
A. Lungs   B. Gamete   C. Screw   D. Polar Air Masses

287. __B__ Community of organisms that live in a particular area.
A. Motion   B. Ecosystem   C. Closed Circuit   D. Sexual Reproduction

288. __D__ Diagram that shows the slow, continuous process of rocks changing from one type to another
A. Transplant   B. Chlorophyll   C. Plasma   D. Rock Cycle

289. __C__ A device that makes work easier by changing the size or direction of a force
A. Troposphere   B. Prokaryote   C. Machine   D. Slope

290. __D__ Able to hold more water vapor
A. Territory   B. Cytoplasm   C. Genetics   D. Warm Air

291. __B__ Accomplishment of completing a job with minimum use of time and effort.
A. Heart   B. Efficiency   C. Cumulus   D. Runoff

292. __B__ Wispy, feathery clouds made mostly of ice crystals that form at high levels
A. Lake Effect Snow   B. Cirrus   C. Variable   D. Sex Linked Gene

293. __B__ Movement of air from land to sea at night.
A. Mitosis   B. Land Breeze   C. Food Chain   D. Marrow

294. __C__ A muscular organ that mixes food and passes it to the small intestine- uses hydrochloric acid
A. Brain   B. Open Circuit   C. Stomach   D. Organelle

295. __B__ A rigid structure that surrounds the cell membrane and provides support to the cell
A. Predator   B. Cell Wall   C. Scientific Method   D. Land Breeze

296. __C__ A group of organs that work together to pump and move blood throughout the body
A. Cirrus   B. Exact Location   C. Circulatory System   D. Paramecium

297. __C__ The end of the large intestine where waste material is compressed into a solid.
A. Thunderstorm   B. Tornado Alley   C. Rectum   D. Skeletal Muscle

298. __A__ Heat energy; occurs due to friction.
A. Thermal Energy   B. Fog   C. Climate   D. Hurricane

299. __D__ Process where wastes are removed from the body or cell.
A. Egg   B. Nervous System   C. Series Circuit   D. Excretion

300. __A__ Liquid part of blood
A. Plasma   B. Multicellular   C. Homeostasis   D. Velocity

From the words provided for each clue, provide the letter of the word which best matches the clue.

301. __D__ Scientific study of heredity
A. Sex Cell   B. Doldrums   C. Volvox   D. Genetics

302. __A__ Smaller branches of the bronchi, located in the lungs
A. Bronchioles   B. Force   C. Community   D. Maritime Polar

303. __B__ The new organisms produced by one or two parent organisms
A. Dew Point   B. Offspring   C. Gamete   D. Genotype

304. __A__ Sprouting of the embryo from a seed; when first leaves are seen
A. Germination   B. Polar Air Masses   C. Kinetic Energy   D. Scientific Method

305. __B__ Process by which a gas changes to a liquid
A. Excretion   B. Condensation   C. Egg   D. Relative Location

306. __C__ Describes a trait that covers over, or dominates another form of that trait.
A. Gene   B. Biotic Factor   C. Dominant   D. Dominant Allele

307. __C__ Equal forces acting on an object in opposite directions
A. Rectum   B. Ecology   C. Balanced Force   D. Ribosomes

308. __D__ A group of similar cells that perform the same function.
A. Constant Speed   B. Isobar   C. Fulcrum   D. Tissue

309. __C__ Diagram that shows the slow, continuous process of rocks changing from one type to another
A. Distance   B. Golgi Body   C. Rock Cycle   D. Carnivore

310. __D__ Organism that makes its own food (generally plants).
A. Oxygen   B. High Pressure   C. Receptors   D. Autotroph

311. __D__ Brings fair skies and clear, nice weather; moves clockwise
A. Lake Effect Snow   B. Precipitation   C. Dominant   D. High Pressure

312. __D__ The rate of change of position in which the same distance is traveled each second
A. Cardiac Muscle   B. Viability   C. Stratus   D. Constant Speed

313. __B__ Community of organisms that live in a particular area.
A. Barometer   B. Ecosystem   C. Thunder   D. Chemical Digestion

314. __D__ Any change made to DNA.
A. Genetics   B. Hybrid   C. Rain Gauge   D. Mutation

315. __C__ Protista that moves by a flagellum.
A. Open Circuit   B. Balanced Force   C. Euglena   D. Predator

316. __C__ Separates the nucleus from the cytoplasm
A. Trachea   B. Artery   C. Nuclear Membrane   D. Ovary

317. __B__ A temporary, "false foot" of cytoplasm that helps a Protista move and eat.
A. Liver   B. Pseudopod   C. Inherited   D. Trait

318. __D__ Loosening soil around plants to allow moisture in and roots to grow.
A. Local Wind   B. Offspring   C. Habitat   D. Cultivate

319. __A__ Measures air pressure
A. Barometer   B. Fibrous Root   C. Conservation   D. Skeletal Muscle

320. C Point deep inside earth where energy is released, causing an earthquake
A. Variable Motion B. Atmosphere C. Focus D. Dominant Trait

321. B Heterotroph that eats only animals
A. Bronchi B. Carnivore C. Chloroplast D. Multicellular

322. A An offspring that was given different genetic information for a trait from each parent
A. Hybrid B. Friction C. Kidney D. Marrow

323. B A blood vessel that carries blood away from the heart
A. Heat Index B. Artery C. Taxonomy D. Deceleration

324. C The energy of motion
A. Bronchioles B. Stratosphere C. Kinetic Energy D. Red Blood Cell

325. D The increased temperature you feel as a result of relative humidity
A. Germination B. Hurricane C. Oral Cavity D. Heat Index

326. D A type of Protista characterized by great flexibility and the presence of pseudopodia.
A. Plant Cell B. Peristalsis C. Tornado D. Amoeba

327. A A violently rotating column of air stretching from a cloud to the ground-turns counterclockwise
A. Tornado B. Dependent Variable C. Jet Stream D. Autotroph

328. D Breaks down food into smaller molecules.
A. Warm Air B. Sexual Reproduction C. Flagella D. Digestive System

329. A A colonial form of live green algae, round in shape.
A. Volvox B. Learned Behavior C. Molecule D. Pulley

330. D A physical characteristic coded by a gene
A. Uterus B. Vein C. Wedge D. Trait

331. A Snow created when cold air flows over relatively warm water then over cold land
A. Lake Effect Snow B. Smog C. Meteorology D. Sperm Cell

332. B An organelle found in plant and algae cells where photosynthesis occurs
A. Clouds B. Chloroplast C. Brain D. Diaphragm

333. B Two or more atoms combine.
A. Large Intestines B. Molecule C. Condensation D. Instinct

334. C A muscular tube that connects the mouth to the stomach.
A. Altitude B. Energy C. Esophagus D. Heterozygous

335. C Enzymes are used to break foods into their smaller chemical building blocks
A. Weather Front B. Bladder C. Chemical Digestion D. Food Chain

336. B Layer above the troposphere where meteors burn up
A. Displacement B. Mesosphere C. Transformed D. Cold Air

337. B Thin hair like roots on the outer layer of the tap root, absorb water and anchor plant
A. Wheel And Axle B. Root Hair C. Nimbus D. Taproot

338. C Measures wind speed
A. Nuclear Membrane B. Plasma C. Anemometer D. Fog

339. A The fixed point about which a lever pivots
A. Fulcrum B. Cilia C. Nucleus D. Telophase

340. D An organism's genetic makeup, or allele combinations.
A. Ionosphere B. Cultivate C. Vacuole D. Genotype

341. C Elevation or height above sea level
A. Mesosphere B. Euglena C. Altitude D. Digestion

342. D A segment of DNA on a chromosome that codes for a specific trait
A. Ecosystem B. Loam C. Thinning D. Gene

343. D Sex cell
A. Cold Front B. Esophagus C. Focus D. Gamete

344. C Cells from two parents unite to form the first cell of a new organism
A. Exosphere B. Chromosome C. Sexual Reproduction D. Epiglottis

345. D Haploid sex cell formed in the female reproductive organs.
A. Stationary Front B. Velocity C. Efficiency D. Egg

346. D A series of events in which one organism eats another to obtain energy
A. Procedure B. Ovule C. Homeostasis D. Food Chain

347. A Second layer of the atmosphere that contains the ozone layer.
A. Stratosphere B. Power C. Cumulus Clouds D. Rock Cycle

348. B Made of a single cell
A. Organs B. Unicellular C. Photosynthesis D. Anemometer

349. B The rate at which work is done.
A. Wind Chill B. Power C. Cell Membrane D. Chlorophyll

350. C The pre-fix for mid-level clouds
A. Air Quality B. Mutation C. Alto D. Work

351. C Brain of the cell, contains DNA.
A. Tissue B. Vector C. Nucleus D. Anaphase

352. A An intense, warm ocean current in the western North Atlantic Ocean.
A. Gulf Stream B. Population Density C. Animal Cell D. Air Mass

353. D Both alleles for a trait are the same and dominant.
A. Radiation B. Sea Breeze C. Cellular Respiration D. Homozygous Dominant

354. C A cell that has half the number of chromosomes found in the organism's body cells.
A. Polar Easterlies B. Skeletal System C. Sex Cell D. Digestive System

355. B The highest atmosphere layer leading to outer space.
A. Smooth Muscle B. Exosphere C. Alveoli D. Humidity

356. C Involuntary muscle found in many internal organs
A. Weather B. Organ C. Smooth Muscle D. Exact Location

357. D A single strand of DNA tightly coiled around special proteins
A. Pseudopod B. Organic C. Nitrogen D. Chromosome

358. D Protecting the environment by not over using or replacing resources
A. Mitosis B. Air Resistance C. Amoeba D. Conservation

359. B All members of one species in a particular area.
A. Water Vapor B. Population C. Motion D. Ingestion

360. B Force that opposes the motion of objects that move through the air
A. Composting B. Air Resistance C. Recessive Trait D. Homozygous Dominant

361. C An organism that has two different alleles for a trait
A. Climate B. Alto C. Heterozygous D. Unicellular

362. A Organic material worked on by decomposers to breaking it down
A. Composting B. Heredity C. Gulf Stream D. Thermosphere

363. C Swollen base of an angiosperm's pistil where egg-producing ovules are found
A. DNA B. Population C. Ovary D. Cumulonimbus

364. A The mass of nerve tissue that is the main control center of the nervous system
A. Brain B. Asthenosphere C. Meiosis D. Series Circuit

365. A Plant process of using water, carbon dioxide and sunshine to make food
A. Photosynthesis B. Neurons C. Root Hair D. Maritime Tropical

366. C Hair-like projections that extend from the plasma membrane and are used for locomotion
A. Organ System B. Eye Spot C. Cilia D. Cytoplasm

367. D Layers of air surrounding the earth.
A. Dew Point B. Warm Air C. Precipitation D. Atmosphere

368. D Blood cells that carry oxygen from the lungs to the body cells.
A. Diaphragm B. Dependent Variable C. Energy D. Red Blood Cell

369. B A collection of tissues that carry out a specialized function of the body
A. Red Blood Cell B. Organ C. Cold Front D. Uterus

370. B Green pigment in chloroplasts of plants and algae needed for photosynthesis
A. Marrow B. Chlorophyll C. Deceleration D. Liver

371. C Wavelike contractions of smooth muscles in the organs of the digestive tract.
A. Force B. Rock Cycle C. Peristalsis D. High Pressure

372. C The measurable effect, outcome, or response in which the research is interested.
A. Maritime Polar B. Instinct C. Dependent Variable D. Velocity

373. D Simple machine that consists of two circular objects of different sizes
A. Hybrid B. Lake Effect Snow C. Homozygous Dominant D. Wheel And Axle

374. D Made of many cells
A. Unicellular B. Organic C. Heredity D. Multicellular

375. B Taking food into the body
A. Oral Cavity B. Ingestion C. Peristalsis D. Stratosphere

376. A Filters waste from the blood like urea, water, salt and proteins.
A. Kidney B. Oxygen C. Thinning D. Weather Front

377. A The ability to live
   A. Viability   B. Dominant Trait   C. Barometer   D. Stratus

378. A A complex molecule containing the genetic information that makes up the chromosomes.
   A. DNA   B. Ovary   C. Polar Easterlies   D. Viability

379. D A cell in an animal
   A. Bronchi   B. Organ System   C. Nimbus   D. Animal Cell

380. C A boundary between air masses that don't move possibly causing rain for several days
   A. Air Quality   B. Esophagus   C. Stationary Front   D. Meiosis

381. A A muscle that is attached to the bones of the skeleton and provides the force that moves the bones
   A. Skeletal Muscle   B. Chromosome   C. Population Density   D. Air Resistance

382. A Allele whose trait always shows.
   A. Dominant Allele   B. Biotic Factor   C. Habitat   D. Taxonomy

383. B Area of low atmospheric pressure and calm westerly winds located at the equator.
   A. Nucleus   B. Doldrums   C. Meteorology   D. Asthenosphere

384. B To change in appearance or character
   A. Rectum   B. Transformed   C. Thermosphere   D. Vacuole

385. D Outer boundary of the cytoplasm and the environment outside; semi-permeable
   A. Anaphase   B. Open Circuit   C. Chloroplast   D. Cell Membrane

386. A The amount of water vapor in the air
   A. Humidity   B. Cold Air   C. Wind Chill   D. Anemometer

387. C Substance in center of bones that makes blood cells
   A. Distance   B. Vein   C. Marrow   D. Ecosystem

388. A Violently swirling winds that are sometimes visible as a funnel-shaped cloud
   A. Tornado   B. Sperm Cell   C. Alto   D. Transformed

389. D A large body of air that has about the same temperature and moisture throughout.
   A. Motion   B. Climate   C. Ionosphere   D. Air Mass

390. B Involuntary muscle tissue found only in the heart
   A. Sexual Reproduction   B. Cardiac Muscle   C. Kinetic Energy   D. Ribosomes

391. D The condition of earth's atmosphere at a particular time and place
   A. Vector   B. Telophase   C. Recessive Trait   D. Weather

392. D All the different populations that live together in an area
   A. Bronchioles   B. Cardiac Muscle   C. Hurricane   D. Community

393. B Cell division that produces gametes
   A. Scientific Method   B. Meiosis   C. Air Mass   D. Epiglottis

394. B A dark cloud whose name means rain.
   A. Skeletal System   B. Nimbus   C. Root Hair   D. Egg

395. A Fluid in a cell that holds all the organelles in place.
   A. Cytoplasm   B. Inherited   C. Offspring   D. Organs

396. __D__ Air sacs in the lungs where gas exchange happens
A. Molecule   B. Trait   C. Tornado   D. Alveoli

397. __C__ Speed and direction of a moving body; velocity equals the displacement divided by the time
A. Radiation   B. Photosynthesis   C. Velocity   D. Local Wind

398. __C__ A form of pollution that is brownish haze resembling fog
A. Receptors   B. Exosphere   C. Smog   D. Kidney

399. __A__ Increased cooling you feel as a result of the wind
A. Wind Chill   B. Volvox   C. Mutation   D. Chlorophyll

400. __D__ Clouds that look like fluffy, rounded piles of cotton and usually mean fair weather.
A. Composting   B. Digestive System   C. Skeletal Muscle   D. Cumulus Clouds

Matching

Provide the word that best matches each clue.

1. _____ Type of cohort study where subjects are sampled after the outcome has occurred.

2. _____ Collection of propositions to illustrate the principles of a subject.

3. _____ Any problem in the design or conduct of a statistical study that tends to favor certain results.

4. _____ The number of times a variable occurs in a data set.

5. _____ Tells how much or many of something there is.

6. _____ Each of the 100 equal groups into which a population can be divided according to the distribution of values of a variable.

7. _____ A very small circular shape.

8. _____ Explain the meaning of information, words, or actions.

9. _____ Make or place alongside something.

10. _____ Increasing by successive addition.

11. _____ Every possible sample of a size has an equal chance of being selected.

12. _____ Actual measurements or observations collected from the sample.

13. _____ The random variable is a statistic based on the results of more than one trial.

14. _____ The relationship between rankings of different ordinal variables.

15. _____ Calculation of the value of a function between known values.

16. _____ A characteristic that differs from one subject to the next.

17. _____ Things who are studied.

18. _____ Sometimes questions are worded in a way that suggest a particular response.

19. _____ All of the information collected.

20. _____ A bias where people who have an interest in the outcome of an experiment have an incentive to use biased methods.

21. _____ Put or add together.

118

22. _____ Descriptive measure for a population represented by Greek letters.

23. _____ Made, done, happening, or chosen without method or conscious decision.

24. _____ Tells how large the standard deviation is relative to the mean. It can be used to compare the spreads of data sets whose values have different units.

25. _____ probability of a success.

A. Experimental Units	B. parallel	C. Variable
D. Coefficient of Variation	E. Theory	F. Self Interest
G. Dot	H. Raw data	I. Interpret
J. Data Set	K. Random	L. Random sampling
M. Parameter	N. Interpolation	O. Frequency
P. Percentile	Q. Leading Question Bias	R. Bias
S. Sampling distribution	T. Cumulative	U. P
V. Quantitative Variables	W. Rank Correlation	X. Retrospective
Y. Compound		

Provide the word that best matches each clue.

26. _____ The act of making and recording a measurement.

27. _____ Explain the meaning of information, words, or actions.

28. _____ A value that does not depend on changes in other values.

29. _____ No relationship exists on the categorical variables in the population.

30. _____ The selection of a random sample.

31. _____ A supposition or proposed explanation based on limited evidence as a starting point for further investigation.

32. _____ Presented in a table that gives the frequency for each category.

33. _____ Expresses the value of a score relative to the mean and standard deviation of its distribution.

34. _____ The probability of correctly rejecting the null hypothesis.

35. _____ A characteristic that differs from one subject to the next.

36. _____ A type of study where two samples are drawn.

37. _____ When the experimental units are people.

38. _____ Any problem in the design or conduct of a statistical study that tends to favor certain results.

39. _____ The assignment to treatment groups is not made by the investigator.

40. _____ Any number of entities members considered as a unit.

41. _____ Probability of a type II error.

42. _____ Extending without break or irregularity.

43. _____ A circular chart divided into triangular areas proportional to the percentages of the whole.

44. _____ A sample is chosen by a method such that every member of the population is equally likely to be selected.

45. _____ A bias where people are reluctant to admit to behavior that may reflect negatively on them.

46. _____ A subset of a population.

47. _____ The collection of all people, objects, or events having one or more specified characteristics.

48. _____ Make or place alongside something.

49. _____ Type of qualitative variable. Have a natural ordering, but have no mathematically value.

50. _____ All of the information collected.

A. parallel
B. Bias
C. Case Control
D. Simple Random Sample
E. Hypothesis
F. Data Set
G. Null Hypothesis
H. Pie chart
I. Continuous
J. Social Acceptability
K. Subject
L. Variable
M. Population
N. Power
O. random sampling
P. Beta
Q. Independent variable
R. Frequency Distribution
S. Observation
T. Group
U. Standard score
V. Ordinal Variables
W. Sample
X. Interpret
Y. Observational Study

Provide the word that best matches each clue.

51. _____ A branch of mathematics concerned with quantitative data.

52. _____ population standard deviation.

53. _____ Descriptive measure for a sample.

54. _____ The difference between the largest and the smallest value.

55. _____ The probability of correctly rejecting the null hypothesis.

56. _____ Each participant in a treatment group has an equal chance of being placed in any of the groups.

57. _____ Descriptive measure for a population represented by Greek letters.

58. _____ The assignment to treatment groups is not made by the investigator.

59. _____ Arranged into groups.

60. _____ Calculating a value outside the range of known values.

61. _____ Bar graph in which categories are represented in order of frequency.

62. _____ Only one mode.

63. _____ All of the information collected.

64. _____ Presented in a table that gives the frequency for each category.

65. _____ Drawing inferences from sample data to a population.

66. _____ Made, done, happening, or chosen without method or conscious decision.

67. _____ Scores that differ so markedly from the main body of data that their accuracy is questioned.

68. _____ A vertical array of numbers or other information.

69. _____ Make a detailed inspection of; for statistical purposes.

70. _____ A value that does not depend on changes in other values.

71. _____ The collection of all people, objects, or events having one or more specified characteristics.

72. _____ Occurs when some members in the population are more likely to be included in the sample than others.

73. _____ The difference between consecutive lower class limits.

74. _____ Make or place alongside something.

75. _____ A bias where people who have an interest in the outcome of an experiment have an incentive to use biased methods.

A. Pareto Chart   B. Sigma   C. Unimodal
D. parallel   E. Self Interest   F. Parameter
G. Outlier   H. Population   I. Class Width

J. Extrapolation
M. Data Set
P. Survey
S. Frequency Distribution
V. Sampling Bias
Y. Independent variable

K. Random assignment
N. Range
Q. Random
T. Statistic
W. Inferential Statistics

L. Statistics
O. Grouped
R. Column
U. Power
X. Observational Study

Provide the word that best matches each clue.

76. _____ Intervals of equal width that cover all values observed in the data set.

77. _____ The probability that is the largest risk a researcher is willing to take of rejecting a true null hypothesis.

78. _____ Descriptive measure for a sample.

79. _____ A random sample that is not drawn by a well-defined random method.

80. _____ A response where the opinions of non-responders tend to differ from the opinions of those who do respond.

81. _____ The least or smallest amount or quantity possible, attainable, or required.

82. _____ An error retaining a false null hypothesis.

83. _____ Longer tail extends to the right

84. _____ Of or relating to or denoting numerals.

85. _____ Only one mode.

86. _____ Ratio of a circle's circumference to its diameter, ≈ 3.1416

87. _____ As great, high, or intense as possible or permitted.

88. _____ Distributions that are asymmetrical.

89. _____ A series of values of a variable at successive times.

90. _____ Tells how much or many of something there is.

91. _____ A distribution that shows the proportion or percent frequency for each interval.

92. _____ The score or qualitative category that occurs with greatest frequency.

93. _____ Make a detailed inspection of; for statistical purposes.

94. _____ When the first class has no lower limit, or the last class has no upper limit.

95. _____ A line on a graph indicating a statistical trend.

96. _____ The population is divided into subpopulations and random samples are taken of each stratum.

97. _____ Type of cohort study where subjects are sampled after the outcome has occurred.

98. _____ Any number of entities members considered as a unit.

99. _____ The selection of a random sample.

100. _____ Put or add together.

A. Open Ended Classes
B. Type II
C. Numerical
D. Stratified sampling
E. Time series
F. Non response
G. Level of significance
H. Survey
I. Skewed distribution
J. Minimum
K. Group
L. Relative frequency
M. Mode
N. Quantitative Variables
O. Retrospective
P. Pi
Q. Sample of Convenience
R. Statistic
S. Classes
T. Compound
U. Positively skewed
V. Maximum
W. random sampling
X. Unimodal
Y. Trend line

Provide the word that best matches each clue.

101. _____ A very small circular shape.

102. _____ Distributions that are asymmetrical.

103. _____ Approximately 68% of the data will be within one standard deviation of the mean.

104. _____ The selection of participants in one sample is affected by the selection of participants in the other sample.

105. _____ The act of making and recording a measurement.

106. _____ Relating to or denoting a statistical method assessing the goodness of fit between observed values and those expected theoretically.

107. _____ Longer tail extends to the left

108. _____ Descriptive measure for a population represented by Greek letters.

109. _____ Bar graph that shows frequencies or relative frequencies in categories for more than one group frequencies within each category.

110. _____ Any number of entities members considered as a unit.

111. Frequency — The number of times a variable occurs in a data set.

112. Double Blind — An experiment where neither the investigator nor the subjects know who has been assigned to which treatment.

113. Bar Graph — A graphical representation of a frequency distribution.

114. Discrete Variable — Type of quantitative variable whose possible values can be listed.

115. Treatments — The procedures applied to each experimental unit.

116. Trend line — A line on a graph indicating a statistical trend.

117. Z Score — Tells how many standard deviations that value is from its population mean.

118. Grouped — Arranged into groups.

119. Correlation coefficient — A number that represents the degree of association or strength of relationship between two variables.

120. Alpha — Significance level; probability of a type I error.

121. ordinal — The number designating place in an ordered sequence.

122. Spread — Distribute or disperse widely.

123. Cumulative frequency — A distribution that shows the number, proportion, or percentage of scores that occur below the real upper limit of each interval.

124. Standard score — Expresses the value of a score relative to the mean and standard deviation of its distribution.

125. Group — Come together and form a group or mass.

- A. Negatively skewed
- B. Frequency
- C. Observation
- D. Bar Graph
- E. Chi square
- F. Stacked
- G. Collect
- H. ordinal
- I. Cumulative frequency
- J. Grouped
- K. Double Blind
- L. Skewed distribution
- M. Alpha
- N. Spread
- O. Dependent samples
- P. Group
- Q. Discrete Variable
- R. Standard score
- S. Parameter
- T. Trend line
- U. Empirical Rule
- V. Z Score
- W. Treatments
- X. Correlation coefficient
- Y. Dot

Provide the word that best matches each clue.

126. The largest value that can appear in that class.

127. _____ A circular chart divided into triangular areas proportional to the percentages of the whole.

128. _____ The selection of participants in one sample is not affected by the selection of participants in the other sample.

129. _____ Group of subjects is studied to determine whether various factors of interest are associated with an outcome.

130. _____ Distribute or disperse widely.

131. _____ Arranged into groups.

132. _____ Studies conducted by a procedure that produces the correct result on average.

133. _____ The procedures applied to each experimental unit.

134. _____ A set containing all points between two given endpoints.

135. _____ A vertical array of numbers or other information.

136. _____ The difference between the largest and the smallest value.

137. _____ A subset of a population.

138. _____ Relating to or denoting a statistical method assessing the goodness of fit between observed values and those expected theoretically.

139. _____ Sometimes questions are worded in a way that suggest a particular response.

140. _____ Cause surprise or confusion, especially by acting against an expectation.

141. _____ A form with a set of queries to gain statistical information.

142. _____ Calculating a value outside the range of known values.

143. _____ A distribution that shows the proportion or percent frequency for each interval.

144. _____ Expresses the value of a score relative to the mean and standard deviation of its distribution.

145. _____ The percentage of the scores of the distribution that fall below that score.

146. _____ People having the same social or economic status.

147. _____ A group.

148. _____ Bar graph that shows frequencies or relative frequencies in categories for more than one group frequencies within each category.

149. _____ An error rejecting a true null hypothesis.

150. _____ Minimum, 1st Quartile, Median, 3rd Quartile, Maximum.

A. Sample
B. Range
C. Five Number Summary
D. Type I
E. Cohort Study
F. Spread
G. Upper Class Limit
H. Chi square
I. Cohort
J. Unbiased
K. Stacked
L. Pie chart
M. Interval
N. Relative frequency
O. Stratum
P. Confounding
Q. Independent samples
R. Standard score
S. Treatments
T. Questionnaire
U. Extrapolation
V. Grouped
W. Percentile rank
X. Column
Y. Leading Question Bias

Provide the word that best matches each clue.

151. _____ Make or place alongside something.

152. _____ A probability distribution that is unimodal and symmetrical.

153. _____ Studies conducted by a procedure that produces the correct result on average.

154. _____ The quantitative relation between two amounts showing the number of times one value contains or is contained within the other.

155. _____ The least or smallest amount or quantity possible, attainable, or required.

156. _____ Explain the meaning of information, words, or actions.

157. _____ Having two variables.

158. _____ Cause surprise or confusion, especially by acting against an expectation.

159. _____ A line on a graph indicating a statistical trend.

160. _____ Descriptive measure for a population represented by Greek letters.

161. _____ Sometimes questions are worded in a way that suggest a particular response.

162. _____ Whiskers out to the lowest or highest values that are not outliers.

163. _____ The region for rejecting the null hypothesis.

164. _____ A procedure for determining how much of the variability among scores to attribute to a range of sources of variation.

165. _____ Type of quantitative variable. Can take on any value in some interval.

166. _____ Intervals of equal width that cover all values observed in the data set.

167. _____ The assignment to treatment groups is not made by the investigator.

168. _____ As great, high, or intense as possible or permitted.

169. _____ The quality of being unsteady and subject to changes.

170. _____ A measure of center in a data set.

171. _____ Distribute or disperse widely.

172. _____ Scores that differ so markedly from the main body of data that their accuracy is questioned.

173. _____ A random sample that is not drawn by a well-defined random method.

174. _____ A number that represents the degree of association or strength of relationship between two variables.

175. _____ Matching each participant in the experimental condition with a participant in the control condition.

A. Analysis of variance
B. Correlation coefficient
C. Sample of Convenience
D. Spread
E. Interpret
F. Continuous Variable
G. Critical region
H. Mean
I. Trend line
J. Parameter
K. Ratio
L. Fluctuation
M. Confounding
N. Modified Boxplot
O. Leading Question Bias
P. Normal distribution
Q. Minimum
R. Matched sample
S. Observational Study
T. parallel
U. Maximum
V. Unbiased
W. Classes
X. Bivariate
Y. Outlier

Provide the word that best matches each clue.

176. _____ Observing the same participants under both the experimental and control conditions.

177. _____ Of or relating to or denoting numerals.

178. _____ The square root of the variance.

179. _____ Its value is not affected much by extreme values in the data set.

180. _____ All of the information collected.

181. _____ Whiskers out to the lowest or highest values that are not outliers.

182. _____ The probability of obtaining a value of the test statistic equal to or more extreme than that observed.

183. _____ Significance level; probability of a type I error.

184. _____ Increasing by successive addition.

185. _____ Probability of a type II error.

186. _____ The act of making something happen.

187. _____ The population is divided into subpopulations and random samples are taken of each stratum.

188. _____ The selection of participants in one sample is affected by the selection of participants in the other sample.

189. _____ A statistic representing how closely two variables co vary.

190. _____ Population mean.

191. _____ probability of a success.

192. _____ Bar graph in which categories are represented in order of frequency.

193. _____ A number that represents the degree of association or strength of relationship between two variables.

194. _____ The number designating place in an ordered sequence.

195. _____ A series of values of a variable at successive times.

196. _____ Relating to or denoting a statistical method assessing the goodness of fit between observed values and those expected theoretically.

197. _____ Things who are studied.

198. _____ A measure of how far the values in a data set are from the mean, on the average.

199. _____ Graphical representation of frequency distribution for quantitative data. Rectangle for each class.

200. _____ The quantitative relation between two amounts showing the number of times one value contains or is contained within the other.

A. Resistant Statistic	B. Correlation	C. Correlation coefficient
D. Chi square	E. Variance	F. Standard Deviation
G. P value	H. Pareto Chart	I. Dependent samples
J. Time series	K. P	L. Repeated measures
M. Histogram	N. Causation	O. Mu
P. Ratio	Q. Stratified sampling	R. Cumulative
S. Numerical	T. Data Set	U. Modified Boxplot
V. Alpha	W. Beta	X. Experimental Units
Y. ordinal		

Provide the word that best matches each clue.

1. RETROSPECTIVE — Type of cohort study where subjects are sampled after the outcome has occurred.
2. THEORY — Collection of propositions to illustrate the principles of a subject.
3. BIAS — Any problem in the design or conduct of a statistical study that tends to favor certain results.
4. FREQUENCY — The number of times a variable occurs in a data set.
5. QUANTITATIVE VARIABLES — Tells how much or many of something there is.
6. PERCENTILE — Each of the 100 equal groups into which a population can be divided according to the distribution of values of a variable.
7. DOT — A very small circular shape.
8. INTERPRET — Explain the meaning of information, words, or actions.
9. PARALLEL — Make or place alongside something.
10. CUMULATIVE — Increasing by successive addition.
11. RANDOM SAMPLING — Every possible sample of a size has an equal chance of being selected.
12. RAW DATA — Actual measurements or observations collected from the sample.
13. SAMPLING DISTRIBUTION — The random variable is a statistic based on the results of more than one trial.
14. RANK CORRELATION — The relationship between rankings of different ordinal variables.
15. INTERPOLATION — Calculation of the value of a function between known values.
16. VARIABLE — A characteristic that differs from one subject to the next.
17. EXPERIMENTAL UNITS — Things who are studied.
18. LEADING QUESTION BIAS — Sometimes questions are worded in a way that suggest a particular response.
19. DATA SET — All of the information collected.
20. SELF INTEREST — A bias where people who have an interest in the outcome of an experiment have an incentive to use biased methods.
21. COMPOUND — Put or add together.

22. PARAMETER — Descriptive measure for a population represented by Greek letters.

23. RANDOM — Made, done, happening, or chosen without method or conscious decision.

24. COEFFICIENT OF VARIATION — Tells how large the standard deviation is relative to the mean. It can be used to compare the spreads of data sets whose values have different units.

25. P — probability of a success.

A. Experimental Units	B. parallel	C. Variable
D. Coefficient of Variation	E. Theory	F. Self Interest
G. Dot	H. Raw data	I. Interpret
J. Data Set	K. Random	L. Random sampling
M. Parameter	N. Interpolation	O. Frequency
P. Percentile	Q. Leading Question Bias	R. Bias
S. Sampling distribution	T. Cumulative	U. P
V. Quantitative Variables	W. Rank Correlation	X. Retrospective
Y. Compound		

Provide the word that best matches each clue.

26. OBSERVATION — The act of making and recording a measurement.

27. INTERPRET — Explain the meaning of information, words, or actions.

28. INDEPENDENT VARIABLE — A value that does not depend on changes in other values.

29. NULL HYPOTHESIS — No relationship exists on the categorical variables in the population.

30. RANDOM SAMPLING — The selection of a random sample.

31. HYPOTHESIS — A supposition or proposed explanation based on limited evidence as a starting point for further investigation.

32. FREQUENCY DISTRIBUTION — Presented in a table that gives the frequency for each category.

33. STANDARD SCORE — Expresses the value of a score relative to the mean and standard deviation of its distribution.

34. POWER — The probability of correctly rejecting the null hypothesis.

35. VARIABLE — A characteristic that differs from one subject to the next.

36. CASE CONTROL — A type of study where two samples are drawn.

37. SUBJECT — When the experimental units are people.

38. BIAS — Any problem in the design or conduct of a statistical study that tends to favor certain results.

#	Term	Clue
39.	OBSERVATIONAL STUDY	The assignment to treatment groups is not made by the investigator.
40.	GROUP	Any number of entities members considered as a unit.
41.	BETA	Probability of a type II error.
42.	CONTINUOUS	Extending without break or irregularity.
43.	PIE CHART	A circular chart divided into triangular areas proportional to the percentages of the whole.
44.	SIMPLE RANDOM SAMPLE	A sample is chosen by a method such that every member of the population is equally likely to be selected.
45.	SOCIAL ACCEPTABILITY	A bias where people are reluctant to admit to behavior that may reflect negatively on them.
46.	SAMPLE	A subset of a population.
47.	POPULATION	The collection of all people, objects, or events having one or more specified characteristics.
48.	PARALLEL	Make or place alongside something.
49.	ORDINAL VARIABLES	Type of qualitative variable. Have a natural ordering, but have no mathematically value.
50.	DATA SET	All of the information collected.

- A. parallel
- B. Bias
- C. Case Control
- D. Simple Random Sample
- E. Hypothesis
- F. Data Set
- G. Null Hypothesis
- H. Pie chart
- I. Continuous
- J. Social Acceptability
- K. Subject
- L. Variable
- M. Population
- N. Power
- O. random sampling
- P. Beta
- Q. Independent variable
- R. Frequency Distribution
- S. Observation
- T. Group
- U. Standard score
- V. Ordinal Variables
- W. Sample
- X. Interpret
- Y. Observational Study

Provide the word that best matches each clue.

#	Term	Clue
51.	STATISTICS	A branch of mathematics concerned with quantitative data.
52.	SIGMA	population standard deviation.
53.	STATISTIC	Descriptive measure for a sample.
54.	RANGE	The difference between the largest and the smallest value.

#	Term	Definition
55.	POWER	The probability of correctly rejecting the null hypothesis.
56.	RANDOM ASSIGNMENT	Each participant in a treatment group has an equal chance of being placed in any of the groups.
57.	PARAMETER	Descriptive measure for a population represented by Greek letters.
58.	OBSERVATIONAL STUDY	The assignment to treatment groups is not made by the investigator.
59.	GROUPED	Arranged into groups.
60.	EXTRAPOLATION	Calculating a value outside the range of known values.
61.	PARETO CHART	Bar graph in which categories are represented in order of frequency.
62.	UNIMODAL	Only one mode.
63.	DATA SET	All of the information collected.
64.	FREQUENCY DISTRIBUTION	Presented in a table that gives the frequency for each category.
65.	INFERENTIAL STATISTICS	Drawing inferences from sample data to a population.
66.	RANDOM	Made, done, happening, or chosen without method or conscious decision.
67.	OUTLIER	Scores that differ so markedly from the main body of data that their accuracy is questioned.
68.	COLUMN	A vertical array of numbers or other information.
69.	SURVEY	Make a detailed inspection of; for statistical purposes.
70.	INDEPENDENT VARIABLE	A value that does not depend on changes in other values.
71.	POPULATION	The collection of all people, objects, or events having one or more specified characteristics.
72.	SAMPLING BIAS	Occurs when some members in the population are more likely to be included in the sample than others.
73.	CLASS WIDTH	The difference between consecutive lower class limits.
74.	PARALLEL	Make or place alongside something.
75.	SELF INTEREST	A bias where people who have an interest in the outcome of an experiment have an incentive to use biased methods.

A. Pareto Chart
B. Sigma
C. Unimodal
D. parallel
E. Self Interest
F. Parameter
G. Outlier
H. Population
I. Class Width

J. Extrapolation
K. Random assignment
L. Statistics
M. Data Set
N. Range
O. Grouped
P. Survey
Q. Random
R. Column
S. Frequency Distribution
T. Statistic
U. Power
V. Sampling Bias
W. Inferential Statistics
X. Observational Study
Y. Independent variable

Provide the word that best matches each clue.

76. CLASSES — Intervals of equal width that cover all values observed in the data set.

77. LEVEL OF SIGNIFICANCE — The probability that is the largest risk a researcher is willing to take of rejecting a true null hypothesis.

78. STATISTIC — Descriptive measure for a sample.

79. SAMPLE OF CONVENIENCE — A random sample that is not drawn by a well-defined random method.

80. NON RESPONSE — A response where the opinions of non-responders tend to differ from the opinions of those who do respond.

81. MINIMUM — The least or smallest amount or quantity possible, attainable, or required.

82. TYPE II — An error retaining a false null hypothesis.

83. POSITIVELY SKEWED — Longer tail extends to the right

84. NUMERICAL — Of or relating to or denoting numerals.

85. UNIMODAL — Only one mode.

86. PI — Ratio of a circle's circumference to its diameter, ≈ 3.1416

87. MAXIMUM — As great, high, or intense as possible or permitted.

88. SKEWED DISTRIBUTION — Distributions that are asymmetrical.

89. TIME SERIES — A series of values of a variable at successive times.

90. QUANTITATIVE VARIABLES — Tells how much or many of something there is.

91. RELATIVE FREQUENCY — A distribution that shows the proportion or percent frequency for each interval.

92. MODE — The score or qualitative category that occurs with greatest frequency.

93. SURVEY — Make a detailed inspection of; for statistical purposes.

94. OPEN ENDED CLASSES — When the first class has no lower limit, or the last class has no upper limit.

95.	TREND LINE	A line on a graph indicating a statistical trend.
96.	STRATIFIED SAMPLING	The population is divided into subpopulations and random samples are taken of each stratum.
97.	RETROSPECTIVE	Type of cohort study where subjects are sampled after the outcome has occurred.
98.	GROUP	Any number of entities members considered as a unit.
99.	RANDOM SAMPLING	The selection of a random sample.
100.	COMPOUND	Put or add together.

A. Open Ended Classes
B. Type II
C. Numerical
D. Stratified sampling
E. Time series
F. Non response
G. Level of significance
H. Survey
I. Skewed distribution
J. Minimum
K. Group
L. Relative frequency
M. Mode
N. Quantitative Variables
O. Retrospective
P. Pi
Q. Sample of Convenience
R. Statistic
S. Classes
T. Compound
U. Positively skewed
V. Maximum
W. random sampling
X. Unimodal
Y. Trend line

Provide the word that best matches each clue.

101.	DOT	A very small circular shape.
102.	SKEWED DISTRIBUTION	Distributions that are asymmetrical.
103.	EMPIRICAL RULE	Approximately 68% of the data will be within one standard deviation of the mean.
104.	DEPENDENT SAMPLES	The selection of participants in one sample is affected by the selection of participants in the other sample.
105.	OBSERVATION	The act of making and recording a measurement.
106.	CHI SQUARE	Relating to or denoting a statistical method assessing the goodness of fit between observed values and those expected theoretically.
107.	NEGATIVELY SKEWED	Longer tail extends to the left
108.	PARAMETER	Descriptive measure for a population represented by Greek letters.
109.	STACKED	Bar graph that shows frequencies or relative frequencies in categories for more than one group frequencies within each category.
110.	GROUP	Any number of entities members considered as a unit.

111. FREQUENCY — The number of times a variable occurs in a data set.

112. DOUBLE BLIND — An experiment where neither the investigator nor the subjects know who has been assigned to which treatment.

113. BAR GRAPH — A graphical representation of a frequency distribution.

114. DISCRETE VARIABLE — Type of quantitative variable whose possible values can be listed.

115. TREATMENTS — The procedures applied to each experimental unit.

116. TREND LINE — A line on a graph indicating a statistical trend.

117. Z SCORE — Tells how many standard deviations that value is from its population mean.

118. GROUPED — Arranged into groups.

119. CORRELATION COEFFICIENT — A number that represents the degree of association or strength of relationship between two variables.

120. ALPHA — Significance level; probability of a type I error.

121. ORDINAL — The number designating place in an ordered sequence.

122. SPREAD — Distribute or disperse widely.

123. CUMULATIVE FREQUENCY — A distribution that shows the number, proportion, or percentage of scores that occur below the real upper limit of each interval.

124. STANDARD SCORE — Expresses the value of a score relative to the mean and standard deviation of its distribution.

125. COLLECT — Come together and form a group or mass.

- A. Negatively skewed
- B. Frequency
- C. Observation
- D. Bar Graph
- E. Chi square
- F. Stacked
- G. Collect
- H. ordinal
- I. Cumulative frequency
- J. Grouped
- K. Double Blind
- L. Skewed distribution
- M. Alpha
- N. Spread
- O. Dependent samples
- P. Group
- Q. Discrete Variable
- R. Standard score
- S. Parameter
- T. Trend line
- U. Empirical Rule
- V. Z Score
- W. Treatments
- X. Correlation coefficient
- Y. Dot

Provide the word that best matches each clue.

126. UPPER CLASS LIMIT — The largest value that can appear in that class.

#	Term	Definition
127.	PIE CHART	A circular chart divided into triangular areas proportional to the percentages of the whole.
128.	INDEPENDENT SAMPLES	The selection of participants in one sample is not affected by the selection of participants in the other sample.
129.	COHORT STUDY	Group of subjects is studied to determine whether various factors of interest are associated with an outcome.
130.	SPREAD	Distribute or disperse widely.
131.	GROUPED	Arranged into groups.
132.	UNBIASED	Studies conducted by a procedure that produces the correct result on average.
133.	TREATMENTS	The procedures applied to each experimental unit.
134.	INTERVAL	A set containing all points between two given endpoints.
135.	COLUMN	A vertical array of numbers or other information.
136.	RANGE	The difference between the largest and the smallest value.
137.	SAMPLE	A subset of a population.
138.	CHI SQUARE	Relating to or denoting a statistical method assessing the goodness of fit between observed values and those expected theoretically.
139.	LEADING QUESTION BIAS	Sometimes questions are worded in a way that suggest a particular response.
140.	CONFOUNDING	Cause surprise or confusion, especially by acting against an expectation.
141.	QUESTIONNAIRE	A form with a set of queries to gain statistical information.
142.	EXTRAPOLATION	Calculating a value outside the range of known values.
143.	RELATIVE FREQUENCY	A distribution that shows the proportion or percent frequency for each interval.
144.	STANDARD SCORE	Expresses the value of a score relative to the mean and standard deviation of its distribution.
145.	PERCENTILE RANK	The percentage of the scores of the distribution that fall below that score.
146.	STRATUM	People having the same social or economic status.
147.	COHORT	A group.

148. STACKED — Bar graph that shows frequencies or relative frequencies in categories for more than one group frequencies within each category.

149. TYPE I — An error rejecting a true null hypothesis.

150. FIVE NUMBER SUMMARY — Minimum, 1st Quartile, Median, 3rd Quartile, Maximum.

A. Sample	B. Range	C. Five Number Summary
D. Type I	E. Cohort Study	F. Spread
G. Upper Class Limit	H. Chi square	I. Cohort
J. Unbiased	K. Stacked	L. Pie chart
M. Interval	N. Relative frequency	O. Stratum
P. Confounding	Q. Independent samples	R. Standard score
S. Treatments	T. Questionnaire	U. Extrapolation
V. Grouped	W. Percentile rank	X. Column
Y. Leading Question Bias		

Provide the word that best matches each clue.

151. PARALLEL — Make or place alongside something.

152. NORMAL DISTRIBUTION — A probability distribution that is unimodal and symmetrical.

153. UNBIASED — Studies conducted by a procedure that produces the correct result on average.

154. RATIO — The quantitative relation between two amounts showing the number of times one value contains or is contained within the other.

155. MINIMUM — The least or smallest amount or quantity possible, attainable, or required.

156. INTERPRET — Explain the meaning of information, words, or actions.

157. BIVARIATE — Having two variables.

158. CONFOUNDING — Cause surprise or confusion, especially by acting against an expectation.

159. TREND LINE — A line on a graph indicating a statistical trend.

160. PARAMETER — Descriptive measure for a population represented by Greek letters.

161. LEADING QUESTION BIAS — Sometimes questions are worded in a way that suggest a particular response.

162. MODIFIED BOXPLOT — Whiskers out to the lowest or highest values that are not outliers.

163. CRITICAL REGION — The region for rejecting the null hypothesis.

164. ANALYSIS OF VARIANCE		A procedure for determining how much of the variability among scores to attribute to a range of sources of variation.
165. CONTINUOUS VARIABLE		Type of quantitative variable. Can take on any value in some interval.
166. CLASSES		Intervals of equal width that cover all values observed in the data set.
167. OBSERVATIONAL STUDY		The assignment to treatment groups is not made by the investigator.
168. MAXIMUM		As great, high, or intense as possible or permitted.
169. FLUCTUATION		The quality of being unsteady and subject to changes.
170. MEAN		A measure of center in a data set.
171. SPREAD		Distribute or disperse widely.
172. OUTLIER		Scores that differ so markedly from the main body of data that their accuracy is questioned.
173. SAMPLE OF CONVENIENCE		A random sample that is not drawn by a well-defined random method.
174. CORRELATION COEFFICIENT		A number that represents the degree of association or strength of relationship between two variables.
175. MATCHED SAMPLE		Matching each participant in the experimental condition with a participant in the control condition.

A. Analysis of variance
B. Correlation coefficient
C. Sample of Convenience
D. Spread
E. Interpret
F. Continuous Variable
G. Critical region
H. Mean
I. Trend line
J. Parameter
K. Ratio
L. Fluctuation
M. Confounding
N. Modified Boxplot
O. Leading Question Bias
P. Normal distribution
Q. Minimum
R. Matched sample
S. Observational Study
T. parallel
U. Maximum
V. Unbiased
W. Classes
X. Bivariate
Y. Outlier

Provide the word that best matches each clue.

176. REPEATED MEASURES		Observing the same participants under both the experimental and control conditions.
177. NUMERICAL		Of or relating to or denoting numerals.
178. STANDARD DEVIATION		The square root of the variance.
179. RESISTANT STATISTIC		Its value is not affected much by extreme values in the data set.

180.	DATA SET	All of the information collected.
181.	MODIFIED BOXPLOT	Whiskers out to the lowest or highest values that are not outliers.
182.	P VALUE	The probability of obtaining a value of the test statistic equal to or more extreme than that observed.
183.	ALPHA	Significance level; probability of a type I error.
184.	CUMULATIVE	Increasing by successive addition.
185.	BETA	Probability of a type II error.
186.	CAUSATION	The act of making something happen.
187.	STRATIFIED SAMPLING	The population is divided into subpopulations and random samples are taken of each stratum.
188.	DEPENDENT SAMPLES	The selection of participants in one sample is affected by the selection of participants in the other sample.
189.	CORRELATION	A statistic representing how closely two variables co vary.
190.	MU	Population mean.
191.	P	probability of a success.
192.	PARETO CHART	Bar graph in which categories are represented in order of frequency.
193.	CORRELATION COEFFICIENT	A number that represents the degree of association or strength of relationship between two variables.
194.	ORDINAL	The number designating place in an ordered sequence.
195.	TIME SERIES	A series of values of a variable at successive times.
196.	CHI SQUARE	Relating to or denoting a statistical method assessing the goodness of fit between observed values and those expected theoretically.
197.	EXPERIMENTAL UNITS	Things who are studied.
198.	VARIANCE	A measure of how far the values in a data set are from the mean, on the average.
199.	HISTOGRAM	Graphical representation of frequency distribution for quantitative data. Rectangle for each class.
200.	RATIO	The quantitative relation between two amounts showing the number of times one value contains or is contained within the other.

A. Resistant Statistic
B. Correlation
C. Correlation coefficient
D. Chi square
E. Variance
F. Standard Deviation
G. P value
H. Pareto Chart
I. Dependent samples
J. Time series
K. P
L. Repeated measures
M. Histogram
N. Causation
O. Mu
P. Ratio
Q. Stratified sampling
R. Cumulative
S. Numerical
T. Data Set
U. Modified Boxplot
V. Alpha
W. Beta
X. Experimental Units
Y. ordinal

Word Search

1.

L	D	N	O	M	I	N	A	L	V	A	R	I	A	B	L	E	S	V	V	C	B	Z
K	S	E	L	F	I	N	T	E	R	E	S	T	H	K	N	T	B	J	A	B	C	O
S	T	A	C	K	E	D	F	L	B	B	Y	Z	X	B	O	Y	C	H	O	K	O	E
A	N	V	A	C	A	D	E	B	H	P	G	I	D	Q	N	Z	M	E	A	N	R	K
P	Q	J	X	V	M	D	Y	T	O	S	T	A	T	I	S	T	I	C	S	D	R	X
S	T	R	A	T	I	F	I	E	D	S	A	M	P	L	I	N	G	C	S	Z	E	I
S	L	E	V	E	L	O	F	S	I	G	N	I	F	I	C	A	N	C	E	O	L	O
S	A	M	P	L	I	N	G	D	I	S	T	R	I	B	U	T	I	O	N	A	A	Z
N	I	N	D	E	P	E	N	D	E	N	T	V	A	R	I	A	B	L	E	C	T	N
H	I	N	D	E	P	E	N	D	E	N	T	S	A	M	P	L	E	S	A	T	I	U
I	T	O	X	X	K	C	X	Z	C	A	S	E	C	O	N	T	R	O	L	U	O	M
U	D	S	R	I	W	D	G	P	B	D	F	C	O	L	U	M	N	X	G	Z	N	E
L	C	Y	Z	Z	P	L	B	N	C	W	C	S	D	D	K	J	V	Q	T	U	C	R
F	S	M	E	V	A	R	I	A	N	C	E	P	O	P	A	W	F	D	V	G	O	I
N	G	M	W	N	L	M	P	M	U	L	D	R	L	Y	H	T	R	G	P	E	E	C
L	U	E	L	Y	H	J	A	E	C	L	W	E	G	T	V	P	A	U	Z	W	F	A
A	P	T	S	Y	T	J	V	I	Q	T	U	A	X	W	I	H	B	S	S	B	F	L
V	O	R	Y	M	M	H	J	E	Q	O	R	D	I	W	D	H	V	G	E	A	I	M
M	A	I	B	D	Z	T	H	J	E	O	N	Z	S	C	N	Y	L	Y	N	T	C	C
K	O	C	P	D	I	S	C	R	E	T	E	V	A	R	I	A	B	L	E	T	I	H
Q	H	W	Q	Q	B	C	G	P	F	A	U	L	Y	S	F	X	F	P	C	O	E	Z
G	J	F	V	W	S	X	B	Y	L	H	W	J	M	K	T	O	N	L	S	C	N	W
N	D	A	Z	U	W	N	J	Z	R	S	Q	B	N	K	U	E	J	I	O	H	T	O

Symmetric
Numerical
Data Set
Nominal Variables
Stacked
Self Interest
Sampling distribution

Spread
Stratified sampling
Column
Mean
Case Control
Discrete Variable
Variance

Correlation coefficient
Level of significance
P
Independent variable
Statistics
Independent samples

2.

M	O	P	G	V	E	R	C	Q	D	W	W	J	V	B	V	D	X	X	B	Q	S	N
R	A	N	D	O	M	I	Z	E	D	D	E	S	I	G	N	I	O	C	L	U	O	Q
D	R	E	T	R	O	S	P	E	C	T	I	V	E	S	K	S	X	L	I	A	C	T
I	B	J	B	O	P	U	Y	R	L	J	O	O	B	I	S	T	X	U	A	L	I	W
U	S	R	A	J	O	Y	H	M	H	A	R	S	D	V	H	R	L	S	X	I	A	V
X	W	X	R	R	T	P	M	H	T	X	D	K	K	N	I	I	J	T	A	L	F
W	O	Q	G	H	X	S	F	Z	U	B	I	P	C	O	S	B	W	E	V	A	A	V
A	L	S	R	D	L	V	D	L	K	L	N	M	Y	T	T	U	Y	R	O	T	C	T
T	C	G	A	U	W	O	F	D	E	A	A	C	S	X	O	T	C	S	S	I	C	Z
K	I	T	P	W	C	P	K	L	C	R	L	X	T	M	G	I	B	A	K	V	E	F
X	K	M	H	U	L	A	L	G	I	N	V	T	O	A	R	O	G	M	Q	E	P	W
L	P	K	E	O	S	A	L	L	A	T	B	D	R	I	A	N	E	P	R	V	T	K
J	B	U	D	S	R	Z	G	P	I	G	N	W	V	J	M	M	O	L	Z	A	A	W
V	Z	N	Q	A	E	C	M	F	C	A	U	S	A	T	I	O	N	I	I	R	B	Z
T	X	R	P	T	U	R	S	C	R	Q	C	M	S	G	D	Q	Q	N	V	I	I	G
S	K	E	W	E	D	D	I	S	T	R	I	B	U	T	I	O	N	G	E	A	L	R
W	O	U	T	L	I	E	R	E	B	Z	L	U	F	W	J	Q	A	I	W	B	I	V
L	D	G	J	Y	P	L	E	T	S	S	J	C	G	P	R	J	X	U	V	L	T	H
O	M	X	T	L	C	O	N	F	O	U	N	D	I	N	G	X	O	Y	I	E	Y	L
Q	U	P	S	A	M	P	L	I	N	G	D	I	S	T	R	I	B	U	T	I	O	N
W	U	C	E	N	S	U	S	Z	J	G	X	R	T	M	D	I	Q	J	N	P	E	A
T	F	M	P	H	Z	G	M	X	B	A	C	O	R	R	E	L	A	T	I	O	N	N
V	I	C	P	M	K	V	S	Z	Q	W	D	O	B	J	P	D	C	J	Y	T	I	S

Time series
Census
Grouped
Sampling distribution
ordinal
Cluster Sampling
Confounding

Skewed distribution
Qualitative Variable
Retrospective
Histogram
Social Acceptability
Causation
parallel

Bar Graph
Random
Randomized design
Distribution
Correlation
Outlier

3.

```
K H A P V T X J W Q F Q U G A X D U M A N C I
F I V E N U M B E R S U M M A R Y I A G O Q R
J V R C U M P R H L U A Y P I C H A M J M K C
O I Q C C E G E G I Q M I N I M U M C C I Y O
L A U I O E C I N T E R V A L O N F O O N L R
E D A F O L T L I T O Y U D I V R V C M A I R
V G R Q K X U N E Z P J L I L V P C W P L O E
E U T U Y Y G M G I T J T S X K E H S O V K L
L V I T C I N R N C U H W T U Q R I X U A Z A
O F L Z J A W Y O R K A N R X T C S O N R T T
F O E X X N M U U U D V G I C Y E Q S D I B I
S G X A H A H D U Z P S B B M A N U Z V A G O
I E S P Y J F J Y H E E C U E C T A E C B X N
G X T F Q D C N Q S H P D T U X A R E L L A T
N U A I P C C U M U L A T I V E G E N Z E J V
I X T Z S D X D B P X V D O G K E W T S S O W
F R I T L M T W D I J U P N B A R G R A P H A
I K S X W U G D U M C A T E G O R I C A L V D
C O T E A J H U J X O W U N B I A S E D N Q I
A P I K K F W A O T H A W L F K Q Q P Y C B N
N E C H L K O J Z L F T N T P G J V Y X M G K
C H S E E Y C K S H Z Y L P U L D Y U I R P H
E B G J R I N T E R P O L A T I O N P D G V R
```

Column   Chi square   Bar Graph
Unbiased   Pi   Compound
Nominal Variables   Interpolation   percentage
Minimum   Categorical   Quartile
Interval   Cumulative   Level of significance
Correlation   Distribution   Statistics
Five Number Summary   Grouped

4.

A	P	V	D	W	C	H	M	L	Y	H	E	G	V	C	E	V	D	V	M	G	W	D
P	V	R	C	G	X	U	G	M	G	L	L	H	X	V	U	Q	O	O	A	O	A	R
I	I	N	T	E	R	V	A	L	W	S	H	C	V	L	G	N	T	U	T	I	D	A
Z	N	K	T	E	A	Q	R	A	N	D	O	M	F	M	F	Z	S	V	C	S	Y	E
X	G	K	E	G	F	V	E	S	P	I	E	C	H	A	R	T	D	H	J	Z	K
L	O	S	R	Y	L	M	R	T	M	C	P	Q	X	V	E	C	W	A	E	M	K	X
Q	U	A	L	I	T	A	T	I	V	E	V	A	R	I	A	B	L	E	D	O	A	D
Q	B	T	T	S	U	S	Q	T	Y	P	E	I	C	O	L	U	M	N	S	U	B	G
T	Y	N	I	Q	T	J	G	F	K	E	U	O	I	K	A	T	V	D	A	W	P	N
X	N	P	S	B	W	R	S	B	U	M	V	O	R	C	F	P	T	O	M	G	C	D
R	E	I	W	C	U	M	U	L	A	T	I	V	E	J	C	O	T	J	P	Z	W
D	H	M	Y	L	T	W	K	X	G	X	R	N	E	P	L	R	Z	Z	L	Q	I	V
C	A	E	G	W	U	M	V	T	R	G	Z	D	I	P	Z	B	A	Y	E	Z	X	D
Y	F	T	V	R	I	J	K	P	N	O	E	J	X	C	C	A	L	Y	U	P	Q	D
Z	X	C	A	T	Q	H	T	J	O	C	N	O	N	R	E	S	P	O	N	S	E	R
S	B	V	S	C	Z	M	Y	N	J	W	B	H	F	N	W	W	H	A	I	B	H	I
J	T	E	A	D	B	B	R	A	N	K	C	O	R	R	E	L	A	T	I	O	N	B
P	B	B	L	L	E	V	E	L	O	F	S	I	G	N	I	F	I	C	A	N	C	E
W	M	I	H	J	X	Y	I	Q	D	U	D	Q	X	F	U	K	S	A	N	V	J	J
I	R	R	Z	X	L	E	X	T	R	A	P	O	L	A	T	I	O	N	X	X	H	V
W	D	I	S	C	R	E	T	E	V	A	R	I	A	B	L	E	I	B	O	P	R	K
C	Y	R	F	Y	B	K	F	W	G	Q	W	B	P	I	N	Q	M	C	Z	P	R	X
A	X	T	G	N	H	T	P	E	F	V	B	Q	K	W	R	D	K	Q	H	U	B	E

Alpha   Rank Correlation   Pie chart   Type I
Matched sample   Mode   Qualitative Variable   Data
Non response   Column   Pi   Level of significance
Extrapolation   Discrete Variable   Chi square   Random
Boxplot   Dot   Cumulative   Interval

145

5.

```
H O R D I N A L V A R I A B L E S A F H F V Y
P A Z D M C B Y Z K T Q Q M R B V R V S L D T
U Z O Y E K D Y S M F H A A O T G E Q T U C D
R P H V T P D A M O D E X X Q E K S D R L F U
D A L B Z A E B O J E I M I U C S I C A X K L
A R N S I V Y N B V O B U M Z N P D A T A N W
C E M D S H P T D O T D N U H J Y U E I O G Z
S T L A O M M I N E Z D M M Z U K A Q F S L T
P O V Z T M F D V H N E O R L T L L Q I W F S
N C H X P C S Q U E S T I O N N A I R E N A O
P H I S D C H A T C E N S U S T J N U D V P D
J A S I O B W E M O W E I A Y Q C G S S W D O
O R T R C V W G D P U O H K M M Z S N A K E U
E T O Q X V H N Q S L T Q R A P L E C M X N B
L L G G Q E S K Z Y A I L J U B L E P P X E L
Q X R T L L I W P P Y M N I B L U E L L C M E
J X A A R O M X F M U Q P G E Z M M S I M M B
B T M W U H G I L B D O R L A R G Q Y N F N L
M G I R H O O S P R E A D I E S S R H G R U I
J E K S A M P L I N G D I S T R I B U T I O N
C D A R E S I S T A N T S T A T I S T I C L D
Z R X N Q V E Y V B E L L S H A P E D X Z U X
Z V V L L F E U E M L E B O B U G U E O W U Q
```

Dependent samples
Bell Shaped
Ordinal Variables
Mean
Outlier
Resistant Statistic
Stratified sampling

Maximum
Census
Pareto Chart
Spread
Matched sample
Mode
Questionnaire

Double Blind
Rho
Random sampling
Residual
Sampling distribution
Histogram

6.

```
G I W L E S I M P L E R A N D O M S A M P L E
T L Q J X V S L W J X E Y I C H N G S P G D D
O D V G A E F O D P U A B S V H C H G W P X N
X W A Q N N D A P H F A P X N S I N Q U O G E
I N T E R P O L A T I O N H G A H S K X O H G
C R I T I C A L R E G I O N O M R E Q I K I A
K N F R G U Q N Q B O N I O Z P L V T U I O T
Q L H J Q R O P S G Y M V F Y L U A N J A F I
N O N R E S P O N S E H S A H I R X F T S R V
Z V Y V T I Q T W C E P A R F N G N S O T E
H J T L P R O S P E C T I V E G C P U A V Q L
E J E X Y P U T K F D E L B S D J U L F P N Y
C Q U A L I T A T I V E V A R I A B L E B A S
O B S E R V A T I O N F V Q A S K P H B E M K
T P E R C E N T I L E R A N K T D I Y V L D E
R A N G E P S S Z S B B R K E R W M P K L O W
W I B C I K V L S T A T I S T I C S O H S N E
D E N W N A S A G Q C V A J H B J Z T J H B D
N D N D Y E S F L L O H N A K U L S H X A N Q
P U O L V O B S X U F K C P E T P Y E C P S G
H X E P Y L I L Y T E S E W E I J Y S V E R U
R E T R O S P E C T I V E L X O F O I M D K A
Y I Q H Z I X S F L Z J B Q C N D K S P H Z B
```

Percentile rank	Prospective	Statistics
Critical region	Retrospective	Nu
Null Hypothesis	Observation	Sampling distribution
Interpolation	Non response	Qualitative Variable
Negatively skewed	Variance	Ratio
Simple Random Sample	Bell Shaped	P value
Chi square	Range	

7.

```
A A Q I X E R U A S K T O A D S L D Z L U E Z
Y C O E F F I C I E N T O F V A R I A T I O N
Y M Q D C I V A R I A B L E N U V Y F L Z X H
Z O Y B P U P E R C E N T I L E D G X E S P P
M R Q Y L E M G Q W F X D B C S P O W E R W H
B D I A F T R U F I P R C W S F R Y H O G V G
I I X D N K I C L O O I I F C W F A G C T C N
X N X Z Y K G X E A N C S A S O Q R W F W O J
Z A E N Y R Q L W N T C N F R M D P E D I F Q
I L V H Y Q G Z H Q T I N Q U P L I R T A I X
D V P C O Z G J N C N I V E K I K G U X Q T N
I A A O I J O K J E Y O L E Q B C B U C U N A
B R O N I O A O R N R C M E F T I L L V A R W
J I Q T C L O C H S T M U R R A I F G R S L
Q A I I T C R X Z U R I G X T A E U Z X T C X
U B R N L C R R Z S Z H O S B G N Q X R I J X
F L B U A V O N X U S T I D T F W K U K L Z N
W E P O C N N L U B T D R J M R A N G E E N P
Q S C U A P Z I L R T Z N O N R E S P O N S E
B O A S Z Z L S O E X T C X P O J I O V J C L
Z G D E K G C O C B C C O N F O U N D I N G Y
S G N T F O U A T C O T O C M V Y G P Y B H U
M D Z S A M P L E O F C O N V E N I E N C E F
```

Range   Continuous   Non response
Percentile   Collect   Power
Quartile   Cumulative frequency   Raw data
Sample of Convenience   ordinal   Plot
Census   Percentile rank   Pi
Ordinal Variables   Confounding   Coefficient of Variation
Variable   Distribution

148

8.

```
T S Y K R P T W Q M F M O D J A O H L M D D H
U I M K A F Y S C U H B U H G C O N O E L A V
W Q M U N R L Y Z A Q L R L O A S D K M A T W
E X H H D T P S D M T V L V V F N C Z J D A A
Q Y E S O R I T N O Z E M D W A A M U T I G I
T A C U M F E E E G U K G P R T E N D D S R J
W Q U N I R C M G C R B V O S Q V A V B C R J
B A U U Z N H A A O Z F L M R S V T K T R A C
D P A L E U A T T R R O R E N I I D H G E N L
S D R L D O R I I N C G E H B B C Z E W T K U
J P K H D A T C V D X F A Q O L A A W J E C S
X Z B Y E U W S E E L H T N G T I T L B V O T
K I R P S Y P A L Q R L O G I G K N J Q A R E
L P D O I M G M Y J J F S M T Z G Z D P R R R
S L Q T G P W P S I P P A R A M E T E R I E S
V G G H N B K L K F Y I S V J M O G A R A L A
Q T N E J S F I E Q E F B E T A N I Q C B A M
S D P S R O A N W A Q J W K V A E L W Z L T P
R J U I L P A G E V W C M Q R K E C B T E I L
U C F S F C E U D L N K I T J R E G I R M O I
V N E M S H T O I N T E R P R E T C J Q L N N
G V R B B F Q W N P I Y E R B N K H J B N P G
F F P Q C O N T I N U O U S M X J P S B W Z B
```

Null Hypothesis	Random	Rho
Rank Correlation	Data	Systematic Sampling
Organize	Beta	Randomized design
Interpret	Parameter	Cluster Sampling
Range	Discrete Variable	Continuous
Negatively skewed	Categorical	Pie chart
Double Blind	Stacked	

9.

```
X R Q D B S U Z G E F I A C O N T I N U O U S
P A R A M E T E R F G E U Z O Y S R P M L L S
T N Y W H B F P E V U E I C J T P T Z A K H L
R C C O R R E L A T I O N L O B X C R I B K I
F E R I Y G B J X D D L B K J M A Q R A E F C
Q L B E H B K N Z F S E F W Q P P R M A T K M
O R A N D O M S A M P L I N G P C O G G E U A
P S B C L U S T E R S A M P L I N G U R G K M
M A X I M U M E V H R T D N B X V O N A K S
K Z F F N U M E R I C A L I U R A N G E D P U
D Q T S N B J V A G L S L S S U O I X E W M H
Z Y N Q N O R M A L D I S T R I B U T I O N Z
E K V E U J X G C U L D U R Q T Y P E I I K H
M U L D R A N D O M A S S I G N M E N T C S Y
W R I B Y H E R F B O W Y B Z V M B U E P Z N
D E D O L A L P H A E M E U B N X M L Y N O M
I Z Z Y C C F C G T L I R T I K I X C Y I T M
F M M C C O R N E N Q K N I A H Z S U T F Q X
X C X U E Z L W V V R E Z O J N F B A G V N W
H O B O P N J U Y H J I R N O R M S A V K H R
M G W S N J S Q M B A V G S W H U J J I W O H
L B P L M Z Q U H N X M K R M A Z E A Q L W O
E Y I Y M D P U S G I C S Y C U V Z G L Q K F
```

Type II   Range   Correlation
Continuous   Distribution   Maximum
Census   Bar Graph   Compound
Random assignment   random sampling   Mu
Causation   Stratum   Parameter
Normal distribution   Column   Cluster Sampling
Numerical   Alpha

150

10.

```
L N D E S C R I P T I V E S T A T I S T I C S
E F S I C D N K O T S G T Y M I J J D D V C D
A R I W O F J P E R C E N T A G E Z U U A R M
D E V Z N Y P Z A Q A M P E K B O W B A R I P
I Q E G T B O X P L O T U N B I A S E D I T P
N U M Q I C H N B J S P R E A D H J J J A I T
G E X T N U U R T X V H X T Z S B T A E N C J
Q N J D U Q N X J I V H M Y H T C G U Q C A D
U C U B O M O D I F I E D B O X P L O T E L G
E Y I W U T G K B H P X D P L H I D Z A T R F
S A K M S Y J H E P Y O O C U N E C X Y Y E X
T A N J V D P T L V K S S L A R Y Q C G B G K
I C K P A H Y O L A I V T A U K Y M N I J I F
O Z M J R C L Q S L B G R S G H Q X R H C O R
N U O J I P B Y H U B H W S S U B J E C T N Z
B A T F A M I B A E O K D W Q U A R T I L E T
I S I R B U N I P B H I A I F V D D V U T U A
A Q X O L H U A E P R A M D L U Z C N N S N K
S J D U E W N S D U Q B C T B W X Y L S T N O
T G S T R A T U M F K N C H D M P W A N B D H
P P L L P A D C C X G S N V D O A L A M O T G
I Z W A Q J Y Y C A Z T G I M Z C D M K R D H
D V O I J B V N O O O I G L P O J U E E U G S
```

P value	Critical region	Modified Boxplot
Spread	Boxplot	Quartile
percentage	Subject	Leading Question Bias
Bias	Dot	Bell Shaped
Class	Continuous Variable	Class Width
Variance	Stratum	Frequency
Unbiased	Descriptive Statistics	

151

1.

L	D	N	O	M	I	N	A	L	V	A	R	I	A	B	L	E	S	V	V	C	B	Z
K	S	E	L	F	I	N	T	E	R	E	S	T	H	K	N	T	B	J	A	B	C	O
S	T	A	C	K	E	D	F	L	B	B	Y	Z	X	B	O	Y	C	H	O	K	O	E
A	N	V	A	C	A	D	E	B	H	P	G	I	D	Q	N	Z	M	E	A	N	R	K
P	Q	J	X	V	M	D	Y	T	O	S	T	A	T	I	S	T	I	C	S	D	R	X
S	T	R	A	T	I	F	I	E	D	S	A	M	P	L	I	N	G	C	S	Z	E	I
S	L	E	V	E	L	O	F	S	I	G	N	I	F	I	C	A	N	C	E	O	L	O
S	A	M	P	L	I	N	G	D	I	S	T	R	I	B	U	T	I	O	N	A	A	Z
N	I	N	D	E	P	E	N	D	E	N	T	V	A	R	I	A	B	L	E	C	T	N
H	I	N	D	E	P	E	N	D	E	N	T	S	A	M	P	L	E	S	A	T	I	U
I	T	O	X	X	K	C	X	Z	C	A	S	E	C	O	N	T	R	O	L	U	O	M
U	D	S	R	I	W	D	G	P	B	D	F	C	O	L	U	M	N	X	G	Z	N	E
L	C	Y	Z	Z	P	L	B	N	C	W	C	S	D	D	K	J	V	Q	T	U	C	R
F	S	M	E	V	A	R	I	A	N	C	E	P	O	P	A	W	F	D	V	G	O	I
N	G	M	W	N	L	M	P	M	U	L	D	R	L	Y	H	T	R	G	P	E	E	C
L	U	E	L	Y	H	J	A	E	C	L	W	E	G	T	V	P	A	U	Z	W	F	A
A	P	T	S	Y	T	J	V	I	Q	T	U	A	X	W	I	H	B	S	S	B	F	L
V	O	R	Y	M	M	H	J	E	Q	O	R	D	I	W	D	H	V	G	E	A	I	M
M	A	I	B	D	Z	T	H	J	E	O	N	Z	S	C	N	Y	L	Y	N	T	C	C
K	O	C	P	D	I	S	C	R	E	T	E	V	A	R	I	A	B	L	E	T	I	H
Q	H	W	Q	Q	B	C	G	P	F	A	U	L	Y	S	F	X	F	P	C	O	E	Z
G	J	F	V	W	S	X	B	Y	L	H	W	J	M	K	T	O	N	L	S	C	N	W
N	D	A	Z	U	W	N	J	Z	R	S	Q	B	N	K	U	E	J	I	O	H	T	O

Symmetric	Spread	Correlation coefficient
Numerical	Stratified sampling	Level of significance
Data Set	Column	P
Nominal Variables	Mean	Independent variable
Stacked	Case Control	Statistics
Self Interest	Discrete Variable	Independent samples
Sampling distribution	Variance	

152

2.

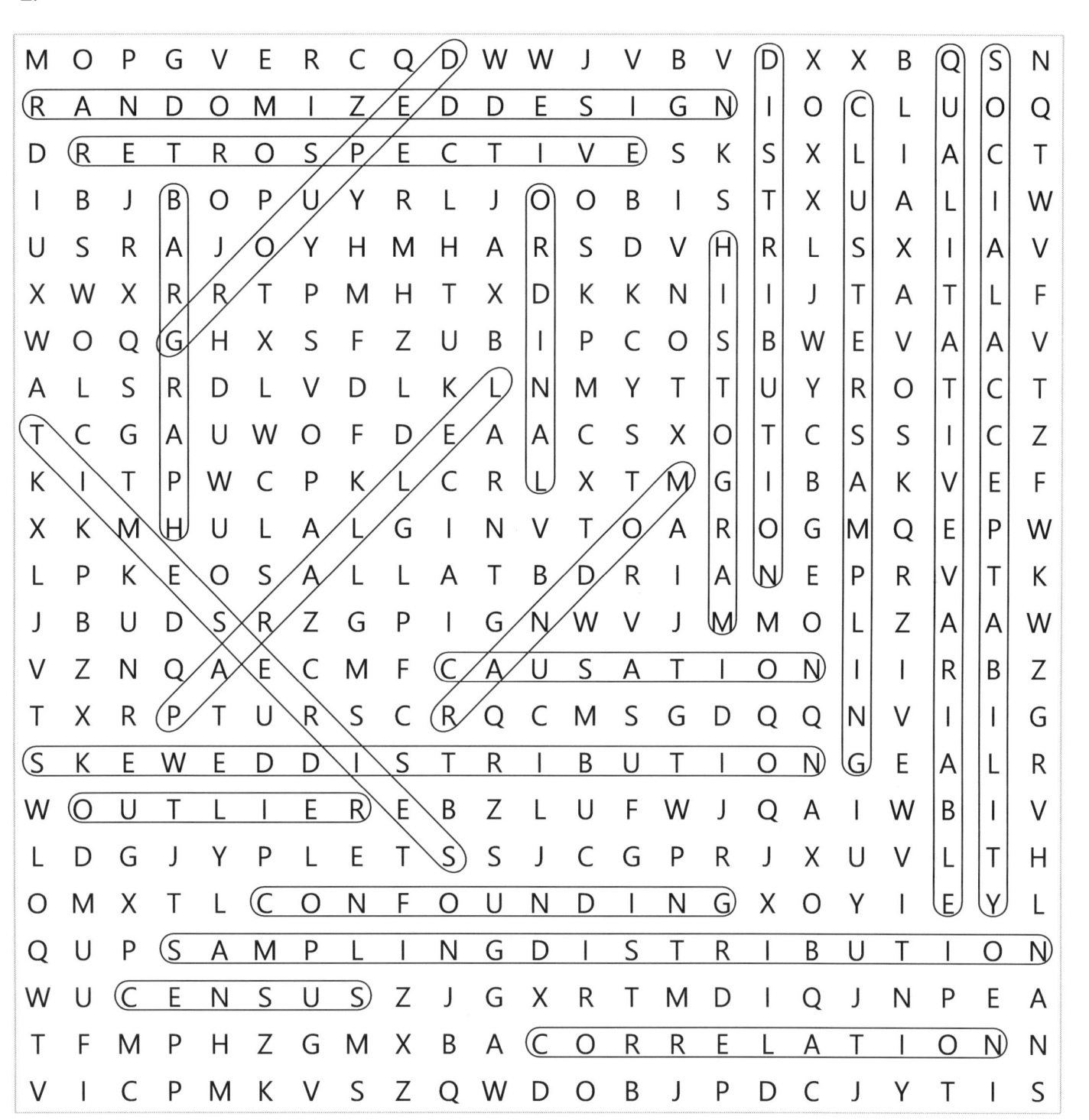

M	O	P	G	V	E	R	C	Q	D	W	W	J	V	B	V	D	X	X	B	Q	S	N
R	A	N	D	O	M	I	Z	E	D	D	E	S	I	G	N	I	O	C	U	O	O	Q
D	R	E	T	R	O	S	P	E	C	T	I	V	E	S	K	S	X	L	I	A	C	T
I	B	J	B	O	P	U	Y	R	L	J	O	O	B	I	S	T	X	U	A	L	I	W
U	S	R	A	J	O	Y	H	M	H	A	R	S	D	V	H	R	L	S	X	I	A	V
X	W	X	R	R	T	P	M	H	T	X	D	K	K	N	I	I	J	T	A	T	L	F
W	O	Q	G	H	X	S	F	Z	U	B	I	P	C	O	S	B	W	E	V	A	A	V
A	L	S	R	D	L	V	D	L	K	L	N	M	Y	T	T	U	Y	R	O	T	C	T
T	C	G	A	U	W	O	F	D	E	A	A	C	S	X	O	T	C	S	S	I	C	Z
K	I	T	P	W	C	P	K	L	C	R	L	X	T	M	G	I	B	A	K	V	E	F
X	K	M	H	U	L	A	L	G	I	N	V	T	O	A	R	O	G	M	Q	E	P	W
L	P	K	E	O	S	A	L	L	A	T	B	D	R	I	A	N	E	P	R	V	T	K
J	B	U	D	S	R	Z	G	P	I	G	N	W	V	J	M	M	O	L	Z	A	A	W
V	Z	N	Q	A	E	C	M	F	C	A	U	S	A	T	I	O	N	I	I	R	B	Z
T	X	R	P	T	U	R	S	C	R	Q	C	M	S	G	D	Q	Q	N	V	I	I	G
S	K	E	W	E	D	D	I	S	T	R	I	B	U	T	I	O	N	G	E	A	L	R
W	O	U	T	L	I	E	R	E	B	Z	L	U	F	W	J	Q	A	I	W	B	I	V
L	D	G	J	Y	P	L	E	T	S	S	J	C	G	P	R	J	X	U	V	L	T	H
O	M	X	T	L	C	O	N	F	O	U	N	D	I	N	G	X	O	Y	I	E	Y	L
Q	U	P	S	A	M	P	L	I	N	G	D	I	S	T	R	I	B	U	T	I	O	N
W	U	C	E	N	S	U	S	Z	J	G	X	R	T	M	D	I	Q	J	N	P	E	A
T	F	M	P	H	Z	G	M	X	B	A	C	O	R	R	E	L	A	T	I	O	N	N
V	I	C	P	M	K	V	S	Z	Q	W	D	O	B	J	P	D	C	J	Y	T	I	S

Time series   Skewed distribution   Bar Graph
Census   Qualitative Variable   Random
Grouped   Retrospective   Randomized design
Sampling distribution   Histogram   Distribution
ordinal   Social Acceptability   Correlation
Cluster Sampling   Causation   Outlier
Confounding   parallel

153

3.

```
K H A P V T X J W Q F Q U G A X D U M A N C I
F I V E N U M B E R S U M M A R Y I A G O Q R
J V R C U M P R H L U A Y P I C H A M J M K C
O I Q C C E G E G I Q M I N I M U M C I Y O
L A U I O E C I N T E R V A L O N F O N L R
E D A F O L T L I T O Y U D I V R V C M A I R
V G R Q K X U N E Z P J L I L V P C W P L O E
E U T U Y Y G M G I T J T S X K E H S O V K L
L V I T C I N R N C U H W T U Q R I X U A Z A
O F L Z J A W Y O R K A N R X T C S O N R T T
F O E X X N M U U U D V G I C Y E Q S D I B I
S G X A H A H D U Z P S B B M A N U Z V A G O
I E S P Y J F J Y H E E C U E C T A E C B X N
G X T F Q D C N Q S H P D T U X A R E L L A T
N U A I P C C U M U L A T I V E G E N Z E J V
I X T Z S D X D B P X V D O G K E W T S S O W
F R I T L M T W D I J U P N B A R G R A P H A
I K S X W U G D U M C A T E G O R I C A L V D
C O T E A J H U J X O W U N B I A S E D N Q I
A P I K K F W A O T H A W L F K Q Q P Y C B N
N E C H L K O J Z L F T N T P G J V Y X M G K
C H S E E Y C K S H Z Y L P U L D Y U I R P H
E B G J R I N T E R P O L A T I O N P D G V R
```

Column   Chi square   Bar Graph
Unbiased   Pi   Compound
Nominal Variables Interpolation percentage
Minimum   Categorical   Quartile
Interval   Cumulative   Level of significance
Correlation   Distribution   Statistics
Five Number Summary Grouped

4.

A	P	V	D	W	C	H	M	L	Y	H	E	G	V	C	E	V	D	V	M	G	W	D
P	V	R	C	G	X	U	G	M	G	L	L	H	X	V	U	Q	O	O	A	O	A	R
I	I	N	T	E	R	V	A	L	W	S	H	C	V	L	G	N	T	U	T	I	D	A
Z	N	K	T	E	A	Q	R	A	N	D	O	M	F	M	F	Z	S	V	C	S	Y	E
X	G	K	E	G	G	F	V	E	S	P	I	E	C	H	A	R	T	D	H	J	Z	K
L	O	S	R	Y	L	M	R	T	M	C	P	Q	X	V	E	C	W	A	E	M	K	X
Q	U	A	L	I	T	A	T	I	V	E	V	A	R	I	A	B	L	E	D	O	A	D
Q	B	T	T	S	U	S	Q	T	Y	P	E	I	C	O	L	U	M	N	S	U	B	G
T	Y	N	I	Q	T	J	G	F	K	E	U	O	I	K	A	T	V	D	A	W	P	N
X	N	P	S	B	W	R	S	B	U	M	V	O	R	C	F	P	T	O	M	G	C	D
R	E	I	W	C	U	M	U	L	A	T	I	V	E	J	C	O	T	J	P	T	Z	W
D	H	M	Y	L	T	W	K	X	G	X	R	N	E	P	L	R	Z	Z	L	Q	I	V
C	A	E	G	W	U	M	V	T	R	G	Z	D	I	P	Z	B	A	Y	E	Z	X	D
Y	F	T	V	R	I	J	K	P	N	O	E	J	X	C	C	A	L	Y	U	P	Q	D
Z	X	C	A	T	Q	H	T	J	O	C	N	O	N	R	E	S	P	O	N	S	E	R
S	B	V	S	C	Z	M	Y	N	J	W	B	H	F	N	W	W	H	A	I	B	H	I
J	T	E	A	D	B	B	R	A	N	K	C	O	R	R	E	L	A	T	I	O	N	B
P	B	B	L	L	E	V	E	L	O	F	S	I	G	N	I	F	I	C	A	N	C	E
W	M	I	H	J	X	Y	I	Q	D	U	D	Q	X	F	U	K	S	A	N	V	J	J
I	R	R	Z	X	L	E	X	T	R	A	P	O	L	A	T	I	O	N	X	X	H	V
W	D	I	S	C	R	E	T	E	V	A	R	I	A	B	L	E	I	B	O	P	R	K
C	Y	R	F	Y	B	K	F	W	G	Q	W	B	P	I	N	Q	M	C	Z	P	R	X
A	X	T	G	N	H	T	P	E	F	V	B	Q	K	W	R	D	K	Q	H	U	B	E

Alpha   Rank Correlation   Pie chart   Type I
Matched sample Mode   Qualitative Variable   Data
Non response   Column   Pi   Level of significance
Extrapolation   Discrete Variable   Chi square   Random
Boxplot   Dot   Cumulative   Interval

155

5.

Dependent samples
Bell Shaped
Ordinal Variables
Mean
Outlier
Resistant Statistic
Stratified sampling

Maximum
Census
Pareto Chart
Spread
Matched sample
Mode
Questionnaire

Double Blind
Rho
Random sampling
Residual
Sampling distribution
Histogram

6.

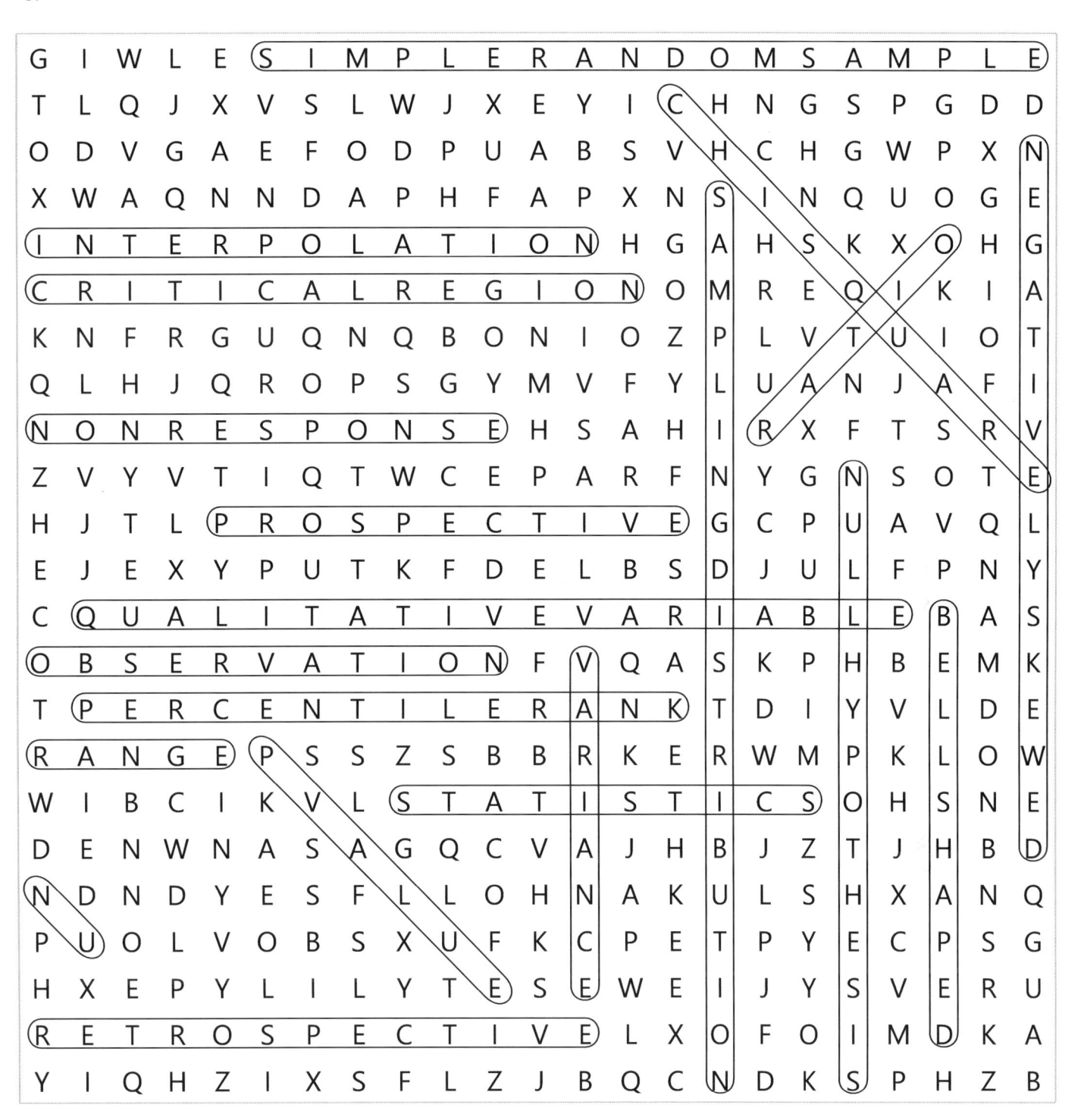

```
G I W L E S I M P L E R A N D O M S A M P L E
T L Q J X V S L W J X E Y I C H N G S P G D D
O D V G A E F O D P U A B S V H C H G W P X N
X W A Q N N D A P H F A P X N S I N Q U O G E
I N T E R P O L A T I O N H G A H S K X O H G
C R I T I C A L R E G I O N O M R E Q I K I A
K N F R G U Q N Q B O N I O Z P L V T U I O T
Q L H J Q R O P S G Y M V F Y L U A N J A F I
N O N R E S P O N S E H S A H I R X F T S R V
Z V Y V T I Q T W C E P A R F N Y G N S O T E
H J T L P R O S P E C T I V E G C P U A V Q L
E J E X Y P U T K F D E L B S D J U L F P N Y
C Q U A L I T A T I V E V A R I A B L E B A S
O B S E R V A T I O N F V Q A S K P H B E M K
T P E R C E N T I L E R A N K T D I Y V L D E
R A N G E P S S Z S B B R K E R W M P K L O W
W I B C I K V L S T A T I S T I C S O H S N E
D E N W N A S G Q C V A J H B J Z T J H B D
N D N D Y E S F L O H N A K U L S H X A N Q
P U O L V O B S X U F K C P E T P Y E C P S G
H X E P Y L I L Y T E S E W E I J Y S V E R U
R E T R O S P E C T I V E L X O F O I M D K A
Y I Q H Z I X S F L Z J B Q C N D K S P H Z B
```

Percentile rank	Prospective	Statistics
Critical region	Retrospective	Nu
Null Hypothesis	Observation	Sampling distribution
Interpolation	Non response	Qualitative Variable
Negatively skewed	Variance	Ratio
Simple Random Sample	Bell Shaped	P value
Chi square	Range	

7.

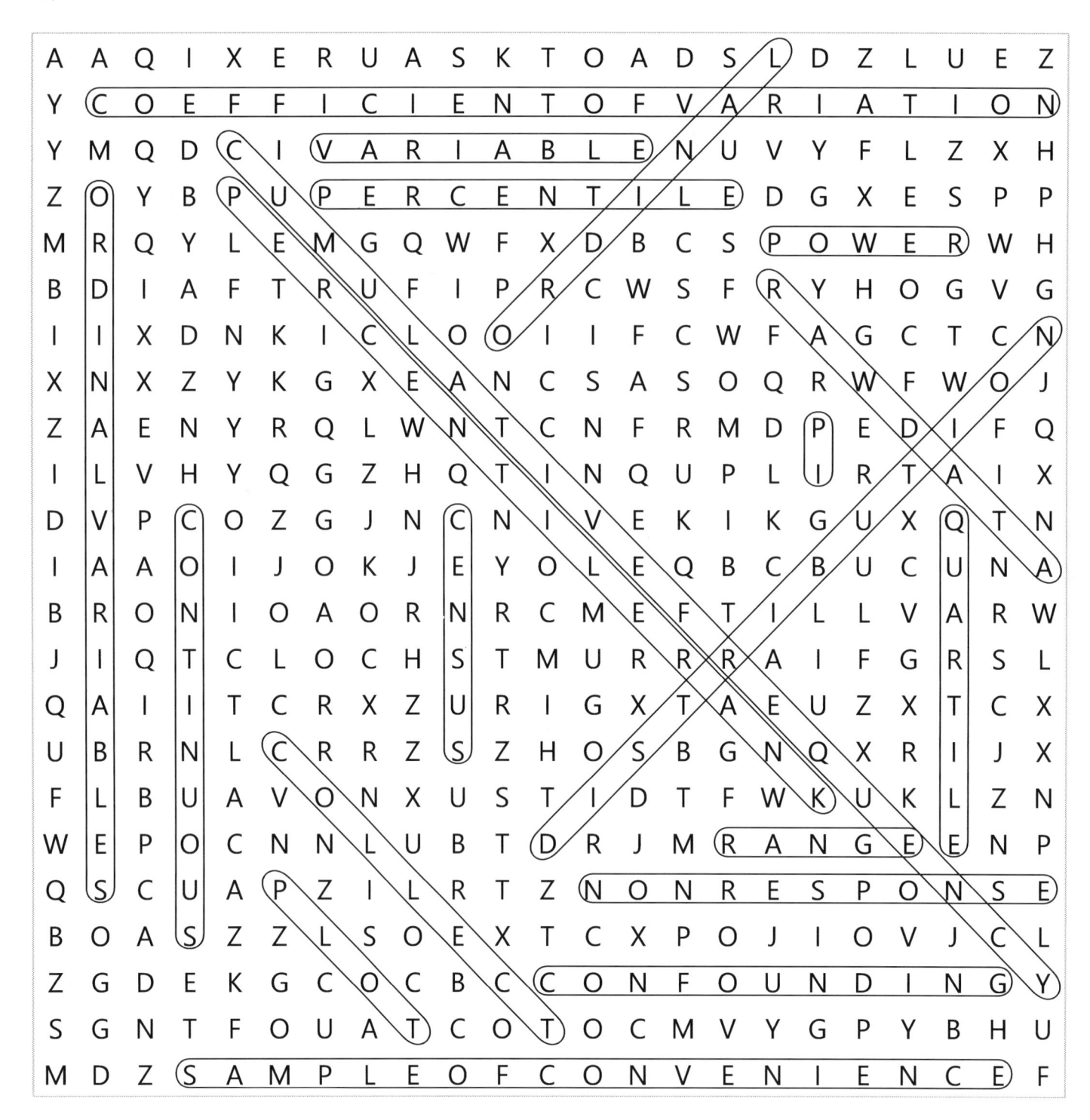

A	A	Q	I	X	E	R	U	A	S	K	T	O	A	D	S	L	D	Z	L	U	E	Z
Y	C	O	E	F	F	I	C	I	E	N	T	O	F	V	A	R	I	A	T	I	O	N
Y	M	Q	D	C	I	V	A	R	I	A	B	L	E	N	U	V	Y	F	L	Z	X	H
Z	O	Y	B	P	U	P	E	R	C	E	N	T	I	L	E	D	G	X	E	S	P	P
M	R	Q	Y	L	E	M	G	Q	W	F	X	D	B	C	S	P	O	W	E	R	W	H
B	D	I	A	F	T	R	U	F	I	P	R	C	W	S	F	R	Y	H	O	G	V	G
I	I	X	D	N	K	I	C	L	O	O	I	I	F	C	W	F	A	G	C	T	C	N
X	N	X	Z	Y	K	G	X	E	A	N	C	S	A	S	O	Q	R	W	F	W	O	J
Z	A	E	N	Y	R	Q	L	W	N	T	C	N	F	R	M	D	P	E	D	I	F	Q
I	L	V	H	Y	Q	G	Z	H	Q	T	I	N	Q	U	P	L	U	R	T	A	I	X
D	V	P	C	O	Z	G	J	N	C	N	I	V	E	K	I	K	G	U	X	Q	T	N
I	A	A	O	I	J	O	K	J	E	Y	O	L	E	Q	B	C	B	U	C	U	N	A
B	R	O	N	I	O	A	O	R	N	R	C	M	E	F	T	I	L	L	V	A	R	W
J	I	Q	T	C	L	O	C	H	S	T	M	U	R	R	R	A	I	F	G	R	S	L
Q	A	I	I	T	C	R	X	Z	U	R	I	G	X	T	A	E	U	Z	X	T	C	X
U	B	R	N	L	C	R	R	Z	S	Z	H	O	S	B	G	N	Q	X	R	I	J	X
F	L	B	U	A	V	O	N	X	U	S	T	I	D	T	F	W	K	U	K	L	Z	N
W	E	P	O	C	N	N	L	U	B	T	D	R	J	M	R	A	N	G	E	E	N	P
Q	S	C	U	A	P	Z	I	L	R	T	Z	N	O	N	R	E	S	P	O	N	S	E
B	O	A	S	Z	Z	L	S	O	E	X	T	C	X	P	O	J	I	O	V	J	C	L
Z	G	D	E	K	G	C	O	C	B	C	O	N	F	O	U	N	D	I	N	G	Y
S	G	N	T	F	O	U	A	T	C	O	T	O	C	M	V	Y	G	P	Y	B	H	U
M	D	Z	S	A	M	P	L	E	O	F	C	O	N	V	E	N	I	E	N	C	E	F

Range   Continuous   Non response
Percentile   Collect   Power
Quartile   Cumulative frequency Raw data
Sample of Convenience   ordinal   Plot
Census   Percentile rank   Pi
Ordinal Variables Confounding   Coefficient of Variation
Variable   Distribution

158

8.

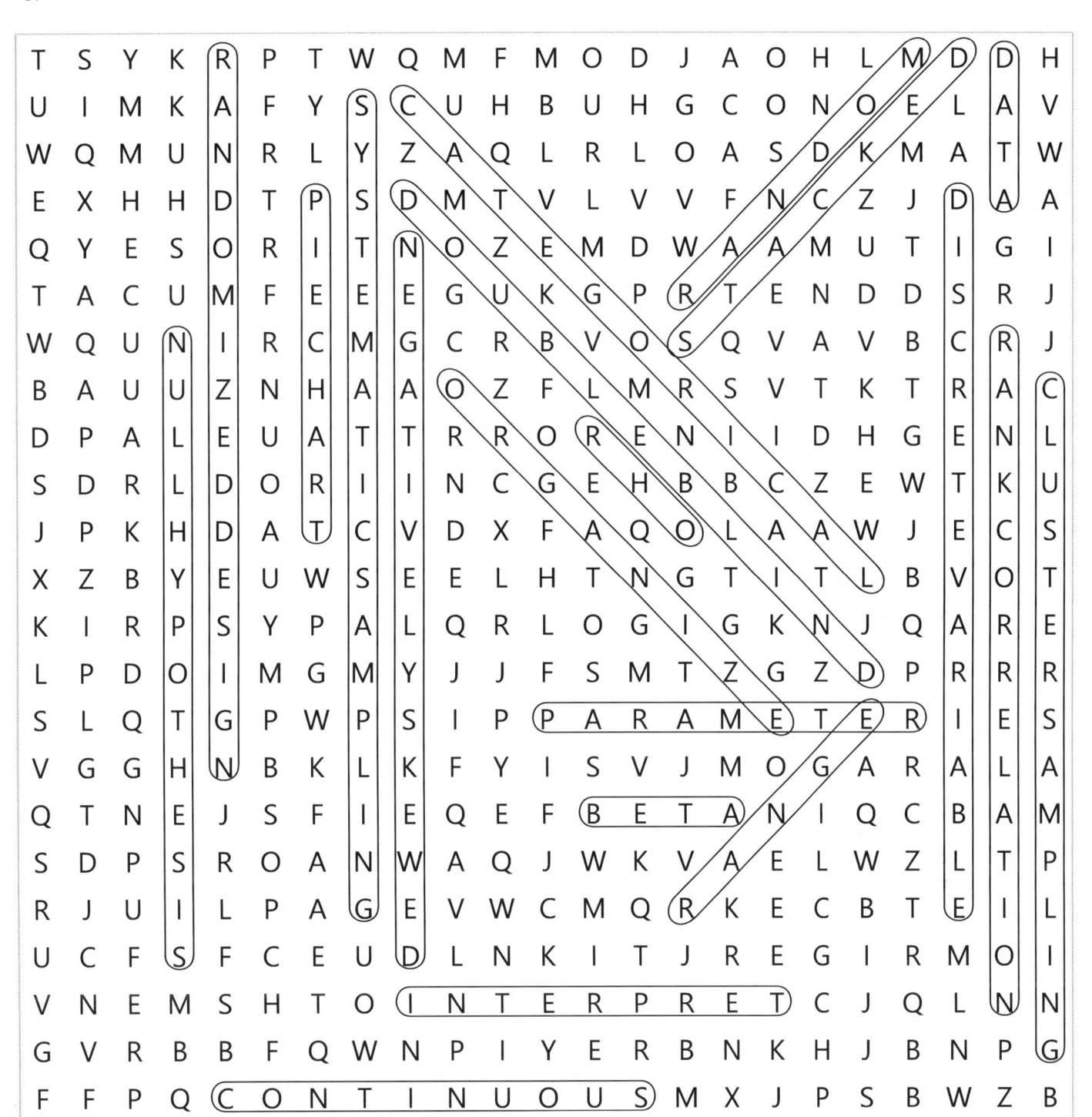

T	S	Y	K	R	P	T	W	Q	M	F	M	O	D	J	A	O	H	L	M	D	H
U	I	M	K	A	F	Y	S	C	U	H	B	U	H	G	C	O	N	O	E	A	V
W	Q	M	U	N	R	L	Y	Z	A	Q	L	R	L	O	A	S	D	K	M	T	W
E	X	H	H	D	T	P	S	D	M	T	V	L	V	V	F	N	C	Z	J	D	A
Q	Y	E	S	O	R	I	T	N	O	Z	E	M	D	W	A	A	M	U	T	I	G
T	A	C	U	M	F	E	E	E	G	U	K	G	P	R	T	E	N	D	D	S	R
W	Q	U	N	I	R	C	M	G	C	R	B	V	O	S	Q	V	A	V	B	C	R
B	A	U	U	Z	N	H	A	A	O	Z	F	L	M	R	S	V	T	K	T	R	A
D	P	A	L	E	U	A	T	T	R	R	O	R	E	N	I	D	H	G	E	A	N
S	D	R	L	D	O	R	I	I	N	C	G	E	H	B	B	C	Z	E	W	T	K
J	P	K	H	D	A	T	C	V	D	X	F	A	Q	O	L	A	A	W	J	E	C
X	Z	B	Y	E	U	W	S	E	E	L	H	T	N	G	T	I	T	L	B	V	O
K	I	R	P	S	Y	P	A	L	Q	R	L	O	G	I	G	K	N	J	Q	A	R
L	P	D	O	I	M	G	M	Y	J	J	F	S	M	T	Z	G	Z	D	P	R	R
S	L	Q	T	G	P	W	P	S	I	P	P	A	R	A	M	E	T	E	R	I	E
V	G	G	H	N	B	K	L	K	F	Y	I	S	V	J	M	O	G	A	R	A	L
Q	T	N	E	J	S	F	I	E	Q	E	F	B	E	T	A	N	I	Q	C	B	A
S	D	P	S	R	O	A	N	W	A	Q	J	W	K	V	A	E	L	W	Z	L	T
R	J	U	I	L	P	A	G	E	V	W	C	M	Q	R	K	E	C	B	T	E	I
U	C	F	S	F	C	E	U	D	L	N	K	I	T	J	R	E	G	I	R	M	O
V	N	E	M	S	H	T	O	I	N	T	E	R	P	R	E	T	C	J	Q	L	N
G	V	R	B	B	F	Q	W	N	P	I	Y	E	R	B	N	K	H	J	B	N	P
F	F	P	Q	C	O	N	T	I	N	U	O	U	S	M	X	J	P	S	B	W	Z

Null Hypothesis
Rank Correlation
Organize
Interpret
Range
Negatively skewed
Double Blind

Random
Data
Beta
Parameter
Discrete Variable
Categorical
Stacked

Rho
Systematic Sampling
Randomized design
Cluster Sampling
Continuous
Pie chart

9.

X	R	Q	D	B	S	U	Z	G	E	F	I	A	C	O	N	T	I	N	U	O	U	S
P	A	R	A	M	E	T	E	R	F	G	E	U	Z	O	Y	S	R	P	M	L	L	S
T	N	Y	W	H	B	F	P	E	V	U	E	I	C	J	T	P	T	Z	A	K	H	L
R	C	C	O	R	R	E	L	A	T	I	O	N	L	O	B	X	C	R	I	B	K	I
F	E	R	I	Y	G	B	J	X	D	D	L	B	K	J	M	A	Q	R	A	E	F	C
Q	L	B	E	H	B	K	N	Z	F	S	E	F	W	Q	P	P	R	M	A	T	K	M
O	R	A	N	D	O	M	S	A	M	P	L	I	N	G	P	C	O	G	G	E	U	A
P	S	B	C	L	U	S	T	E	R	S	A	M	P	L	I	N	G	U	R	G	K	M
M	A	X	I	M	U	M	E	V	H	R	T	D	D	N	B	X	V	O	N	A	K	S
K	Z	F	F	N	U	M	E	R	I	C	A	L	I	U	R	A	N	G	E	D	P	U
D	Q	T	S	N	B	J	V	A	G	L	S	L	S	S	U	O	I	X	E	W	M	H
Z	Y	N	Q	N	O	R	M	A	L	D	I	S	T	R	I	B	U	T	I	O	N	Z
E	K	V	E	U	J	X	G	C	U	L	D	U	R	Q	T	Y	P	E	I	I	K	H
M	U	L	D	R	A	N	D	O	M	A	S	S	I	G	N	M	E	N	T	C	S	Y
W	R	I	B	Y	H	E	R	F	B	O	W	Y	B	Z	V	M	B	U	E	P	Z	N
D	E	D	O	L	A	L	P	H	A	E	M	E	U	B	N	X	M	L	Y	N	O	M
I	Z	Z	Y	C	C	F	C	G	T	L	I	R	T	I	K	I	X	C	Y	I	T	M
F	M	M	C	C	O	R	N	E	N	Q	K	N	I	A	H	Z	S	U	T	F	Q	X
X	C	X	U	E	Z	L	W	V	R	E	Z	O	J	N	F	B	A	G	V	N	W
H	O	B	O	P	N	J	U	Y	H	J	I	R	N	O	R	M	S	A	V	K	H	R
M	G	W	S	N	J	S	Q	M	B	A	V	G	S	W	H	U	J	J	I	W	O	H
L	B	P	L	M	Z	Q	U	H	N	X	M	K	R	M	A	Z	E	A	Q	L	W	O
E	Y	I	Y	M	D	P	U	S	G	I	C	S	Y	C	U	V	Z	G	L	Q	K	F

Type II Range Correlation
Continuous Distribution Maximum
Census Bar Graph Compound
Random assignment random sampling Mu
Causation Stratum Parameter
Normal distribution Column Cluster Sampling
Numerical Alpha

160

10.

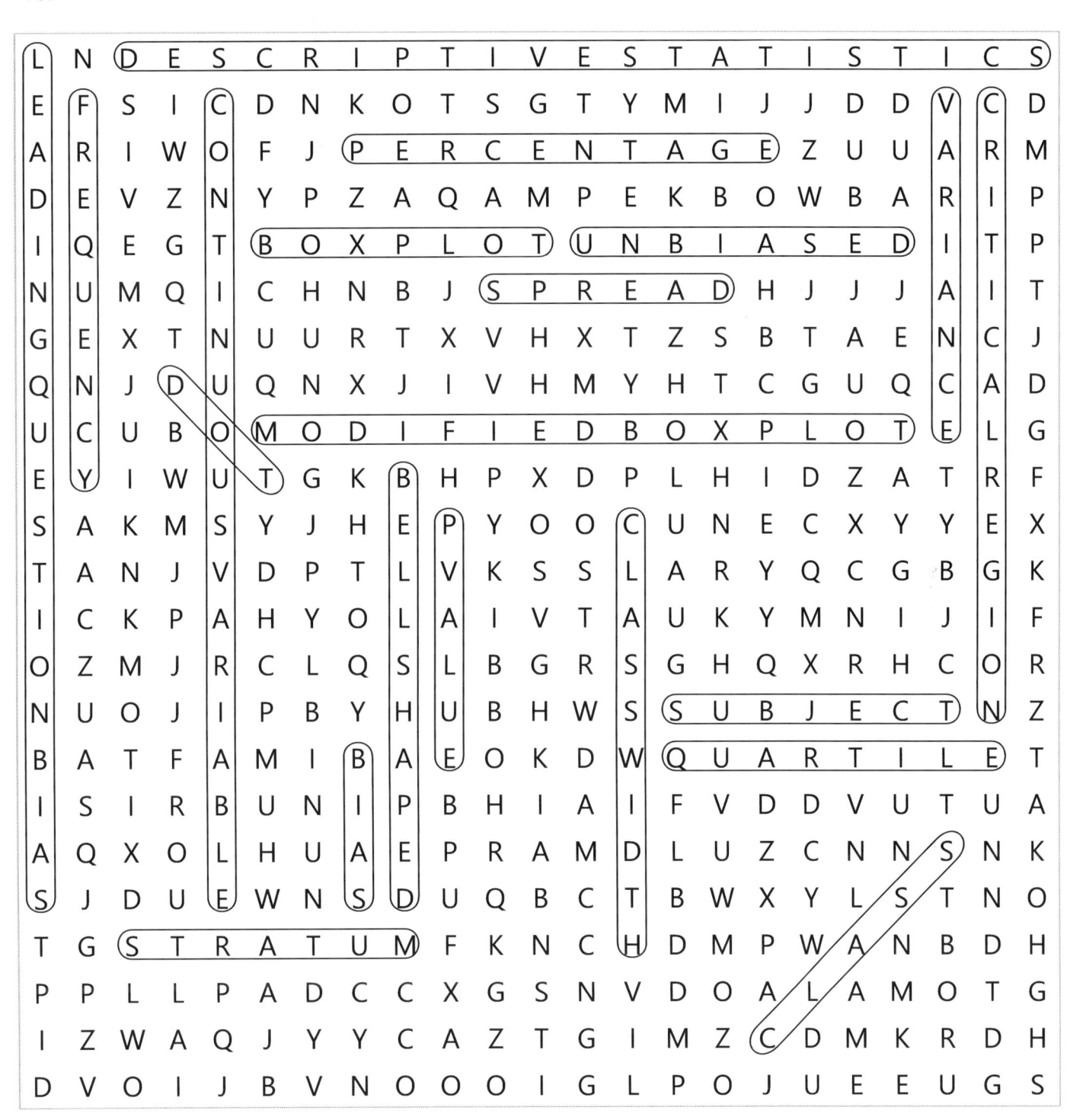

L	N	D	E	S	C	R	I	P	T	I	V	E	S	T	A	T	I	S	T	I	C	S
E	F	S	I	C	D	N	K	O	T	S	G	T	Y	M	I	J	J	D	D	V	C	D
A	R	I	W	O	F	J	P	E	R	C	E	N	T	A	G	E	Z	U	U	A	R	M
D	E	V	Z	N	Y	P	Z	A	Q	A	M	P	E	K	B	O	W	B	A	R	I	P
I	Q	E	G	T	B	O	X	P	L	O	T	U	N	B	I	A	S	E	D	I	T	P
N	U	M	Q	I	C	H	N	B	J	S	P	R	E	A	D	H	J	J	J	A	I	T
G	E	X	T	N	U	U	R	T	X	V	H	X	T	Z	S	B	T	A	E	N	C	J
Q	N	J	D	U	Q	N	X	J	I	V	H	M	Y	H	T	C	G	U	Q	C	A	D
U	C	U	B	O	M	O	D	I	F	I	E	D	B	O	X	P	L	O	T	E	L	G
E	Y	I	W	U	T	G	K	B	H	P	X	D	P	L	H	I	D	Z	A	T	R	F
S	A	K	M	S	Y	J	H	E	P	Y	O	O	C	U	N	E	C	X	Y	Y	E	X
T	A	N	J	V	D	P	T	L	V	K	S	S	L	A	R	Y	Q	C	G	B	G	K
I	C	K	P	A	H	Y	O	L	A	I	V	T	A	U	K	Y	M	N	I	J	I	F
O	Z	M	J	R	C	L	Q	S	L	B	G	R	S	G	H	Q	X	R	H	C	O	R
N	U	O	J	I	P	B	Y	H	U	B	H	W	S	S	U	B	J	E	C	T	N	Z
B	A	T	F	A	M	I	B	A	E	O	K	D	W	Q	U	A	R	T	I	L	E	T
I	S	I	R	B	U	N	I	P	B	H	I	A	I	F	V	D	D	V	U	T	U	A
A	Q	X	O	L	H	U	A	E	P	R	A	M	D	L	U	Z	C	N	N	S	N	K
S	J	D	U	E	W	N	S	D	U	Q	B	C	T	B	W	X	Y	L	S	T	N	O
T	G	S	T	R	A	T	U	M	F	K	N	C	H	D	M	P	W	A	N	B	D	H
P	P	L	L	P	A	D	C	C	X	G	S	N	V	D	O	A	L	A	M	O	T	G
I	Z	W	A	Q	J	Y	Y	C	A	Z	T	G	I	M	Z	C	D	M	K	R	D	H
D	V	O	I	J	B	V	N	O	O	O	I	G	L	P	O	J	U	E	E	U	G	S

P value   Critical region   Modified Boxplot
Spread   Boxplot   Quartile
percentage   Subject   Leading Question Bias
Bias   Dot   Bell Shaped
Class   Continuous Variable   Class Width
Variance   Stratum   Frequency
Unbiased   Descriptive Statistics

161

Printed in Great Britain
by Amazon